PATTERNS *of* PERFORMANCE

THE INEFFECTIVE SOLDIER

Lessons for Management and the Nation

THE LOST DIVISIONS

BREAKDOWN AND RECOVERY

PATTERNS OF PERFORMANCE

PATTERNS *of* PERFORMANCE

by Eli Ginzberg

James K. Anderson, Sol W. Ginsburg, M.D.,

John L. Herma

ASSISTED BY DOUGLAS W. BRAY, WILLIAM A. JORDAN, FRANCIS J. RYAN, MAJOR, MSC, USA

With a Foreword by

Howard McC. Snyder, Major General, MC, USA

GREENWOOD PRESS, PUBLISHERS
WESTPORT, CONNECTICUT

Library of Congress Cataloging in Publication Data

Ginzberg, Eli, 1911-
The ineffective soldier.

Reprint of the ed. published by Columbia University Press, New York.
"Investigation ... undertaken by the staff of the Conservation of Human Resources Project."
Includes bibliographies and indexes.
CONTENTS: [1] The lost dividions.--[2] Breakdown and recovery.--[3] Patterns of performance.
1. United States. Army--Recruiting, enlistment, etc. --World War, 1939-1945. 2. United States. Army--Personnel management. 3. Psychiatry, Military--Cases, clinical reports, statistics. 4. Soldiers--United States. 5. Manpower--United States. I. Columbia University. Conservation of Human Resources Project. II. Title.
[UB323.G5 1975] 355.2'2 75-29042
ISBN 0-8371-7812-6

Originally published in 1959 by Columbia University Press, New York

Reprinted with the permission of Columbia University Press

Reprinted in 1975 by Greenwood Press, a division of Williamhouse-Regency Inc.

Library of Congress Catalog Card Number 75-29042

ISBN 0-8371-7812-6 (Set)
ISBN 0-8371-8469-X (Vol. III-Patterns of Performance)

Printed in the United States of America

P

To

Dwight David Eisenhower

CONSERVATION OF HUMAN RESOURCES

The Conservation of Human Resources Project was established at Columbia University by General Eisenhower in 1950. It is a cooperative research undertaking involving the University, the business community, foundations, trade unions, and the Federal Government. Since 1955 the Project has been under the administrative supervision of Dr. John A. Krout, Vice President of the University.

SPONSORING ORGANIZATIONS

American Can Company
Bigelow-Sanford Carpet Company
Cities Service Company
Cluett, Peabody and Company
Columbia Broadcasting System
Consolidated Edison Company of New York
Continental Can Company
E. I. du Pont de Nemours and Company
General Dynamics Corporation
General Electric Company
General Foods Corporation
Radio Corporation of America
Standard Oil Company (New Jersey)
The Coca Cola Company
The New York Community Trust

In addition to the foregoing, the Ford Foundation has also contributed toward the financing of the Conservation of Human Resources.

STAFF

DIRECTOR

Eli Ginzberg, PH.D., *Economics*

ADVISOR

Howard McC. Snyder, *Major General, MC, USA*

CONSULTANT

Sol W. Ginsburg, M.D., *Psychiatry*

RESEARCH ASSOCIATES

James K. Anderson, A.B., *Manpower and Personnel*
Douglas W. Bray, PH.D., *Social Psychology* (1951–55)
Henry David, PH.D., *Labor History* *
John L. Herma, PH.D., *Psychology*
John B. Miner, PH.D., *Industrial Psychology* (1956–57)
Robert W. Smuts, M.A., *Economic History*

RESEARCH ASSISTANT

William A. Jordan, M.S., *Statistics* (1957–58)

ADMINISTRATION

Bryna Ball **

SECRETARIAL AND STATISTICAL

Edith Garshman, *Secretary* (1952–57)
Judith Nadelmann, *Statistical Assistant* (1955–57)
Gloria Tofano, *Secretary* (1952–57)
Jeanne Tomblen, *Secretary to the Director*

* Executive Director, ** Associate Director, National Manpower Council

ACKNOWLEDGMENTS

MUCH of the material considered in this volume was also utilized in its two companion volumes, *The Lost Divisions* and *Breakdown and Recovery*. The individuals and organizations who rendered assistance in the preparation of those volumes therefore also contributed to the present volume. We wish to note here, however, the outstanding assistance given by the Department of the Army, which made available to us the extensive data outlined in Chapter Two and the Appendix.

The Medical Statistics Division of the Surgeon General's Office, the Statistical and Accounting Branch of the Adjutant General's Office, and the Army Personnel Records Center each made a major contribution. Official reports of World War II were located and made available to us and we were given access to the file copies of statistical worksheets and other backup material. Many special tabulations and detailed rosters were prepared at our request. Many individuals throughout the Department of the Army, a number of them unknown to us by name, worked conscientiously and competently to fulfill our many requests.

The Veterans Administration authorized our access to the veterans' case records and made available a number of unpublished statistical tabulations. Creighton Hays coordinated our early requests for information; and Daniel I. Rosen, Director, Reports and Statistics Service, Department of Medicine and Surgery, and Milton C. Forster, Director, Reports and Statistics Service, Office of the Controller, reviewed our analysis of these data as well as the manuscript chapters pertaining to the Veterans Administration program.

The manuscript was also read by Eugene L. Hamilton and Bernard D. Karpinos of the Medical Statistics Division of the Office of the Surgeon General and by Lieutenant Colonel Lester C. Bieler in the Office of the Under Secretary of the Army.

The Department of the Army aided us in still another way. It assigned an officer with combat experience trained in social work to temporary duty with the Conservation Project for a two-year period to assist us in the preliminary analysis of the case records.

During the initial phases of our inquiry, Edith Beck, a psychiatric social worker, was associated with the Project, during which time she aided in the evaluation of the military case records and explored similar case records of veterans undergoing psychiatric treatment as outpatients at several large psychiatric clinics in New York City. Edward G. Epstein assisted in the final statistical analyses and preparation of tables.

Although the data in this volume were derived from official sources and the aforementioned agencies and individuals assisted us in their interpretation, final responsibility for their accuracy and interpretation rests with the authors.

Ruth Szold Ginzberg greatly improved the readability of the material through her careful editing of the manuscript. Jeanne Tomblen had the major responsibility for typing the successive drafts of the manuscript.

CONTENTS

TABLES

FIGURES

FOREWORD

WITH the publication of *Patterns of Performance*, the Conservation of Human Resources staff completes its comprehensive investigation into *The Ineffective Soldier: Lessons for Management and the Nation*, on which it has centered its primary efforts ever since the Project was first established by General Eisenhower at Columbia University in 1950.

In the first of the complementary volumes, *The Lost Divisions*, the Conservation staff set out to evaluate the mass statistical evidence about the manpower problems of the U. S. Army during World War II as they related to the millions of men who were rejected for service for mental or emotional defects and the hundreds of thousands who failed after induction because of these same defects. The central concern in that volume was to trace in detail the interaction between the performance of men and the Army's military manpower policies and procedures.

In the second, *Breakdown and Recovery*, the Conservation staff selected from its carefully controlled sample of more than 500 cases seventy-nine case histories to illustrate the strategic factors that played a major role in the breakdown of these men while in the Army and in their rehabilitation after their return to civilian life.

In the present study, *Patterns of Performance*, the Conservation staff has sought to integrate within a single volume the mass statistical data which formed the center of *The Lost Divisions* and the clinical materials which were the essence of *Breakdown and Recovery*. It has also developed new data and more powerful means of analysis to probe more deeply into the nature and determinants of effective and ineffective performance.

The importance of this study lies first in its careful sorting out and weighing of the individual factors and constellations of factors in the individual, the Army, and the larger environment that were responsible for the breakdown of the cohort group of 72,700 soldiers who were inducted in the last four months of 1942. No one who reads the first eight chapters with care will ever again assume that one or another single factor can adequately explain why these soldiers broke down.

Another significant contribution presented in this volume is the careful study that the Conservation staff made of the postwar adjustment of these men, and in particular the analysis of why some men recovered early, others after a delay, and some not at all.

By splicing together the evidence of how men performed prior to their entrance into the Army, between induction and breakdown, and after their return to civilian life, the Conservation staff was also able to secure new and important perspectives on the complex problem of performance. It was able to delineate four distinct life patterns of performance, from the adjusted to the poor, and to account in large measure for the differences among them.

Important as these and other contributions to the theory of personality and performance may be—and I consider that they are very important—the strength of this volume and of the entire investigation lies elsewhere. When General Eisenhower established the Conservation of Human Resources Project, he charged it with undertaking basic research, but his interest went beyond. He hoped that to the extent that the Conservation Project would be able to find answers to important questions a firmer basis would be laid for constructive action which would result in the fuller development and improved utilization of the nation's human resources. The subtitle of the entire investigation—*Lessons for Management and the Nation*—underscores the belief of the Conservation staff that it has been able to extract from the rich experience of World War II important lessons of value to the Armed Services, business, and the community at large.

While there are important leads to policy in each chapter the major recommendations emerging from this comprehensive investigation have been summarized and highlighted in Chapters Eight, Thirteen, and Fourteen.

There is one final observation that I should like to make now that the study of *The Ineffective Soldier* is completed. As with life itself, research comes to an end only to begin anew. Much that was obscure about personality and performance has been clarified by this investigation, which has been carried out at once so conscientiously and so imaginatively. And the clarifications which have been achieved should lead—as they already have even prior to the publication of the results—to important improvements in policy. But the gap between what we know and what we need to know about human resources remains wide, very wide. It can be closed only by research. And research to be effective must be continuous. It must be soundly planned and soundly financed. Above all, it must be soundly staffed.

The greatest contribution that General Eisenhower made in inaugurating the Conservation of Human Resources Project was to provide a demonstration of the potency of research in the field of human resources where new knowledge can contribute so much to the fuller realization of the potentialities of the individual and the nation.

HOWARD McC. SNYDER
Major General, MC, USA
Personal Physician
to the President

The White House
Washington, D. C.
March 1959

Part I: THE STUDY OF PERFORMANCE

Chapter One: WHY STUDY THE INEFFECTIVE SOLDIER?

ONE OF THE LESSONS of World War II was the realization that, although American history is studded with outstanding achievements, the nation had failed to meet important challenges. High in the list of revealed shortcomings was the fact that millions of young Americans were either rejected for military service or were separated prior to the termination of hostilities because of mental or emotional defects.

As General Howard Snyder has recalled, General Eisenhower first became aware of manpower shortages during the North African campaign. During the Battle of the Bulge the shortage of reserves gave him great concern. And when he returned to the United States as Chief of Staff of the U.S. Army in 1946 he learned the extent of the deficiencies in the nation's human resources that the war had revealed.

Shortly after accepting the presidency of Columbia University in 1947, General Eisenhower explored the possibility of instituting a major research effort "in the hope of assisting in finding some kind of an answer to this national problem—the wastage of manpower through mental and emotional factors." In his exploratory letter to a group of leading citizens he emphasized that in his opinion the time was particularly propitious to begin a thorough study of the matter because of the existence of the records of the 2 million men lost to the Armed Services in World War II. General Eisenhower also pointed out that most of these men were still alive and could provide a large body of follow-up information.

General Eisenhower stated that the evidence indicated that

another great emergency would find our manpower in limited supply but that "the basic problem is far broader in scope. Manpower losses of this kind imply tremendous costs and inefficiencies for our economy." While recognizing the value of continuing scientific research into various aspects of the question, General Eisenhower stressed the need for developing at an early date "helpful practical methods that will contribute, much more than past procedures, to the efficient utilization of human resources." He took note of the view of some experts that a large percentage of ineffective manpower "is inescapable and is a natural result of our particular civilization," but he refused to accept "such a conclusion until we have done our best to prove or disprove the case."

Indicative of the type of questions which he hoped research might illuminate were the following:

1. Were most of these men from the undereducated groups?

2. Were most of them from urban or from rural backgrounds?

3. How did these men spend their leisure time?

4. Were they underfed or otherwise definitely underprivileged?

5. Did they show a long history of emotional instability, or did these defects come out only under fear or other stress?

6. What has happened to them? Are they now a charge upon society or are they leading useful lives?

7. How accurate were our wartime yardsticks for measuring "mental deficiency"?

8. What can industry, trade unions, the school, the church do to help reduce the volume of loss?

The charge he gave to the Conservation of Human Resources Project was at once very simple and very complex. We were to organize, analyze, and evaluate the great mass of personnel information assembled during World War II in the hope that the findings would point the way to preventing such grievous manpower wastage in the future. The objective was simple; its accomplishment complex. No investigation of this problem of comparable magnitude had been previously undertaken and though we were able to borrow from those who had studied the problem before us, we had to find our own way through the great mass of material.

WHY DID MEN FAIL?

There was no shortage of theories about why so many young Americans had failed to perform effectively during World War II, but most of these reflected the experiences of one man—a general, a psychiatrist, or a writer. But more than 20 million men were screened and more than 14 million served, so that no one individual's personal experiences could possibly provide a sound foundation for valid generalizations.

A few theories were more broadly based. Some investigators had studied a few score or even a few hundred cases which they had personally collected; some had also made use of the data released by the Armed Services and the Selective Service System. These investigations illuminated many aspects of personality and performance, but they did not clarify the major question of why so many men had proved ineffective for military service.

The theories ranged all the way from blaming the way in which American mothers reared their children to concluding that military discipline was too lax. Many held to the theory that General Eisenhower refused to accept without further proof—that a high level of emotional instability is inherent in our modern industrial society. Others saw the roots of adult weakness in the deficiencies and handicaps experienced by children who grew up in underprivileged environments.

Ministers found a direct connection between the decline in religious training of youth and the unwillingness of many soldiers to endure hardships when their country was in danger. Others pointed to the hidden toll resulting from the inroads of pacifism which had swept the country after World War I—if the waging of war is pronounced by many leaders to be totally unjustified, young people will not rush to the colors when their country is attacked.

Some psychiatrists insisted that the evidence of widespread mental and emotional instability in the population revealed by World War II did not surprise them—they had suspected it all along.

There were critics of contemporary society who believed that the manpower deficiencies revealed by World War II reflected a general softening of the population. They placed the blame on the long-term rise in the standard of living which had resulted in a situation where men had increasingly lost the capacity for hard work and sacrifice and had become increasingly addicted to creature comforts.

There is little profit in outlining additional theories which had wide currency during and after the war. The galaxy of theories and the conflict among them reinforced the need for an objective study of the problem. Remedial policies could not be intelligently initiated until there was some agreement as to the nature and causes of manpower wastage. Those in a position to act—in government, in business, and in the community—needed guidelines.

The great diversity of theories is easier to understand when we recognize the many different vantage points from which the causes of ineffective performance can be studied. One approach is to identify shortcomings within the individual which result in his ineffective performance. If a person fails to acquire the rudiments of an education or rejects the basic obligations and values of our society—the obligation to support himself, to take care of his dependents, to stay within the law—the immediate cause of his ineffective performance can in most instances be traced directly to these major shortcomings. It is embedded within himself.

But a considerable number of men who proved ineffective had graduated from high school or even college and had held good jobs in the civilian economy. Their failure was not readily explainable in terms of major personal defects but was more likely to be related to their military experience. When a 36-year-old recruit, the father of two adolescent children, was suddenly uprooted from his civilian environment and sent to a combat unit that was following an accelerated training schedule, he might fail to make the grade, no matter how hard he tried. His failure would reflect a defect in the military assignment system, not in himself.

To take another example: Negroes born and educated in the North were assigned to segregated units, frequently under white Southern officers, located in training centers in the deep South. On duty and particularly off duty they were exposed to the full brunt of discriminatory practices. This occurred during a war fought by the United States in the name of democracy against the racialism and fascism of Hitler and Hirohito. When these Negroes failed, it was in large measure a reflection of the failure of American democracy.

When a much decorated flyer was returned to the United States on rotation after completing fifty combat missions and was assigned to a unit which had no proper assignment for him because it was already overstrength, it was understandable if he suddenly stopped trying to be a good soldier. To see this as an individual shortcoming rather than at least partially as a reaction to an organizational shortcoming would be wrong.

The complex nature of performance in military service can be further indicated by the fact that many educated and strongly motivated men who were properly trained and properly assigned also broke down. The cause of their failure can be found neither within themselves nor within the military organization; but it lies, rather, in the excessive stresses to which they were exposed as a result of the exigencies of war. The experiences of the soldiers who fought on Guadalcanal or with Merrill's Marauders represent only extreme examples of troops who were driven to the limits of their endurance and beyond.

The lesson that every man has his breaking point was learned slowly, but it was learned. No comprehensive study of performance in military service can fail to include a consideration of how excessive stress contributes to breakdown. The troops who pushed the Germans from the boot of Italy to the Po or from the hedgerows of Normandy to the Remagen Bridge on the Rhine were forced to fight under very adverse conditions, not for a few hours or even a few days, but for weeks and even months. As they saw their officers and their buddies killed or wounded, they realized that they could not hope to escape much longer becoming casualties themselves. Nearing exhaustion from fighting both the enemy and the elements, many finally broke down. They kept going as long as they could, but a day came when they could fight no more. They were spent.

What happened to the soldiers who proved ineffective? Did they become, in General Eisenhower's words, "a charge upon society or are they leading useful lives?" While many students have speculated about the reasons why men broke down while the war was still under way, few have explored the postwar adjustment of these ineffective soldiers. But a broader understanding of the men who broke in the service requires not only an evaluation of their background prior to entering upon active duty, but also and particularly an appraisal of what happened to them when they were able to return to civilian life. The severity of a physical illness can often be measured by its duration and by whether the patient is left with disabling effects once he has recovered from the acute phase. Likewise, the seriousness of an emotional disturbance can be judged in many instances only by the later history of the individual—whether he recovered quickly or slowly, whether he was again able to do a day's work and to meet his family and community responsibilities or whether he was able to live only in a sheltered environment.

THE FOCUS OF THE INVESTIGATION

What was the real justification for undertaking such an elaborate investigation into the causes of ineffectiveness among soldiers in World War II and five years after the end of that war at a time when there was little likelihood that this country would again be forced to fight a major war—an investigation that has taken eight years to complete and which has required the full cooperation of the Department of the Army, the Veterans Administration, and many hundreds of veterans? The answer to this question is basic to the analysis presented in this volume and underlies its relationship to *The Lost Divisions* and *Breakdown and Recovery*, the three of which together contain the major results of this investigation.

One way of answering this question is to outline some of the issues with which we were *not* concerned. While we were definitely interested in learning about the success or failure of various military manpower policies, both to understand better what transpired during World War II and to learn how the Armed Forces might profit in the future from a re-evaluation of this experience, neither military history nor the improvement of military manpower policy was our primary objective.

Similarly, while we were interested in learning whether the experience of the Selective Service System and the Armed Forces in the assessment and utilization of millions of young men could contribute new knowledge about the mental health of the American people and particularly about their vulnerability to emotional breakdown, our primary concern was not with psychiatry in its preventive, therapeutic, or rehabilitative aspects. What we might uncover in this area, as in military manpower policy, was ancillary to our major quest, which has been, as the title of our research project suggests, The Conservation of Human Resources. Our central concern has been to broaden knowledge about the nation's human resources in order to provide a sounder foundation for actions aimed at the better development and utilization of this most valuable resource.

Social scientists have always been handicapped in their search for new knowledge by the very great difficulty of designing experiments on human beings and on the social institutions which exercise so great an influence on their behavior. This helps to explain why they often developed theories based on little more than personal experience or generalizations based on a handful of cases.

The personnel data of World War II represented a mine of information for the research investigator. Here were records not of tens or hundreds of individuals, but millions and even tens of millions. Of course, most of the material had been collected as a byproduct of the work of the Selective Service System and the Armed Forces. The basic information had been developed at the time when a man was being evaluated for induction and if he was accepted, the record was expanded by including the principal facts of his military service. In general, materials collected for one purpose do not readily lend themselves to another, especially to research. This constituted a serious limitation because most of the data provided information about how men performed under the special conditions of service in the Army during a major war. But the availability of records of men functioning within such a homogeneous environment represented a great research boon, since the proper study of performance requires a careful assessment of the environment within which people perform.

But we must still search for an answer to the question of how a study of the performance of men in the Armed Services, particularly in time of war, can contribute much that is of value to an understanding of their performance in the normal pursuits of life—in their jobs, in their homes, in their civilian communities.

Our study of the ineffective soldier has been structured to provide information about a man's pre-military and post-military experience as well as his military service. By broadening the focus to include an evaluation of a man's performance prior to his entrance into the Army, his military performance prior to breakdown, and his performance after his return to civilian life, a much more comprehensive evaluation can be made of the factors determining the level of his performance in a military or civilian environment.

There is the other side of the picture. Hundreds of thousands of young men had never been away from home for a single night until they were drafted. During the next twelve to eighteen months they saw more of the country than most people do in a lifetime. Millions also had an opportunity to spend time in foreign lands, and although it was usually under difficult circumstances, this was an experience which most of their fellow citizens never have.

Moreover, for the first time in their lives, many men were offered opportunities for education or training. Thus many profited by their military experience in that it broadened their horizons and helped them to acquire knowledge and skills which stood them in good stead once they returned to civilian life. This was true for many who were discharged prematurely just as it was for the vast majority who served until they were demobilized.

This suggests why the study of the men who proved ineffective in World War II has direct bearing on the understanding of our civilian economy and society. Since nearly 2 million men between the ages of eighteen and thirty-seven out of the 18 million screened in this age range were rejected for military service because of an emotional or mental defect (true mental deficiency and educational deprivation)* and another three quarters of a million were prematurely separated for the same reasons, the total ineffective group includes approximately 1 out of every 7 young men who were called for service. This is a significant sector of the nation's manhood.

There is continuity to men's lives; what happens to a man in one period is certain to influence his performance in another. Hence, a better understanding of the experiences of the many hundreds of thousands who served in the Army during part if not all of World War II cannot fail to add insight and perspective about their actions and reactions in civilian life.

But important as these links are between these men who served in World War II and our contemporary economy and society, they do not form the principal justification for such an ambitious investigation of the ineffective soldier. The answer lies elsewhere. It is found in the lessons that can be learned about the management of men in large organizations. It may not be possible in every or even in the majority of instances to transfer directly the experiences of the Armed Services to civilian life. There are significant

* See *The Uneducated* for a detailed analysis of the illiterate and poorly educated who were screened for military service and those who actually served during World War II.

differences between an army at war and a large corporation or a large nonprofit organization such as a university, a hospital, or a civilian government agency. But, great as are these differences, there are sufficient points of similarity between them to justify the effort of distilling the experience of the army in the hope that it can contribute to the better operation of other large organizations.

While the objective of an army in war is to engage and defeat the enemy in combat, no more than 3 out of every 10 men in uniform ever participate directly in the actual fighting. The rest are engaged in the procurement, distribution, storage, and transportation of materiel, and in providing the wide range of services that the troops require in connection with their processing, housekeeping, medical care, training, and transportation. Much of an army's operations, even in time of war, is logistical rather than combat.

An army can succeed in accomplishing its missions only by the skill that it develops in selecting, training, and utilizing the men who alone can defeat the enemy. There are unique characteristics of a military organization during hostilities: the ever-present compulsion on the individual, the relative immutability of the situation, the risks to life and limb. Yet there is one important bridge between military and civilian experience, between the Army and large organizations in civilian life. Irrespective of its specific mission or of the environment within which it operates, every large organization is constantly confronted with the challenge of making more effective use of its manpower.

In World War II, the Army, which then included the Air Corps, reached a peak strength of more than 8 million men. At that time it was more than double the size of the army which we had mustered in World War I and over ten times as large as the work force of the largest private employer today—the American Telephone and Telegraph Company.

When an organization has expanded to a point where its work force is counted in the tens or hundreds of thousands, it must rely primarily on company-wide policies and procedures for in no other way can it deal effectively with such large numbers. The fact that the Army had a peak strength of more than 8 million and was operating throughout the world means that it had to rely to an even greater extent than other large organizations on formal rules and regulations.

LESSONS FOR LARGE CIVILIAN ORGANIZATIONS

Large organizations are characteristic of our contemporary society and there is no evidence as yet that our largest units have reached their maximum. At this point we will only suggest some of the major areas in which the Army's experience may contain important lessons for large civilian organizations.

The Army did not induct every man who was subject to call any more than a large employer, even in a very tight labor market, will take everybody who shows up at the hiring gate. In point of fact the Army rejected a total of about 5¼ million men out of the 18 million between the ages of eighteen and thirty-seven whom it screened—or roughly 3 out of every 10. There has never been a selection effort of this magnitude in this country. In *The Lost Divisions* a critical review was made of this ambitious screening operation and of the strengths and weaknesses with which it was carried out. In addition, general recommendations for the personnel policy of the Armed Forces and other large organizations arising out of this review were set forth. In this volume we will explore more deeply the problems of screening by considering not only the process of initial selection but the repeated screening in depth that was conducted and by relating these findings to soldiers' pre-military performances and to the differing orders of stress to which they were exposed.

With only minor exceptions the men who enlisted or were drafted into the Army in World War II had had no prior military experience. This meant that the Army was faced with a tremendous training task which it had to carry out under the greatest possible pressure, for each day that it delayed in sending divisions overseas meant that the enemy was able to entrench himself further and so increase the cost of eventually dislodging him.

While there is no direct parallel in civilian industry to such a stupendous training effort, certain points of similarity can be found. Every year approximately one million young men complete their schooling and enter upon full-time employment. While the break between school and work is less than that between civilian and military life, it is still a substantial readjustment. Moreover, while most large corporations do not usually train large numbers of new workers all at once, they nevertheless face a continuously expanding training effort to which they are devoting more and more resources.

Among the most difficult problems that the Army faced was to expand more than 30-fold within a five-year period and at the same time to develop the additional leaders that it required. Starting with a hard core of about 15,000 Regular Army officers, the Army was able to call into service some 150,000 additional officers who had had at least some prior military experience, ranging from active participation in World War I to a minimum of reserve officer training during their college days. But the more than 700,000 others who were commissioned during the war consisted for the most part of graduates of Officer Candidate Schools, most of whom were rushed through a three-months program, and Aviation Cadets who were commissioned upon the successful completion of their flight training.

The Army had long known the importance of developing a strong officer group on whose integrity, competence, and devotion to duty it would so largely have to depend. But it had no alternative to improvization during World War II to obtain the large number of officers it required. While civilian industry is seldom, if ever, confronted with a task of multiplying its leadership personnel more than 45-fold within a five-year period, it has recently been faced with the need of rapidly increasing its executive and supervisory ranks, both because of its continued expansion and because its efforts to cope with this expansion through decentralization usually result in sizable increases in executive staff. The connection between military and civilian experience in this area derives from the increasing reliance of large corporations on formal education and training for each level of its executive group—executive trainees, middle management, and the senior group. Since the Army has long relied upon a complex system of formal training for its regular officer personnel, it has served increasingly during the past decade as a stimulus and a model for industry.

In civilian life only a small percentage of men put forth their best efforts despite the benefits that might accrue to them. The majority are much more likely to do what is required of them and no more. And they take care to see that the work norms are not altered without their consent. But no organization, surely no large organization, has found it possible to rely solely on the workers' self-discipline. They have found it necessary to establish standards and to assign responsibility to a supervisory group to see that the standards are met. Unless those who perform poorly are penalized, others will soon become slipshod.

The Army was faced with a particularly difficult challenge in establishing and enforcing effective discipline. The civilian employer usually holds the threat of discharge over the head of the recalcitrant or ineffective worker. But an army at war which would resort to discharging indiscriminately those who failed to perform effectively would be rewarding inefficiency by insuring that those who failed would no longer have to risk life or limb. In addition to the inequity involved in such a perverted system of reward and punishment, the army would run a much greater risk. By letting the troublesome soldier return to civilian life, it would inevitably encourage others to slacken their efforts and to seek escape.

Again, despite marked differences between a military and a civilian organization, there is much in the Army's experience with discipline that has applicability for the problems of a nonmilitary organization. Every large organization must develop criteria for differentiating acceptable from nonacceptable performance. Next, it must develop methods for instructing its key personnel as to how the criteria are to be applied. Further, it must help those in supervisory positions to distinguish between different types of ineffective performers—between the individual who is sick and the one who is recalcitrant. Thus, every large organization must have a set of policies governing rewards and punishments; it must instruct its supervisors in applying them and insure that punitive action is restricted to those who can be held responsible for their ineffective behavior.

We have suggested how the Army's experience with problems of selection, training, leadership, and discipline have relevance to the problems of large civilian organizations. Many more points of contact, such as the factors that can contribute to high morale and an esprit de corps, could be delineated, but we hope that the above will enable the reader to understand what led us to undertake a comprehensive study of the ineffective soldier. It was our firm conviction that, despite the marked differences which exist between the challenges that an army at war faces and those which are the common concern of large civilian organizations engaged in pecuniary or eleemosynary activities, there are many important points of parallelism between them growing out of the necessity of each to devise policies and procedures for managing large numbers of men. Additional proof that many of the key problems of large organizations are inherent in size itself is the ease with which certain, but by no means all, executives can move effectively between the Armed Services and large civilian organizations.

It may be useful to make one final point. Democracies have never been able to rely exclusively on professional armies to defend themselves. While the United States has long supported a small professional officer corps to provide leadership and direction, it has always looked to the citizenry to respond to the call to arms in an emergency. At such times younger men must lay aside their civilian work and don a uniform which they can take off only when victory has been won. The ability of a democracy such as ours to survive in a world of power conflicts depends in the first instance on the quality of its manpower to perform effectively in peace as in war, on the civilian as on the military front.

The military sector of our national life can never be completely separated from the civilian. Just as the Armed Services depend for their materiel on civilian industry, so they depend for their manpower on the skills and competences in the population. This being so, the experience of the Armed Forces with materiel or manpower always mirrors the conditions prevailing in the society at large. This appraisal of the manpower experience of the Army in World War II, focused on the ineffective soldier, cannot fail to yield new and significant knowledge about the strengths and weaknesses of the American people. And such knowledge must in turn prove helpful as we seek to strengthen the underpinnings of our society in the civilian as in the military sector. For the welfare as well as the security of the nation rests on the quality of the people.

Chapter Two: THE DESIGN OF THE STUDY

AS WE HAVE SUGGESTED, the initial design of our project was greatly influenced by two controlling circumstances. The first, a major asset, was the availability of a tremendous body of information which had been collected about the men who were screened and those who served during World War II. The second, a major liability, was the nature of these materials—they had been collected by the Selective Service System, the Armed Forces, and the Veterans Administration primarily for operational rather than research purposes. The challenge which we faced was to develop a design within the limits of staff, money, and time that would permit us to find as many significant answers as possible to major questions about ineffective performance through the utilization of these materials.

BASIC QUESTIONS

In Army slang an ineffective soldier was an "eight ball." And in the midst of the war few officers had either the time or the inclination to differentiate among the hundreds of thousands who proved ineffective—they were all "eight balls" and that was that. After the war, psychiatrists and other experts referred to the "two million neuropsychiatric casualties" of World War II, a figure which had been derived by adding the total number of men who had been rejected for military service because they were adjudged to have a mental, emotional, or behavioral defect to the number who were discharged prior to demobilization for the same reasons.

We first had to decide whom to include within the term "ineffective soldier." One possible approach would have been to review the great mass of individual records and to determine on the basis of a set of objective criteria which soldiers had failed to perform effectively. But such an effort would have fallen of its own weight since the Army's record center maintained files containing the individual personnel and medical records of the approximately 12 million men who were separated between 1939 and 1946.

Moreover, there was no need for us to engage in such a tremendous undertaking since the Army had evaluated each soldier whom it discharged. While we might want to review at some later stage of the research the evaluations reached by the members of disposition boards, there was every reason to assume that their judgment, reached after talking with the soldier, would be sounder than any attempt on our part to second-guess them. Since we would have available information about the postwar adjustment of the soldier we might occasionally be in a position to re-evaluate some of the decisions made under the pressure of war, but this would be merely a refinement.

As a starting point, then, it appeared reasonable to define ineffectiveness in terms that could be tied to the decision which the Army made about a soldier when it discharged him. To this end we defined an ineffective soldier as any man whom the Army discharged prior to demobilization for reasons of psychoneurosis, psychosis, inaptitude, or traits of character which made him unsuitable for retention in military service. These were the major categories under which soldiers suffering from mental or emotional defects were separated.

We did, however, make some minor adjustments. We omitted from our analysis some of the men who were discharged without honor (this was indicated by blue discharge certificate), such as those who concealed disqualifying factors at the time of enlistment and those who had been convicted by a civil court. We also eliminated a relatively small number of men who had received a medical discharge for "neuropsychiatric illness" when the cause of their failure was organic rather than functional, such as combat veterans who had sustained peripheral nerve injuries.

We excluded two related groups. We omitted approximately 30,000 men who were convicted by general courts-martial. In most instances a general court-martial conviction carried a prison sentence as well as a dishonorable discharge (yellow discharge certificate) from the Army. We also omitted soldiers who were discharged because of a physical disability, although their symptoms frequently pointed to an underlying emotional disorder, such as men who were released because of a peptic ulcer or lumbar pains. Because of the inherent limitations of differential diagnosis, there is no way of determining exactly how many of the soldiers separated during World War II actually had a mental, emotional, or behavioral defect. However, the procedures which we adopted provide a reasonable first approximation of the total number whose release from the Army was the direct result of an emotional or mental defect.

The second problem was to determine the number of soldiers who were ineffective according to the definitions which we adopted. We found that 470,000 men were discharged under these four categories during the period 1942 to 1945. Those discharged because of psychoneurosis accounted for 256,000 or slightly more than half of the total. The next largest category consisted of those separated for inaptitude—122,000, or just over a quarter of the total. Those suffering from a psychosis totaled 55,000, or 12 percent; and 37,000, or 8 percent, were adjudged to have undesirable habits or traits. Except for this last group, all of these men received an honorable discharge. Those who were adjudged to be suffering from a psychosis or psychoneurosis received a medical discharge which the Army called a Certificate of Discharge for Disability (CDD). The inapt group were discharged honorably through administrative channels.

The next question was to determine the range of ineffectiveness represented by the four major discharge categories. Within these groups was the illiterate farm boy from the Georgia backwoods who slipped through the screen at the Armed Forces Induction

Station and was sworn in, only to be separated sixty days later when his sergeant and commanding officer concluded that he simply did not have the intelligence required to absorb basic training and cope with demands of Army life; but also included was the soldier with 27 months of service who had flown scores of missions over Europe and who had won several decorations, but who was discharged early in 1945 as "inapt" because he refused to perform the menial tasks to which he was assigned after his return to the United States.

The next challenge—and from many points of view the central one—was to develop background information about representative groups of ineffective soldiers in the hope of determining the major factors which had led to their becoming ineffective. As we suggested in the preceding chapter, many experts had deliberated about these causes, but there was no agreement among them. Men equally learned in their respective fields, which ranged from psychiatry to religion, held diametrically opposed views. As long as their theories were not subject to statistical testing, it was possible that each was right in that his explanation helped to illuminate the causes of ineffectiveness in a particular soldier or small group of soldiers.

But we wanted to achieve a more solid understanding of the factors responsible for ineffectiveness not of one or a few soldiers, but of the many hundreds of thousands who failed. To that end we set out to design an investigation that would include the entire range of major determinants that were likely to contribute to ineffectiveness—those within the individual, within the organization, and within the environment.

While we had no doubt that the ineffective performance of many men was largely a reflection of their personal deficiencies, such as in the case of the illiterate farm boy from Georgia, we knew that actions of the Army itself also contributed to the ineffectiveness of many others. We have previously noted the likely consequences of assigning an older man who had been following a sedentary civilian occupation to a combat unit that was being readied for shipment overseas and the particular stresses and strains that a Northern college-trained Negro faced when shipped to a training center in the deep South.

Finally, a design for a study of ineffectiveness had to make provision for the special pressures that men experienced by virtue of being in the Army and particularly of engaging in combat. Any man, no matter how strong in body and spirit, if put under enough pressure for a sufficiently long period of time may break.

Those who had firsthand knowledge of the evacuation of psychiatric casualties from overseas theaters in World War II recall how startled they were to find that by the time the men disembarked in the United States, many of them, including some who at breakdown had been severely disturbed, were almost completely recovered. Here was dramatic evidence of the caution which had to be exercised in generalizing about a soldier's eventual condition on the basis of a single reading. A comprehensive study of ineffectiveness should therefore include information not only about a soldier at the time of breakdown but about his performance in civilian life prior to and after his service in the Army.

Thus the design of this investigation was developed to provide answers to five basic questions: Who were the ineffective soldiers of World War II? How many were there? How ineffective were they? Why did they become ineffective? And finally, did they remain ineffective after returning to civilian life?

POLICY ORIENTATION

Since our major objective was to find answers that could contribute to the conservation of the nation's human resources, we developed a design that would enable us to assess how organizational policies affect the way in which manpower is utilized. This approach can be illustrated by contrasting it with the way in which a psychiatrist deals with an ineffective person. He relies primarily on the clinical approach, seeking thereby to gain as much knowledge and understanding as possible about the specific factors in the life history of his patient in order to help him.

While we have made extensive use of biographical materials, it was to deepen our understanding of the interaction among the personal characteristics of individuals, the policies and practices of the organizations to which they were attached, and the environmental stresses with which they were confronted. We have considered in detail the policies that the Army followed, or might have followed, that could have influenced the effectiveness with which soldiers performed.

BASIC MATERIALS

One way to describe the design of the investigation is to review briefly the kinds of materials to which we had access or which we developed as we went along and which provided the basis for this study.

At an early stage of the planning General Eisenhower discussed the investigation with James M. Forrestal, then Secretary of Defense, who expressed an interest in it and a willingness to cooperate in the effort. The Director of the Conservation of Human Resources Project had an opportunity to talk with Mr. Forrestal as the plans matured, at which time the type of assistance which the project needed from the Armed Forces had been clarified: access to the confidential records and help in abstracting the case records, which involved a considerable amount of clerical work.

General Eisenhower also talked with the senior Army staff who likewise offered to help. On 13 December 1950, the Office of the Chief of Staff, Department of the Army, issued a memorandum, the first paragraph of which read:

> As a specific exception to the memorandum of the Joint Statement of Policy on the Release of Information from Medical Records of members and former members of the Armed Forces, dated 18 October 1949, and to current Department of Army policies relative to the use of mili-

tary personnel records and other records in the files of the Department, access to such records will be authorized to designated representatives of Columbia University engaged in the project "The Conservation of Human Resources."

Paragraph four of this memorandum stated:

It is directed that individuals designated by Columbia University be given every assistance practical by all concerned.

The agencies of the Army whose help we enlisted did everything they could to fulfill the directive. This study could never have been completed without the Army's wholehearted cooperation.

We used primarily three bodies of materials—gross statistical information about the flow of manpower into and out of the Army, individual case records of soldiers who proved ineffective, and follow-up materials about the adjustment of these men after their return to civilian life.

The Selective Service System had tabulated a 20 percent sample of the first examination records of all men screened at induction stations between 1940 and 1944. These data were organized not only by state and county but also by the 6,000 local boards which had forwarded the men for examination. Moreover, the data differentiated Negro from non-Negro. Thus, these materials made it possible for us to study in considerable detail the regional patterns of rejections for military service because of mental or emotional defects.

In an earlier study, *The Uneducated*, we used these rejection data to illuminate aspects of illiteracy. In our current investigation these data were further exploited by comparing the numbers rejected for service because of educational or psychiatric deficiencies with the numbers prematurely separated for these same reasons in order to test the efficiency of the screening operation. (See Chapters Ten and Eleven of *The Lost Divisions*.) We did not, however, find it practical to go back to the stored records of the Selective Service System to study the detailed backgrounds of men who were rejected for military service.

A considerable body of gross statistics was also available on soldiers who were separated during the war, including information on the numbers discharged each month and the categories under which they were separated. It was possible to relate these gross separation data to known historical events, such as intense combat and changes in Army discharge policy, and thereby to gain preliminary knowledge about the broad pattern of ineffective performance during World War II. (See Chapter Five of *The Lost Divisions.*)

But useful as these gross statistics were as a point of departure, they by themselves illuminate only a fraction of the complex problem of ineffectiveness. Fortunately we were able to make use of the individual personnel records which the Army retained. During the course of the war the Army had built up a personnel file for each man which included such documents as his induction records, qualification forms, service record, medical records, and board proceedings. When a soldier's discharge had been approved, he was given a final physical examination—in part to see whether he required any immediate medical attention which he should receive prior to being mustered out and in part to provide the Veterans Administration with a preliminary basis for judging any claim for disability compensation. This final physical examination record was placed in his personnel file which was then closed and sent to dead record storage for permanent retention. In each personnel file—called the 201 file—was the information which enabled us to reconstruct the background and the performance in military service of any man who had been on active duty.

It would have been next to impossible, however, to use these personnel folders directly for research purposes. To have built up a reliable sample from millions of individual folders would have been so time-consuming as to have been impractical. Fortunately, however, we were able to tap this rich repository because the Department of the Army had realized the value of retaining a sample of the separation cards which had been punched. Several years after the war, most of these cards were destroyed, but a 5 percent sample of the cards on the approximately 12 million men who had been separated between 1939 and 1946 was kept.

Each of these 600,000 IBM separation cards contained biographical data, such as a man's race, his date and state of birth, his state and county of residence at the time he entered the Army, the date he entered, his grade, the branch in which he served, whether he had served overseas, the date and category of his discharge. These separation cards made it possible for us to construct the sample from which to draw case materials for intensive analysis.

The third major body of data concerned the postwar adjustment of the soldiers who had proved ineffective. This was drawn from two sources—the detailed records of the Veterans Administration and the questionnaire which we sent to all about whom adequate information was not available in the files of the Veterans Administration.

The material made available to us by the Veterans Administration included three basic folders. The *claims folder* contained the detailed reports of the periodic physical and neuropsychiatric examinations that the veteran had to undergo to determine his eligibility for disability compensation. If a social worker had carried out a survey of his family and occupational circumstances to assess the extent to which he was readjusting, this too was included. The *vocational rehabilitation and education folder* contained reports of aptitude and other test scores as well as a detailed record of the training which the veteran had undertaken and his progress. The *medical treatment folder* included reports of all hospital and outpatient treatments received by the veteran.

COHORT ANALYSIS

Had we been primarily concerned with writing the history of ineffective soldiers in World War II rather than with broadening our understanding of personality and performance, we would probably have selected a random sample drawn from all who came on active duty during the course of the war. But in light of our objective, at once broader and more narrow than an appraisal of ineffectiveness of military personnel in World War II, we decided to use a cohort approach in deriving a sample for intensive study.

Therefore, instead of selecting a sample of men who were inducted at different periods of the war, we concentrated on the experiences of a specific group of enlisted men who entered active duty during the same period—the last four months of 1942. The reasons for this decision can be briefly stated. Since we were primarily interested in studying the interaction between the individual, the Army organization, and the situational pressures exerted by the war, particularly combat, it would be desirable for our analysis to eliminate as much as possible differences in the military environment. By concentrating on a group of men who entered service at about the same time, we took a major step in limiting the number of factors that might influence the outcome.

This cohort approach enabled us to trace specifically how changes in situational pressures were likely to contribute to breakdown. The longer a man was in the Army, the greater was the strain he faced, especially since his chances of being sent overseas and into combat increased with his length of service.

A word about the cohort period is necessary. Between July 1940 and December 1945 Army enlisted accessions numbered 10.2 million; in the last four months of 1942, there were 1,764,900. Thus more than one out of every six men who served during the war mobilization came on active duty during these four months. We selected this period not only because so many were accepted but because the Army was selecting at this time from a very wide range in the population—it accepted older men (over thirty-eight), and enlistees as young as seventeen, until December 5 of that year, and it had started to accept selected numbers of illiterates and men classified as "limited service." The only two major groups in the population who were still protected were the eighteen- and nineteen-year-olds who did not want to enlist (Congress made them liable for service on November 13, but they were not drafted in large numbers until after the turn of the year) and fathers, who did not lose their deferred status until 1943.

Our selection of the last third of 1942 as the cohort period was also in part determined by a desire to study performance at a time when the Army was no longer in the throes of improvization, such as characterized the months immediately after Pearl Harbor. However, the fact that 975,000 men entered the Army in October and November of 1942—the heaviest intake of any two-month period throughout the war—placed an extreme strain on the Army's personnel system and increased the probability of errors in screening and assignment. These were the days when a large induction station might process up to 3,000 men between 7 a.m. and 4 p.m., when a psychiatrist was allotted three minutes or less to determine whether a man was emotionally sound.

Despite the difficulties growing out of the size and rate of the inflow, this period appeared to us to have the fewest peculiarities that might skew the results.

PREPARATION OF MATERIALS

The reader who is interested in more detail about our research design will find a fuller description of our procedures in the Appendix. At this point we will call attention only to the most important steps which we followed in processing the data.

At our request the Adjutant General's Office processed all the separation cards of men who were prematurely separated for medical reasons, for inaptitude, or undesirable habits and traits, who had entered on active duty during the cohort period. It was only through a complicated matching of these Adjutant General's cards with the individual medical cards retained by the Surgeon General that we were able to ascertain the diagnosis for which men received a Certificate of Discharge for Disability and thereby to single out those separated for psychiatric illness. There were a total of 3,854 men whose discharge cards had been retained by the Army in the four categories which we had selected for intensive study—those prematurely separated for psychoneurosis, psychosis, inaptitude, and undesirability. This cohort sample was slightly more than 5 percent of the 72,700 who were prematurely separated for these reasons from among those who had entered on active duty during the cohort period—the last four months of 1942.

For reasons that have already been suggested, we did not deal with the cohort sample as an entity but introduced four distinctions based upon the length of time that soldiers were in the Army and the amount of stress to which they were subjected before they were separated. These distinctions are as follows:

Situation I: Men with no foreign service who were separated before the end of a year's service;

Situation II: Men with more than a year's service but all within the continental United States;

Situation III: Men with noncombat overseas service;

Situation IV: Men with overseas service who had been in combat.

The Adjutant General's Office prepared rosters which included a wide range of basic information about the 3,854 men who comprised the cohort sample. After considerable exploratory testing which involved the review of about 250 case records selected from special stratified samples, we drew random samples from the rosters, and requested the Army to abstract the materials in the personnel folders of these soldiers. We did not commit ourselves to a predetermined number of cases. However, we had reason to believe that about 100 cases per situation would probably prove adequate. In point of fact our experimental cases totaled 534, although actually we studied intensively over 1,000 records.

By agreement with the Department of the Army we designed the forms to be used in abstracting the case materials, and the Army made available the clerical and supervisory personnel to carry out the assignment. The basic records were stored in St. Louis at the Army Personnel Records Center. Our basic biographical form included 41 items, half of which covered the man's background before he came on active duty, the other half the salient facts of his military service.

We asked for all of his assignments while on active duty together with his military occupational specialties and his efficiency ratings. Similarly, we tried to get as complete a picture as possible of each soldier's hospitalization and outpatient visits, including the length of hospital stay, diagnosis, and any special records. Provision was made for the Personnel Records Center to photostat the final board hearings or the complete final clinical records—which detailed the reasons for the man's separation. Most of the photostats alone were from five to ten pages long, and a number of them were more than twenty pages. In addition, in order to have as complete a picture of a man's service as possible, we asked the Personnel Records Center to have their Decorations and Awards Section determine whether a soldier was entitled to service stars or other awards even though there was no official entry in his service record. Two clerks were assigned for about two years to abstracting the materials we needed, and they had assistance both from their supervisors and from personnel in various sections. Our instructions, developed in collaboration with key personnel at the Center, covered eight single-spaced pages. Considering the tremendous amount of detail involved, the abstracting effort was carried out with remarkable accuracy and efficiency according to checks which we made from time to time.

The cooperation which we received from the Veterans Administration was just as outstanding. We supplied the Veterans Administration with a roster of names with supplementary identifying data such as the veteran's Army serial number, his grade, and, when available from his military records, his Veterans Administration's claim number. The Veterans Administration checked its Central Location Directory to ascertain the last known address of the veteran in order to determine the regional office in possession of the claims folder. This information was then turned over to the New York Regional Office, which by teletype requested the different regional offices to forward the relevant documents to the New York Office temporarily so that we could review and abstract them. The voluminous nature of these documents is suggested by the fact that they often ran to 500 pages or more per case, and it took us six months to go through the materials.

We sent a questionnaire to all men about whom we did not have adequate information. We also sent questionnaires to a representative group of the other men in order to see whether the replies to the questionnaire would be consistent with the information available from the Veterans Administration, which, indeed, it turned out to be.

The covering letter was simple and direct:

August 10, 1954

Dear Mr. Brown:

I am writing to you because you are one of the men who had Army service during the Second World War. General Eisenhower asked us to find out what has happened to men who had been in the Army and how they have made out since they returned home.

You are one of the veterans whose name was chosen in connection with this study. You can help us by answering the few questions enclosed with this letter. We never use anybody's name in our reports, so you don't have to sign your name unless you want to.

Write your answers on the question pages and just mail them back to us in the stamped envelope. If you want to write anything extra about how you felt when you were in the Army or after you got out, please do so. We would like to hear all you have to say.

Very truly yours,

To those who did not answer, we sent follow-up letters. In order to increase the probability that this second letter would reach them we registered each letter and requested a return receipt. Of the 284 individuals to whom we sent the questionnaire, 160 replied. Since a minimum of 50 could not be reached (letters to all known addresses were returned to us), the response was remarkable.

The questionnaire was limited to two pages and included space for the replies. There were seven basic questions: What kind of a job do you now have? What other jobs have you had since the war? Are you married now? Did you go back to school or get any training after you left the Army? Have you been in good health since you left the Army? Did you ever ask the Veterans Administration for anything? Looking back now on your time in the Army, tell us how you feel about what happened to you in the Army.

The quality of the replies is worthy of note. In the vast majority of cases the men took pains to write fully and honestly. Some sought help from more literate members of their family and dictated their replies.

In the early stages of the work we devoted some effort to learning about the experiences of other armies with ineffective soldiers in World War II so as to broaden our perspective. In this connection the Director of the Project spent some time with the War Office in London, during which he saw in manuscript an excellent appraisal of British experience which has recently been published, *Psychiatry in the British Army in the Second World War*, by Robert H. Ahrenfeldt. In 1951, through the assistance of Major General Howard Snyder, then Head of the Medical Section of the Supreme Headquarters, Allied Powers, Europe, an opportunity was afforded the Project to learn how various European armies had handled certain groups of ineffective soldiers. Through the then Surgeon General of the Army the Project also had the opportunity to learn how the Army treated soldiers who broke down after the outbreak of hostilities in Korea, which afforded yet another vantage point from which to appraise the experience of World War II.

PRESENTATION OF FINDINGS

The Project's access to such rich collections of materials, while a great boon, presented certain problems. For some time it was our intention to write a single volume. However, as we completed more and more sections of the analysis, it became clear that we would not be able to condense the materials into a single book. Hence, we incorporated the comprehensive analysis of the gross data into a volume entitled *The Lost Divisions* in which we considered the problem of ineffectiveness by relating the mass data to the major changes in Army personnel policy which were found to have so marked an effect on the utilization of manpower.

We prepared a second volume, *Breakdown and Recovery*, based exclusively on case materials, for the purpose of delineating the range of strategic factors within the individual, the Army, and the environment that helped to explain why soldiers broke down, as well as the factors, personal, familial, occupational, and cultural, which contributed to the rehabilitation of so many men after their return to civilian life.

Each volume is independent, yet it is a companion to the others. While the total of what we have learned about personality and performance can be extracted only from a perusal of the three, we present in this volume the heart of our findings as well as the major policy recommendations that flow therefrom. The next chapter surveys what we have learned about performance from our earlier analysis and sets out the major questions which we will seek to analyze in this volume.

Chapter Three: FACETS OF PERFORMANCE

AS WE HAVE SUGGESTED earlier, the study of performance requires an approach broad enough to evaluate the capacities of individuals, the organizational policies and procedures under which they work, and the larger environment to which both they and the organization must respond. The following selective summary will present some of the more important findings that have emerged from our evaluation of the statistical data and the case materials. For convenience the findings have been grouped around three main determinants that affect performance—personality factors, organizational policies, and environmental pressures and supports.

Every large organization must take into account that while the potentialities of the available manpower supply in large measure determine whether newly hired employees will find it easy or difficult to meet its performance standards, there are other relevant factors. The policies of the organization, particularly those related to the processing and orientation of recruits, will have a significant influence on their performance. The hypothesis that all an organization need do is to give a man a chance may hold for many but not for those who are close to the margin of effectiveness and whose eventual success will largely depend on whether they are helped at the beginning. As we shall see in the analysis of soldiers who failed within a year, many probably could have served effectively had the Army been able and willing to help them at the start.

In addition to the influence of organizational policies the performance of individuals can be affected by excessive or unusual environmental pressures. Good men who feel that they have been forgotten, as did some soldiers assigned to distant outposts, will begin to lose their will to perform after a time, just as competent soldiers will become ineffective if they are forced to remain in combat until all their reserves have been spent.

PERSONALITY FACTORS

One important question about performance is whether men who do well in one situation at one time in their lives are likely to do well at other times in other situations. Is the individual's performance characterized by substantial stability, or is there considerable variability?

A more careful consideration of this problem will be undertaken later in connection with the analyses of life patterns of performance. But a few tentative conclusions from our companion studies can be presented at this point. To the extent that a man's performance is influenced by his intellectual-educational background, there is likely to be a substantial stability to his performance, regardless of the differences in the tasks to which he is assigned. But since physical and emotional factors also influence his ability to work—and these are subject to change—there may be a corresponding change in his performance. When many illiterates first learned how to read and write in the Army, the basis was laid for a major change in their subsequent performance growing out of a marked improvement in their educational level. But such a change, in adulthood, is rare.

A man's intellectual-educational background looms particularly important when, as in the Army, he is forced to adjust to a wholly different environment. His ability to understand the system, to absorb instruction and training, to avoid being overwhelmed by the new and the strange depends in considerable measure on his intellectual capacity. To a lesser degree similar problems are encountered by individuals who migrate from depressed agricultural regions where they have grown up to a large metropolitan center with its much more intense pace and complex demands. Our earlier analyses have demonstrated this much—soldiers with only a few years schooling or with limited intellectual endowment faced particular hardships; their rate of failure was disproportionately high.

The Army appreciated the importance of intellectual-educational competence and until the latter part of 1942 sought to avoid accepting illiterates or poorly educated men, fearing that it would be difficult to convert them into effective soldiers. Following the suggestions of psychiatric consultants, the Army also rejected men who were adjudged to have some degree of emotional instability on the ground that they, too, could not be readily converted into good soldiers.

But it was not possible for the Army to maintain these high standards indefinitely; the manpower pool was not oversupplied with well-educated, emotionally sound, and physically strong young men. To meet its requirements the Army had to accept increasingly large numbers of men whose qualities and characteristics were less good—who had weaknesses as well as strengths. For this reason the Army searched for prognostic criteria which would enable it to distinguish, prior to induction, between those who would probably perform effectively and those who would probably fail. While the Army had little difficulty in recognizing and rejecting men with patently severe handicaps, it was not able to refine the screening procedures to a point where it could readily distinguish among the large numbers with less severe handicaps. The eventual performance of this latter group depended more on what happened to them after induction than on their innate qualities.

One of the more striking facts about personality and performance that we have found is that even seriously disturbed men were frequently able to function effectively in the Army for remarkably long periods of time. This finding was in sharp contrast to the Army's own attitude towards psychotic individuals and to the prevailing civilian view of the performance potential of seriously disturbed individuals. Army directives prescribed that any person who had ever been diagnosed as psychotic was not to be accepted for service and any person who developed psychotic symptoms was to be immediately discharged. The divergence between our finding and the assumption underlying the regulations is the more remarkable since in the Army, in contrast to civilian life, a man is under surveillance not only during working hours but throughout twenty-four hours of the day. The aberrant behavior of some of these seriously disturbed men came to the attention of the authorities so inadvertently and so belatedly that we can be reasonably certain that many others managed to remain on active duty throughout the entire war. These cases suggest the desirability of reappraising prevailing attitudes towards certain types of seriously disturbed people in order to explore whether, and to what extent, some of them may be able to perform effectively in spite of their unquestioned pathology.

The foregoing is suggestive of some of the relationships which we noted between the qualities and characteristics of people and their current and potential performance. Further aspects of performance can be illuminated by considering the impact of organizational policies.

ORGANIZATIONAL POLICIES AND PERFORMANCE

One of the research opportunities growing out of the large bodies of statistical information collected during and after World War II was the chance to test relationships between organizational policies and performance. On the basis of the evidence presented in *The Lost Divisions* there can be no question that as the Army loosened or tightened its criteria governing discharge, significant changes occurred in the numbers separated as ineffective.

But the full impact of such policy changes was more subtle than a periodic adjustment of the yardstick for determining whom the Army was willing to retain and whom it was ready to discharge. As the Army made it easier for men to be discharged, it indirectly encouraged large numbers who had previously been trying to meet its demands to slacken their efforts. Such directives placed a premium on ineffectiveness because soldiers who could show that they had even minor defects were likely to be discharged—honorably and even with a presumption in favor of their later receiving compensation.

Policy is an instrument for facilitating the accomplishment of an organization's mission. As situations change, an organization must adjust its policies accordingly. But the Army did not fully realize until near the end of the war the need for exercising great caution in changing its personnel policies because of the unexpected repercussions that could occur throughout the organization.

When the Army liberalized its discharge policies in the spring of 1943, it did not expect to open the floodgates to discharges, and when it suddenly tightened them towards the end of the year it was not with the intention of thereafter preventing the return to civilian life of men whose usefulness was clearly at an end. Yet this is what happened in each instance. The Chief of Staff had stated at the time when the easy discharge policy was reversed that soldiers who could do a day's work were not to be separated. Some months later an inspection team from the Surgeon General's Office found in a camp close to Washington a large contingent of clearly ineffective soldiers. Upon inquiring why they had not been discharged, the inspectors were told that General Marshall had prohibited the release of any man who could do a day's work. This had been interpreted locally to mean the equivalent of one day's work per week!

A major challenge to organizational planners is to identify eventualities that may have an adverse effect on future performance and, while there is still time, to take preventive action. Early in the war the Army underestimated the number of reserves it would need to permit men in combat units to be rotated for rest and rehabilitation. Inadequate reserve troops meant that men were kept in the line until they became exhausted and had to be taken out because of ineffectiveness. Their further usefulness as combat soldiers, or even as any other kind of soldier, was questionable. Relief prior to actual breakdown would, in most cases, have avoided this loss.

Another challenge that every organization faces is to coordinate and integrate its separate and discrete plans so that they will on balance contribute to the accomplishment of its major mission. The Army entered World War II convinced that the nation's manpower reserves were ample. This helps to explain why in getting its divisions ready for overseas shipment it acted so lavishly with respect to manpower. If after a short trial a soldier could not meet the training pace, he was discharged and another put in his place.

Had the manpower resources of the country been as unlimited as they were assumed to be, such a policy might have been justified in view of the need to get trained divisions into battle at the earliest possible time. But when the men who were being discharged were at least as able as many of the replacements whom General Hershey was able to furnish, such a policy was unwarranted. It would have been sounder, as the Army came to realize by June 1943, to help marginal recruits to adjust to military life through such aids as the Special Training Units where the illiterates and the poorly educated could receive instruction immediately after induction, and through mental hygiene clinics which could offer emotional support to the soldier at the first sign of difficulty. Although these supportive efforts required the use of scarce personnel, and as such represented a drain on critical manpower resources, the Army was right in concluding that the costs, now that general manpower reserves were low, would be repaid by enabling many to continue in service who might otherwise fail. As we showed in *The Uneducated*, 85 percent of all those who went through these Special Training Units later performed satisfactorily as soldiers.

Another aspect of the impact of policy on performance has already been illustrated by the way in which the local military commander interpreted the directive from headquarters concerning the conservation of manpower. Policies never implement themselves. They can be carried out only by people. Thus, in a large organization such as an army at war—scattered over the globe and officered largely by men with little experience in military affairs—it is essential in promulgating new policies to take into account possible misinterpretations of their meaning as well as the effects of passive or overzealous compliance by people in the field.

Two major implications flow from this observation. A change in major policy is likely to be effective only if the organization orients its key personnel at various echelons as to the objectives and implications of the new directive. Unless this is done, much time will elapse before the new policy becomes fully effective, if it ever does. If the exigencies of the situation make it difficult or impossible to make such an effort, careful consideration should be given to continuing, if at all possible, the operation within existing policies. Since major policy changes involve turmoil and confusion they frequently lead a short-run reduction in the effectiveness of the organization as a whole.

In developing new policies an organization should consider whether such policies are likely to prove acceptable to its members. Even an army at war cannot ignore the basic values and expectations of its soldiers, since it must rely primarily on each individual's understanding and self-discipline and only incidentally on punishments and rewards to insure compliance with its policies. Every citizen and every soldier, especially in a democracy such as the United States, holds certain basic values concerning justice and equity, and an organization that violates them, wittingly or unwittingly, runs the risk of precipitating recalcitrant behavior which will result in a marked lowering of performance. In a matter which affected every soldier, namely, the conditions under which men were to be demobilized, the Army took great pains to elicit the opinions of representative groups prior to promulgating discharge criteria. It recognized the need to follow as closely as possible the preferences of the soldiers themselves as to who should go first, who last.

There are many more ways, as we shall see later, in which the Army's organizational policies affected performance. But these few observations should help to establish the importance of this relationship.

ENVIRONMENTAL PRESSURES AND PERFORMANCE

Combat commanders have often said that they feared the arrival of letters from home almost as much as an enemy barrage. When a soldier received a "Dear John" he was likely to feel that all his tribulations and sacrifices were in vain. Why should he endure the great hardships of combat when he no longer had a wife or sweetheart to come home to if perchance he were lucky enough to escape injury or death? Of course, most men received mail which helped to sustain them and reassure them that their efforts were worthwhile since their loved ones at home looked with pride and admiration on their sacrifices, and wrote cheerfully of their own efforts to contribute to the war. But the many who did not justified the commanders' complaint.

There is no need to illustrate with specific examples that a man's performance is greatly affected by the supports on which he can draw. For men facing death, far away from home, the knowledge that their family cared about them, loved and admired them, was a source of great support and enabled many to keep going who otherwise might have faltered.

The importance of family ties was no less important for the many single men who gained support just from looking forward to the end of the war when they would return home, find a girl, and settle down to start a family. We know that many single men shared the letters which their married or engaged buddies received.

Another way in which the social environment can affect performance is by making it difficult or impossible for a man to live in accordance with his values. In *Breakdown and Recovery* we present several case studies of men who, because they could not live in accordance with their values, were unable to perform effectively in the Army. Some had been so strongly indoctrinated with the commandment that killing is a sin that, even though they were not conscientious objectors, they were still unable to function in combat. Others had been brought up in a family and community with such strict morals that when they were faced with the promiscuity of some of their barracks mates they reacted with revulsion and isolated themselves from the group with whom they felt they had nothing in common.

Group living in the Army was particularly difficult for the enuretic and the homosexual. In civilian life these men could usually make the adjustments that their condition required. In the Army many of these men broke down either immediately after induction or after they had tried without success to cope with their problems in what was a demanding and unsympathetic environment.

The outstanding illustration of the influence of the environment on performance in military service was the way in which the pressures of combat could mount to a point where they led to the temporary or permanent incapacitation of a soldier. To face injury or death required the mobilization of all of a man's physical and moral resources. To do so without sleep, without regular meals, and in inclement weather greatly increased the strain on a man's reserves. To live under such adverse conditions for weeks and months would eventually sap a man's strength until, enervated and depleted, he became ineffective.

The recognition of this danger relatively early in the war led the Air Corps to establish a maximum number of combat missions for each man, after which he would be rotated either temporarily or permanently to a position of relative safety. This provided the airman with a goal and further made it likely that he would be able to stop flying before he collapsed or was killed.

One of the more striking findings about the relation between pressure and performance is that a considerable number of men were able to complete their combat tour of duty only to break down after they were out of danger. Apparently they were able to draw on reserves while they were in combat and to gain special support from being a member of a closely knit fighting unit. But once they were sent to the rear many collapsed because they were overwhelmed by the great fears which they had been able to suppress as long as they had been in combat.

Some men collapsed even before they got into combat. Many soldiers admitted that, horrible as combat was, it frequently was less bad than what they had imagined it would be. A considerable number became so anxious about combat they were unable to complete their training; others became upset when their unit was alerted for overseas shipment; and still others when they were about to enter the line. When the general environment contains a threat to life or limb, some people become ineffective long before they actually enter the danger zone. Their reserves have been eaten away by their fears.

Other soldiers were able to cope with the danger and deprivation which they were forced to endure up front until they had an opportunity to contrast it with the safety and comparative luxury of the hospital to which they were admitted after being wounded or after taking ill. Many soldiers, once they recognized the enormity of the gap between the two environments, were unable to contemplate returning to their units. They developed various types of emotional difficulties which necessitated a prolongation of their hospital stay. In a literal sense the favorable hospital environment was the precipitant of their ineffectiveness.

These illustrations show how pressures in the environment contribute to ineffective performance. Others could have been selected which would demonstrate how a supportive environment can contribute to the rehabilitation of previously ineffective persons. In a later section these positive elements will be stressed in connection with the successful civilian readjustment of a large number of ineffective soldiers.

OPEN QUESTIONS

The foregoing has suggested some of the more important findings that we were able to distill about performance from our studies of the mass statistical data and of the case materials presented in the companion volumes. But there is much about performance that these earlier approaches did not illuminate. We shall now call attention to some of the important open questions in order to indicate the direction of the following analysis, which has been undertaken to answer as many of these questions as possible.

The identification of the relevant factors in a situation is always a step forward in understanding. Hence, the identification of personal, organizational, and environmental determinants of performance was a major advance. Now a second step is necessary—an evaluation of their relative importance. To quantify the major factors in breakdown and readjustment is a major objective of the chapters that follow. Since the experimental cases were drawn so that they could be related to all cohort ineffectives and in turn to the total ineffectives in the Army during World War II, the basis was laid at the outset of our inquiry for a statistically grounded analysis into the causes of ineffectiveness.

Another important question, as we have suggested, is whether a man's performance remains on the same level over time, or whether it tends to vary. In addition to the important social implications of whether soldiers who failed in World War II remained ineffective or were able, after a period of time, to adjust to civilian life, the study of their postwar record can illuminate the important question of whether, and to what extent, ineffective performance tends to be chronic and to what extent it is reversible. These and related questions are considered in the chapters on readjustment.

A third major area of inquiry involves an extension and deepening of the foregoing. This question asks whether different life patterns of performance among the ineffective group can be delineated both as to level and continuity. Since we have information about the men before they entered military service, about their performance on active duty, and about what happened to them after they returned to civilian life, we can search for distinctive patterns. Such life history material is exceedingly scarce and usually exists only for pathological groups, such as mental patients and criminals. Since our information relates to men who were accepted for military service, their life histories are likely to be much closer to those of the general population.

The final open area relates to the policy recommendations that can be precipitated from the several levels of analysis that hold out promise of contributing to the more effective utilization of the nation's human resources. While concern with policy was to the forefront throughout the entire investigation, little more could be done in the companion volumes than to flag the crucial issues. Not until the multiple facets of performance had been studied and their quantitative significance ascertained could sound policy recommendations be formulated. With performance, as with other key aspects of human life, sound policy requires a weighing of possible gains against possible costs. This could be done only after the entire analysis had been completed.

'art II: BREAKDOWN IN THE ARMY

Chapter Four: VARIETIES OF INEFFECTIVENESS

THE PRECEDING CHAPTER set out the three major vantage points from which performance can be studied. During the war some simple, some even naive, views were held concerning ineffective performance. Among the most prevalent was the belief that the principal defect of most ineffective soldiers was that they were not motivated to work or fight; that they were "malingerers." An almost opposite view contended that those who were ineffective were emotionally ill. This second belief came to determine the Army's approach and had a major influence on shaping its manpower policies.

Emotional illness was first linked to malperformance at the end of the nineteenth century, which had witnessed major advances in the understanding of mental illness. The experience of World War I led to a broadening of the concept of mental illness to make room for the many victims of "shell shock"—men who had been well in civilian life but who collapsed under the stress of fighting. But even then, when many medical officers first encountered these battle casualties they sought an organic cause for these breakdowns. Only with the accumulation of experience did they come to realize that they were dealing with functional disorders which had an emotional rather than a physical origin.

The following decades saw such rapid gains in the psychiatric orientation of the public as well as the medical profession that it was generally accepted by the outbreak of World War II that soldiers who became ineffective for other than physical reasons had to be considered emotionally ill. It is an oversimplification however to assume that merely because the same word, illness, is used in the emotional as in the physical realm it has the same meaning. Emotional disturbance cannot be divorced from motivational considerations, even though the latter may not be readily apparent and may operate in devious or hidden ways. Consequently the relationship between emotional disturbance and performance is seldom simple and direct.

We were impressed, for example, by the fact that our sample of ineffective soldiers included many who had proved thoroughly competent prior to their breakdown in the Army while others were incapable of meeting the demands made by the Army from the day of their induction and had to be separated as quickly as possible. While both groups were properly classified as ineffective because the Army had to discharge them before the end of hostilities, there were obvious reasons for distinguishing between them in a study seeking to probe the nature of performance.

The Army labeled each soldier whom it discharged prematurely, making use primarily of psychiatric nomenclature: the soldier's records specified, for example, "psychosis," with some further identifying terms as to the type of psychosis; "psychoneurosis," usually with further elaboration such as "anxiety state, severe"; those discharged for undesirability were frequently described as having a "psychopathic personality."

Since the focus of our study was on performance, not on the individual, such refined clinical classifications could not serve as an adequate basis for our investigation. The fact that many of the medical officers who served as psychiatrists in World War II were graduates only of a short course in psychiatry and the fact that even experienced psychiatrists were frequently forced to work under such pressure of time that their classifications could not be better than first approximations constituted additional reasons for not placing substantial weight on these clinical classifications.

We were not concerned, as psychiatrists have to be, with discovering the origins of the emotional problems and conflicts in individual soldiers. Instead, we had to structure the investigation so as to delineate the entire range of major factors that might have contributed towards or militated against soldiers' being able to meet their duty assignments.

We therefore studied with special care the demands and pressures in the military environment which seemed to have exercised so great an influence on the ability of men to perform. It quickly became clear that soldiers who proved ineffective in their first months of service because they could not tolerate being separated from their families, or because they had too little intelligence to follow instructions, or because they could not tolerate the restraints of military discipline—that such men had to be differentiated from others who broke down only after they had served for eighteen months in an isolated post such as Iceland, or had been in the line for ninety consecutive days fighting a stubborn enemy, or had completed their overseas assignment and collapsed after they had been returned on rotation to the United States.

Such variations in the timing of breakdown emphasized the necessity of an approach that would avoid dealing with ineffective soldiers as a homogeneous group. All were ineffective in the sense that they were prematurely discharged, but this common factor is perhaps less significant than the marked differences among them in the quality of their performance both before and after breakdown.

In our attempt to differentiate among the ineffective soldiers in terms of conditions and pressures to which they were exposed and to which they responded, we were faced with the problem of how to establish a sufficient number of categories so that significant differences could be recognized and at the same time avoid elaboration which would unduly compound the difficulties of the analysis. After several trials we decided to use four discrete situations which would enable us to distinguish in gross terms between the kinds of pressures to which the soldiers were subjected. The basic distinctions, as noted in Chapter Two, were among service in the Zone of the Interior for less than one year, service in the Zone of the Interior for more than one year, overseas service in other than combat duty, and overseas service in combat.

Situation I (discharged during the first year while in the Zone of the Interior) consists largely of men who broke down in training. While some remained in the Army long enough to receive a duty assignment, duty in the United States for most soldiers was primarily training preparatory for overseas duty. Since Army personnel policy did not remain stable over the course of the war, it is important to recall that the first year of service of the cohort group coincided with the period of "easy discharge" policy. The Army was not only willing but anxious at that time to release men whose future usefulness was doubtful.

While the men in Situation I had to cope with the sharp break between civilian and military life, their Army service was of sufficiently short duration that most of them did not experience the depletion of emotional reserves which affected those who served for long periods, particularly under arduous conditions. Of the 72,700 men represented by the cohort sample who were inducted during the last four months of 1942 and who proved ineffective almost 38,300, or 53 percent, were discharged within their first year of service.

Situation II (domestic duty only but of more than one year) was composed of many soldiers who served only a few months more than those in Situation I. But others remained in the Army until after demobilization was well under way. Since the Army tried to get all competent men overseas, those with long domestic service represent a group who were "left behind." The Army had decided that, by and large, they were poor risks for overseas duty.

Some of the personnel changes that occurred between 1941 and 1945 reflected the altered requirements for the Zone of the Interior. In 1942 and 1943 there were large numbers of housekeeping jobs to be done but as the divisions moved overseas these decreased radically. A considerable number of the men in Situation II were released because of this shift. They had been able to handle a simple housekeeping assignment but were not capable of doing more demanding work. Then, in the latter part of the war many capable soldiers were returned on rotation from overseas, and many others who had been hospitalized had recovered to the extent of being able to perform limited duties. The Army, with a surplus of experienced personnel, had no need to retain less capable men. About 18,200 of the 72,700 cohort ineffectives, or roughly 25 percent, fell into Situation II.

Situation III was composed of men who served overseas but not in combat. Since the Army tried to send all men overseas and undertook repeated screenings to this end, men in this Situation were presumably superior to those in Situation II. While this group did not see combat, many had difficult assignments. Some were frequently in a danger zone and therefore subject to surprise attack, such as soldiers assigned to unloading ships or moving ammunition up to the troops in the line.

Others were at outposts where the climate and living conditions were most adverse and where there was no break to the monotonous routine. Many of these men felt that they were the forgotten men of World War II. Mail from home was infrequent; even the enemy did not bother to take note of them by sending over an occasional bomber. And when they did not worry about being forgotten, they could worry whether the boredom of today might be replaced by a surprise enemy landing tomorrow. Better off than the combat soldiers, this group nevertheless was under more severe stress than those who served only within the United States. They accounted for slightly over 8,100, or approximately 11 percent, of the total cohort ineffectives.

Situation IV was composed of men who had been in combat. While there were great variations in the amount and severity of the fighting which they had experienced, the fact that these men had been in combat sets them apart, for combat makes special demands on a man. Moreover, the longer a soldier is in combat the more he will worry that his "number will soon be up" for that is the rule of war—if a man stays in the line long enough the enemy will get him.

In addition to the constant threat to his life and limbs, the combat soldier was exposed to inclement weather, mud, poor food—all of this on the other side of an ocean that separated him from his loved ones. Just under 8,100 or 11 percent of the 72,700 ineffective soldiers in the cohort saw combat.

These summary comments should help the reader to differentiate among the orders of stress which soldiers in the four Situations encountered. The extent to which these military environments differed and the importance of taking these differences into account in assessing the performance of these soldiers is illustrated by the following case histories. The first is taken from among the group who were separated within the first year (Situation I) and the second from among those who served in combat (Situation IV).

A.B. was one of twelve children born into a Midwestern family. He completed one year of high school and then worked as a house painter. When he was inducted at the age of twenty-four he was still living at home. He had been in good health until he received his induction notice. Then he began to have stomach pains, nausea, and vomiting. Although these symptoms were not acute enough to lead the Army to reject him, they became steadily worse during basic training. He could eat only cereal, milk and fruit without extreme discomfort. Because of poor vision he had been classified as fit for limited duty only and had been assigned to a casual service unit. Although this was an easy assignment, substantially free of stress except that inherent in service in the Army, his symptoms grew more severe and in addition he developed a bad case of hives. He was given a medical discharge for psychoneurosis, neurasthenic type, severe, after nine months of service. He returned home and again took up work as a painter. Some time later he married. His stomach trouble cleared up shortly after his discharge from the Army although the hives persisted for several years.

B.C., a high school graduate who was born and brought up in the Midwest, married shortly before induction. Before being drafted at the age of twenty he had worked on an automobile assembly line. He was immediately assigned to an armored infantry unit with which he trained and with which he later served in the European Theater, first as a machine gunner and later as a rifleman. While on maneuvers before going overseas, he began to suffer from stomach pains, nausea, and vomiting. Hospitalized for three weeks he improved and was able to return to his unit. In the Rhineland campaign his buddy was killed and he himself wounded in the leg and testicle in offensive action during the drive from the Moselle to the Saar. While hospitalized his stomach trouble returned but he again improved, was returned to duty and sent to a replacement depot for reassignment. Two weeks later, while still at the depot, his gastric symptoms, which now included almost continuous vomiting, grew so severe he was again hospitalized. He also began to have violent headaches and became increasingly nervous. He was evacuated to the United States and discharged for psychoneurosis, anxiety state, severe. Although his condition improved only slowly, he has been able to hold a good job as inspector with a major electrical manufacturer. Ten years after the war he was still bothered with headaches and stomach disorders and was drawing 30 percent disability compensation from the Veterans Administration.

The distribution of the ineffective soldiers in the cohort by the four situations can be summarized as follows:

Situation	*Weighted* Number*	*Percent*
I. Domestic duty: less than one year	38,294	52.6
II. Domestic duty: one year or more	18,228	25.1
III. Overseas: non-combat	8,121	11.2
IV. Overseas: combat	8,057	11.1
Total cohort	72,700	100.0

* The method of weighting cases is given in the Appendix.

The table shows more than 38,000 men (or more than 1 out of 2 cohort ineffectives) failed to complete 12 months of active duty. When the number who failed during the first year are added to the number who never got overseas because the Army considered them to be poor risks, we find that over 56,500 of the 72,700 broke down in response to stresses and strains in the Army at home. They were never subjected to the more severe pressures of distance, isolation, and danger which the overseas group had to face. Thus, more than 3 out of every 4 men were "domestic casualties."

The soldiers who broke down overseas, however, are under-represented in our cohort, for we know that for the Army as a whole men with overseas service accounted for 42 percent of the total ineffective group. A fuller explanation of the difference is set out in the Appendix. Here it is sufficient to note that it results largely from the selection of the cohort period which was followed immediately by the institution of the Army's easy discharge policy, which meant that many inductees were separated as soon as they showed the first signs of faltering. But among ineffective soldiers who served overseas, however, we have no basis for believing that the proportion in the cohort who were in combat would differ significantly from that in the Army as a whole. This means that only about a fifth of all who became ineffective in the Army during the course of the war had seen combat. The literature on military ineffectiveness which emphasizes the problem of the combat soldier gives an incomplete and distorted picture.

The situational analysis helps to clarify important differences about ineffectiveness as seen in terms of both the individual and the organization and has important managerial implications. The discharge of a soldier after only three months of service, while troublesome and costly to the Army and the nation, had a different order of significance from the discharge of a combat veteran who broke down after three months in the line. In assessing the cost of discharging the latter the Army had to weigh its investment in the man of two years or more of training against the difficulty of securing a replacement for him which depended on the stage of the war and the theater. It was much more difficult to get replacements for the South Pacific than for the European Theater; and the need for replacements in the European Theater, for instance, was much greater during the Battle of the Bulge than before or after.

A situational analysis also facilitates the evaluation of how differences in assignment and location affected the ability of soldiers to perform and helps in a general way to assess the pressures which may have contributed to their breaking down. But a fuller exploration of performance requires an extension of this line of analysis. Provision must also be made for assessing the nature and severity of the soldier's breakdown, particularly in terms of his further performance. The Army was able to provide considerable medical and other types of assistance to all who broke down but it had to determine rather quickly whether the soldier could be returned to duty, even to a restricted assignment, or whether he should be discharged. And if he were discharged, society had a real interest in whether his ineffectiveness would be of short duration or whether he would remain a charge on the nation for a long time or indefinitely.

The Army not only had to decide whether to retain or discharge a man; if he were to be discharged, it had to decide under which category he was to be separated. Because of the importance of this decision, both to the Army and to the soldier, every man who was discharged prematurely for ineffectiveness had to come before a board of officers which heard expert testimony, reviewed his records, and in most instances interrogated the man himself before reaching a decision. The Army's discharge categories, however, do not permit a differentiation among the men as to their potential usefulness for further military service. Included under the same label were soldiers who were completely inadequate and others who had only minor defects. This is true particularly for the two largest categories; those whom the Army separated for psychoneurosis and those discharged because of inaptitude, who together accounted for almost 80 percent of the total number discharged prematurely for ineffectiveness.

We therefore developed a threefold classification of the men in each Situation. Category 1 included men whose incapacitation at the time of breakdown was "major," which meant that there was convincing evidence that the soldier could not have been of any further use to the military. Category 2 included those with "moderate" incapacitation—men with demonstrable defects which, however, were not so severe as to make them clearly of no further use. Such presumptive usability was, in many instances, contingent upon how much effort the Army was able or willing to make to rehabilitate them and whether it could place them in suitable assignments. Men in Category 3 had only "minor" incapacitation. They were soldiers whom the Army had decided to discharge, not because they had clearly proved themselves to be ineffective but because they might become so or because the Army no longer had need for them in the kinds of jobs they had been doing and the men were unable or unwilling to do anything else; or if the need existed, it was believed that the Army could secure better replacements. This group can be thought of as "logistical losses" since their separation was more a result of the Army's personnel policies than their own deficiencies. More detailed background on these categories is provided in the Appendix.

It should be noted that our placing a man in Category 2 or 3 does not mean that we disagree with the Army's decision to discharge him. Our retrospective evaluation simply implies that on the basis of the soldier's record he was not clearly of no further use to the Army. We have no doubt that the Army was usually right in deciding not to make the investment that would have been required to return many Category 2 men to duty; and we do not even question the Army's judgment in separating many who had only minor incapacitation for further service—Category 3—on the grounds that it did not need them or could get superior replacements. Our purpose in establishing the categories was to evaluate the severity of a man's breakdown and his performance potential.

The 72,700 ineffectives were distributed among the three categories as follows:

Category	*Degree of Incapacitation*	*Weighted Number*	*Percent*
1	Major	34,112	46.9
2	Moderate	22,038	30.3
3	Minor	16,550	22.8
		72,700	100.0

The table shows that about 34,100, or 47 percent, fell into Category 1; that is, they were soldiers with major incapacitation and therefore were adjudged to be of no further use to the Army. Men with moderate incapacitation, Category 2, totaled about 22,000, or 30 percent of the total. About 16,600, or 23 percent, were in Category 3, which means that their incapacitation for further service was adjudged to be minor.

To illustrate the differences in the degree of incapacitation among ineffective soldiers, the following cases have been selected —all from among men who served for less than one year (Situation I):

Major Incapacitation

C.D., a common laborer, had completed the seventh grade and had married at the age of twenty-two shortly before induction. His childhood showed no signs of abnormal behavior. Yet within one month after being assigned to an infantry training battalion, he began acting in a bizarre manner, developed paranoid delusions, and became violent. Hospitalized at once, he was discharged to the custody of his parents with a diagnosis of dementia praecox, hebephrenic type, with paranoid delusions. Some years later he was committed to a state mental institution.

Moderate Incapacitation

D.E. was a high school graduate who at the age of thirty was managing his own grocery store. After induction, he trained with an infantry unit for almost a year during which he received superior ratings before he was given a medical discharge for neuro-circulatory asthenia, severe. Although his symptoms had existed before induction they had not incapacitated him. However, after induction they seemed to bother him considerably. He became fatigued easily, was short of breath, and suffered from pains around his heart. He lost 45 pounds despite a high caloric diet and special vitamins. For a time he was given limited duty, but finally a medical disposition board decided his condition prevented his serving further. His commanding officer spoke highly of him and observed that while he never complained and was rarely on sick call, it was quite apparent that the soldier suffered whenever he exerted himself physically. Following discharge, D.E. returned to running his grocery store and some time later stated that he was again in good health.

Minor Incapacitation

E.F. was a 23-year-old service-station attendant who had had two years of high school and was married. Upon his induction he was assigned to an anti-aircraft training unit. Three weeks after his induction he was hospitalized for acute bronchitis which cleared up after five days. During his illness the medical personnel noted that he appeared to be nervous, and upon questioning him they elicited the information that he had been feeling nervous for several months and that he had a particular fear of hypodermics, doctors and hospitals, and injured people. The staff kept him in the hospital for another five weeks and discharged him for psychoneurosis, mixed type. After discharge E.F. first worked in a steel mill and later as a heavy duty truck driver. In his questionnaire he reported that he had been in good health since his discharge and commented that in the Army he had been very homesick.

We found relatively little difficulty in classifying the cases according to the category scheme. Occasionally we were uncertain about whether a soldier's incapacitation was major or moderate, or moderate or minor. But the number of uncertain cases was not large and in reaching a decision about them we had certain special advantages over the members of an Army Disposition Board. We did not have the man before us and were therefore less likely to respond to his personality and become either unduly sympathetic or harsh. Nor did we need to concern ourselves, as did the Board members, with the impact on others in the unit of a decision to discharge a soldier or not. Furthermore, we were able to establish and hold to a more objective scheme of evaluation since we were able to apply the same criteria to the entire group. Finally, we had more complete information than was available to most Boards.

We added one refinement to the category scheme to facilitate the analysis. We further differentiated the men in Category 1—those with major incapacitation for further military service. There were some men whose records contained clear indications of ineffectiveness prior to their induction which, had they been recognized by the examining officers and acted upon, should have led to their being rejected for military service. For instance, Army regulations provided that no man who had ever had a psychosis should be inducted. Yet a number who had been hospitalized in state mental institutions slipped through the screen. We placed such men, and others like them, in Category 1a, but only when their induction records clearly demonstrated that they should not have been inducted according to the Army's own regulations.

There were many others, however, who had to be discharged after they broke down but whose induction records gave no clear evidence of major defect and they may in fact have actually been free of any serious defect. Yet they responded so acutely to their Army experience that they were of no further value to the military. These men we placed in Category 1b. The following cases illustrate the difference between these two sub-categories, F.G. being an example of Category 1a and G.H. an example of 1b.

Shortly after induction, F.G. began to engage in bizarre behavior such as saluting everyone he met, including civilian workers, and jumping out from behind trash cans to frighten passers-by. When hospitalized, he was found to be suffering from visual and auditory hallucinations and as a result he was later discharged for dementia praecox, hebephrenic type. An investigation of his background revealed that he had never been effective. Raised in extreme poverty on a small, isolated Southern farm and blind in one eye, he had been born club-footed and did not walk until he was seven. He left the fourth grade at age sixteen. Described as a mentally dull person who drank to excess, he was completely unaccustomed to normal social relationships and rarely left his mother's side. Because of his many handicaps, he was indulged and protected by the rest of the family. Several of his many siblings were also abnormal: one brother was a hermit, another mentally deficient, and a third was described as being "off his rocker" ever since he fell into a fire when drunk. According to the neighbors, the entire family has always been considered "rather peculiar." After discharge F.G. returned home where his mother continued to care for him; when she died some years later, a brother took over the responsibility.

After two months service in an Air Corps unit, G.H. was discovered by the Military Police early one morning lying naked in a muddy ditch. When hospitalized, he was found to be very excited, proved difficult to handle, and escaped on one occasion after tearing the screen from his window. He was discharged to the custody of his father with a CDD for psychosis, manic depressive type, manic phase. Since then he has been in and out of several state mental hospitals. Prior to induction at the age of twenty he had given no indication of ineffectiveness. He graduated from high school in the upper fourth of his class and had been business editor of the school paper. For a year and a half he had worked as an apprentice in a caterpillar-tractor factory. Injured in an automobile accident in the spring of 1942, he did little work that summer, but by fall had recovered and enlisted.

We also took special note of certain soldiers who were separated from the Army not because of their incapacity to perform but because the Army had a firm policy which disqualified them for military service. The most important groups were the homosexuals and the enuretics; these we placed in Category 1c. The justification for including this group in Category 1 lies in the fact that had the examining physicians been in a position to evaluate the presence or severity of their condition they would not have been accepted for service according to induction standards. Then there were a number of cases whose ineffectiveness upon later evaluation turned out to have been primarily a result of a physical disability, although they were discharged for psychiatric reasons. Such men were placed in Category 1d, of which H.I. is a good example.

H.I. was discharged at the end of the war with a diagnosis of psychoneurosis, conversion reaction, which was manifested by stomach pains and vomiting. Within two weeks after discharge he was admitted to a VA hospital because of stomach trouble. He was operated upon and found to have had a duodenal ulcer with marked edema and inflammation causing pyloric obstruction. Since then he has been free of his previous symptoms.

The distribution of the 34,112 men with major incapacitation for further service (Category 1) among the four sub-categories that have just been reviewed follows:

	Sub-Category	*Weighted Number*	*Percent*
1a	Men with pre-military indications of ineffectiveness	16,797	49.3
1b	Men with no pre-military indications of ineffectiveness	10,883	31.9
1c	Homosexuals and enuretics	3,182	9.3
1d	Men with major physical disability	3,250	9.5
		34,112	100.0

The foregoing distribution sheds light on two important aspects of ineffectiveness. It permits us to determine the relative importance of those who fell within the special sub-groups. But, more importantly, it emphasizes that about half of all the soldiers who at the time of their breakdown were adjudged to have major incapacitation for further military service should never have been inducted in the first place. Their records contained information about such serious prior incapacity or malperformance that according to Army regulations they were disqualified for service.

While the variability of military stress would have justified using more than four Situations and while the condition of men at the time of breakdown and their potential for further performance could have been refined beyond a threefold gradation, elaboration in either direction would have greatly compounded the difficulties of analysis and particularly of retaining an overall view.

The following figure provides an overview of the entire cohort in terms of the interrelations between the two major dimensions—situational stresses and degree of incapacitation for further military performance.

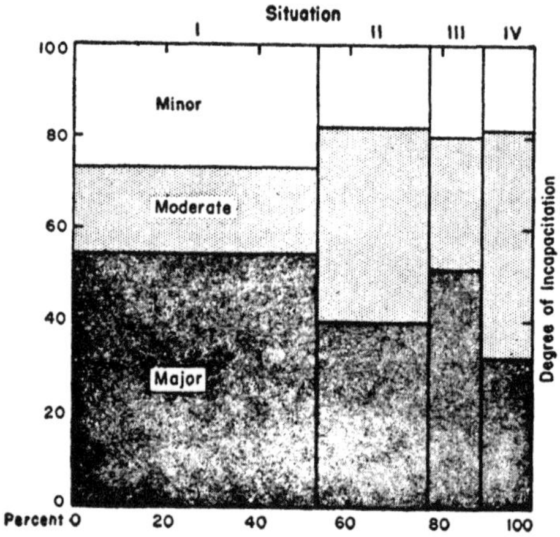

DISTRIBUTION OF COHORT INEFFECTIVES
BY SITUATION AND BY DEGREE OF
INCAPACITATION, IN PERCENT

When the degree of the men's incapacitation for further military service is considered simultaneously with their type of service (Situation), a number of interesting facts become apparent. We have seen earlier that almost half of the entire group manifested such major incapacitation at the time of breakdown that they could offer no further useful service to the Army. But we see now that this was more characteristic of men who broke down early and less of those who had been through combat. Part of the explanation is to be found in the fact already demonstrated that many who broke down early did not belong in the Army in the first place. They had slipped through the screen. While the combat group was exposed to the most severe stress, it shows relatively fewer cases of severe incapacitation. This group was made up of men who had been screened not only at induction but during training in the United States and then again when their units were being readied for overseas shipment. Moreover, those who went through combat only to break later on—and there were many such—were tested anew in each battle so that we can conclude that they represented an inherently stronger group.

The figure also points up the fact that more than 3 out of every 5 men who were discharged with only minor incapacitation are found among those who served for less than a year. The explanation for this is ready at hand. During this period the Army followed an easy discharge policy. The assumption was that it was better to discharge soldiers whose potential performance was doubtful, and in whom there was not yet a substantial investment, and take a chance on getting a better replacement. The more the Army invested in a man, the more reluctant it was to discharge him unless he proved himself to be clearly ineffective. There was one exception. A considerable number of soldiers in Situation IV—Combat—were discharged with only minor incapacitation. This can be explained by the fact that as the war came to the end, the Army's manpower requirements eased greatly and it was again willing to discharge men, particularly those who had seen combat, at the first sign of trouble.

It is more difficult to interpret the intermediate group, men whose incapacitation at the time of breakdown was moderate. They accounted for about a third of the total. Many of these men could have remained on active duty had the Army been willing or able to offer them the help they needed—either treatment at a mental hygiene clinic or an assignment more nearly within the scope of their capabilities. But for a variety of reasons the Army decided not to do so. Sometimes it could not spare the specialist personnel; at other times it had no suitable assignments; and toward the end of the war its manpower requirements were eased.

We classified the cohort sample in terms of the Situation in which men broke down and the degree of their incapacitation for further military service with the aim of giving an over-all view of the types of ineffective soldiers. It may add clarity to the picture if the analysis in terms of Situations and Categories is related to the Army's method of classifying soldiers whom it discharged.

The men in the cohort sample were discharged for the following causes:

Reason for Separation	*Weighted Number*	*Percent*
Psychoneurosis	40,603	55.9
Psychosis	6,620	9.1
Undesirability	5,268	7.2
Inaptitude	20,209	27.8
	72,700	100.0

Somewhat more than half were given medical discharges for psychoneurosis and slightly more than one quarter were discharged administratively for inaptitude. About 1 in 11 was separated because of a psychosis and about 1 in 14 was a behavioral problem and was discharged without honor (blue certificate) for undesirable habits or traits of character.

The degree of incapacitation for further military service, according to our evaluation scheme, of the men in each discharge category is shown in the following table.

The outstanding fact revealed by this table is that the clinical diagnostic categories used by the Army do not by themselves provide a clear indication of the soldier's incapacitation for further

DEGREE OF INCAPACITATION BY REASON FOR SEPARATION, IN PERCENT

REASON FOR SEPARATION	TOTAL	DEGREE OF INCAPACITATION *Major*	*Moderate*	*Minor*
Psychoneurosis	100.0	34.4	44.5	21.1
Psychosis	100.0	95.4	2.0	2.6
Undesirability	100.0	80.5	10.2	9.3
Inaptitude	100.0	47.4	16.3	36.3
Total Cohort	100.0	46.9	30.3	22.8

service. The only exception was the group discharged because of psychosis where, except for a few errors in diagnosis, all who were discharged were clearly no longer of use to the Army. The largest proportion of those separated because of psychoneurosis had a moderate degree of incapacitation for further military service. Nevertheless, a considerable number of these cases fell into the other two categories. It is surprising that such a high proportion of the disciplinary cases were also characterized as having major incapacitation for further service. The inapt group also contained a considerable proportion of men with major incapacitation, but more than half had only moderate or minor incapacitation for further service.

The following table sets out the percentage distribution of the cohort ineffectives by Situation for each reason for separation.

SITUATION BY REASON FOR SEPARATION, IN PERCENT

REASON FOR SEPARATION	TOTAL	SITUATION *I*	*II*	*III*	*IV*
Psychoneurosis	100.0	52.4	20.0	10.4	17.2
Psychosis	100.0	43.5	13.9	31.5	11.1
Undesirability	100.0	37.0	48.2	13.0	1.8
Inaptitude	100.0	60.3	32.9	5.6	1.2
Total Cohort	100.0	52.6	25.1	11.2	11.1

Several significant facts are revealed by this distribution. As could have been anticipated, most of the inapt soldiers were separated relatively early in their military service and certainly before they got overseas. The fact that so small a percentage of soldiers in Situation IV were discharged for undesirability reflected Army policy to avoid disciplining combat veterans who became difficult to manage late in the war, especially if their combat service had been acceptable or good. Ninety-six out of every 100 men in the cohort with combat service were discharged medically, which meant that as veterans they would be more likely to be favorably considered for disability compensation by the Veterans Administration.

The relatively larger number of soldiers who were separated for undesirability in Situation II reflected the Army's policy of giving a man who presented disciplinary problems a second and even a third chance before taking punitive action. The Army was particularly indulgent towards the alcoholic. Moreover, some homosexuals who had slipped past the initial screen were able to meet the strenuous demands of the military environment for a limited time but as the length of their service increased, many were unable to continue or otherwise attracted attention and were discharged as undesirable.

Another point worth noting is the large proportion, nearly 43 percent, of the men who were separated for psychosis who had overseas service. Apparently many of these men who were eventually separated for serious mental disturbance gave indications of their condition only after they had been on active duty for a considerable time. It is of interest in this connection to consider men in the cohort whom we adjudged at breakdown to be severely incapacitated for further service. The following summary table shows, for each reason for separation, the percent of those men who had shown pre-military indications of ineffectiveness.

PRE-MILITARY INDICATIONS OF INEFFECTIVENESS BY REASON FOR SEPARATION

Reason for Separation	*Percent of those with major incapacitation who revealed pre-military indications of ineffectiveness*
Psychoneurosis	26.0
Psychosis	41.2
Undesirability	70.3
Inaptitude	79.1
Total Cohort	49.2

The foregoing suggests that the records of soldiers who were judged to be severely handicapped for further service at discharge and who were discharged as inapt or undesirable gave more evidence of pre-military ineffectiveness than did the records of those who were separated through medical channels. Perhaps the most surprising fact, however, is that the records of only about 4 out of every 10 men separated for psychosis contained indications of any disqualifying characteristics prior to their induction.

The data presented in this chapter support the premise which served as our point of departure: that ineffectiveness in military service cannot be considered a homogeneous phenomenon; that it is, on the contrary, a composite of many facets, reflecting characteristics of the individuals, differences in the degrees of stress to which they were exposed, and policies followed by the organization of which they were a part. These elements cannot be singled out for factorial analysis and expressed quantitatively, but if the entire group is viewed through the double grid of situational and incapacitation categories, many aspects of ineffectiveness can be clearly delineated.

Thus it appears that at the time of their breakdown less than half of all the cohort ineffectives were sufficiently incapacitated that they had to be returned to civilian life. In fact almost 1 out of every 2 of these men should never have been inducted in the first place since their records contained evidence that they fell below the Army's standards of induction.

As to the rest, about 23 percent were adjudged at separation to have had only minor incapacitation for further service and an additional 30 percent were moderately incapacitated. If we estimate, perhaps somewhat arbitrarily, that about half of those with moderate incapacitation could have been rehabilitated and then add this number to those with minor incapacitation, it appears that 40 percent of all the men in our cohort who were separated because of ineffectiveness had potential for further military service. Since the Army took in less qualified men during the cohort period than during the rest of the war, this is a minimum percentage of potential usability and can be safely applied to all Army ineffectives. Inasmuch as the total number of ineffectives during World War II totaled half a million, the number who could have continued to serve had the Army wanted them or had it been willing and able to make certain adjustments to facilitate their doing so was approximately 200,000 men, or the equivalent of over 12 combat divisions, almost one-seventh of the total combat divisions that the United States raised in the war.

Chapter Five: PERFORMANCE OF INEFFECTIVE SOLDIERS

IN DISCHARGING SOLDIERS prior to demobilization the Army took note of differences among them. The vast majority were discharged honorably, indicating the Army's belief that their ineffectiveness did not result from willful action. Those who were judged to be poorly motivated, who appeared to be unwilling to put forth the required effort to meet the demands made on them, or who became disciplinary problems, received a discharge without honor.

In making these distinctions the Army sought to differentiate among men according to the quality of their effort. The Army did take account of a soldier's service prior to his breakdown, but this was primarily for the purpose of gaining additional perspective on whether he had made a serious effort to do his duty or not.

Although considerations of purpose and intent were clearly important in distinguishing between the sick and the delinquent in order to determine the grounds for discharge, they did not provide an adequate basis for delineating the range of differences in the performance of those who were discharged. For a study of performance we must raise a much broader group of questions about the military records of men who were prematurely discharged.

How long did these soldiers serve? Did they serve overseas? Did they serve in combat? We have already answered these questions in part but they require a more detailed study. While some men who served only in the Zone of the Interior made valuable contributions to the war effort, the fact that the enemy had to be defeated overseas meant that the Army's greatest continuing need was for combat soldiers.

A second important criterion of a soldier's effectiveness was the rank which he achieved. While rank was in some measure a function of the length of time that a man served, it also reflected his abilities and leadership potential. During the Army's period of rapid expansion and later when it suffered large combat losses, there was a constant need for men to fill noncommissioned as well as commissioned officer positions.

As we pointed out in *The Lost Divisions*, the grade distribution of all enlisted men for the period 1942 to 1945 showed that about 2 out of every 5 men achieved a noncommissioned rank of corporal or higher. In considering the military effectiveness of the cohort sample as reflected by rank, it will be necessary to differentiate between the highest grade that a soldier achieved during his military service and the rank which he held at separation, since some men who had been advanced in grade were later demoted.

While the length of time that a soldier served, where he served, and the rank which he achieved will provide a rough measure of his effectiveness, there are other indices which will help to round out the evaluation. For instance, how much of a soldier's time was nonproductive in that he was absent without leave, confined to the guardhouse, or in the hospital? In this connection time spent in the hospital is the most revealing index for all except the chronic delinquent. But other indices such as the soldier's efficiency ratings, decorations and awards, and the number and types of courts-martial are relevant. We combined all of these factors into a rating scheme which allows us to estimate a soldier's overall performance up to his breakdown. The method used to develop these performance ratings is described in the Appendix.

The analysis which follows makes use of materials that relate to the soldiers' length of service, their foreign service, their rank, the time that they spent in the hospital and, for those who saw combat, their decorations, and finally our own evaluation of their overall performance prior to breakdown.

LENGTH OF SERVICE

Before a soldier was assigned to overseas duty he normally had completed basic training and usually had gone to a technical school or had had some advanced training or on-the-job training with his unit; if a member of a combat unit he had often participated in divisional training and in maneuvers. Depending on the period of the war and the timing of the next major campaign, such a cycle of training required a minimum of a year and usually a year and a half. Hence, a soldier who served for only a few months or even for a year was not likely to have been of much real value to the Army. But we cannot conclude that all who served longer were. The Army, operating under great pressures, sometimes carried poor soldiers for a long time, a few right up to demobilization. On the other hand we have already had indications that a considerable proportion of those who were discharged early were not truly ineffective. The following table shows the distribution of the entire cohort by months of service.

LENGTH OF SERVICE OF COHORT INEFFECTIVES

Months Completed	*Percent*
0 - 5	22.5
6 - 11	30.4
12 - 17	17.2
18 - 23	6.9
24 - 29	5.9
30 - 35	13.5
36 - 41	3.2
42 - 47	.4
	100.0

Of the 72,700 ineffectives represented by the cohort sample, 38,294, or 53 percent, were discharged in Situation I—before they had served a year. Moreover, 8,752, or 48 percent, of the 18,228 who were separated in Situation II—domestic duty of more than a year—served for less than 15 months and were therefore still likely to be in training at the time of separation. If these 8,752 are added to the 38,294 in Situation I, we see that a total of 47,046, or 65 percent, served for less than 15 months and then only in the Zone of the Interior. The easy discharge policy of the Army, which was not officially reversed until November 1943, was reflected by the number of men released early in Situation II as well as by those released in Situation I. Both of these groups tended to be part of the same pattern.

Length of service is an arbitrary criterion of performance. Yet in view of the time required to train a soldier it is reasonable to contend that men who served for less than a year contributed little to the Army. As the previous table shows, 53 percent of the cohort ineffectives were in this category. On the other hand, men who served for at least a year and a half—30 percent of the cohort—could be presumed to have been of some value to the Army, since during this period Army personnel policy permitted and good management demanded the discharge of men who were clearly deficient. For those who served at least a year but less than a year and a half, length of service alone is not an adequate criterion for evaluating their usefulness.

Since we started with a definition of ineffective soldiers as men separated prior to demobilization the reader may wonder how it happened that some of this group served until late in 1945, or even into 1946. The explanation of this apparent anomaly is twofold: first, some men who had not accrued sufficient points for early demobilization became ineffective after the fighting had ceased; secondly, and more typically, many men were, at war's end, already on the route to discharge through medical or administrative channels because they had proved to be in one way or another ineffective. Since this route was, as we shall see, sometimes quite prolonged, especially for men who were initially hospitalized overseas, some few of the cohort group were not separated until after V-J Day.

More significant than the general distribution are differences in the proportions of men in each Situation that served at least 18 months.

LENGTH OF SERVICE BY SITUATION, IN PERCENT

	SITUATION		
MONTHS COMPLETED	*II*	*III*	*IV*
Less than 18	60.0	19.4	2.8
18 - 23	18.2	18.1	2.7
24 - 29	3.7	17.7	26.8
30 - 35	14.0	37.5	52.3
36 and over	4.1	7.3	15.4
	100.0	100.0	100.0

The foregoing reveals that while 40 percent of the men discharged in Situation II served 18 months or more, this was true of more than 80 percent in Situation III and 97 percent in Situation IV. Closer inspection shows that of those in Situation II who served 18 months or more, one large group went out before completing 2 years of service, while the other large group served between 2½ to 3 years. Of the men in Situation III the greatest number served between 2½ to 3 years. For men in Situation IV the average length of service was even longer than for men in Situation III. Men entering the Army during the cohort period and serving 30 to 35 months would have been separated between March and November 1945; hence, their separation virtually coincided with the end of hostilities.

The explanation of these differences reflects three circumstances. First, as we noted in the last chapter, the Army conducted a secondary screening of men whom it sent overseas. They were usually the more capable soldiers and we would expect them to have served longer—even those who eventually proved ineffective. Secondly, the Army's logistical position played a role in the large number of discharges of Zone of the Interior men with between 1½ to 2 years service. With most of the divisions moving overseas, the Army did not require so many in housekeeping positions at home and let many marginal soldiers go. In contrast, once it transported a man overseas, it usually did not want to send him back unless he was clearly a liability. It had made a sizable training investment in him and shipping was a serious bottleneck. Moreover, for every soldier returned home a replacement had to be sent to the theater of war; otherwise units would have to operate understrength. As to the men who had been in combat (Situation IV), their breakdown came late, since it was coincidental with, or followed upon, their being in combat, and the majority did not fight until the campaigns of 1944. Also all men discharged in Situation IV spent some time in the hospital, much of which was immediately prior to discharge.

A further refinement of the length of service criterion is to consider those who served overseas and note the amount of time which they spent outside of the United States. The following table gives the length of overseas service for men in Situations III (noncombat) and IV (combat).

LENGTH OF OVERSEAS SERVICE BY SITUATION, IN PERCENT

	SITUATION	
MONTHS COMPLETED	*III*	*IV*
0-5	17.7	9.8
6-11	35.1	38.6
12-17	26.8	34.7
18-23	15.3	13.5
24 and over	5.1	3.4
	100.0	100.0

On the average, ineffective soldiers in Situation III spent 46 percent of their Army service overseas; those in Situation IV, 40 percent. Furthermore, approximately half the soldiers in these two Situations spent a year or more overseas. Relatively few failed during their first six months of overseas service. Even allowing for the unwillingness of commanders to send men home for fear that they would not receive replacements, these figures suggest that a considerable proportion of soldiers serving overseas who eventually broke down and had to be prematurely discharged performed adequately for considerable periods of time.

The length of time an ineffective soldier served before being discharged depended upon many factors—the stage of the war, the Army's overall manpower requirements at the time, the specific personnel policies then in effect, and the soldier's reactions to stress.

Some men were not able to perform within the Army at all and had to be discharged soon after induction. Other were able to meet the demands which were made on them but only at increasing cost. Each month the pressure became greater, for it was cumulative.

The steady increase of ineffectives in Situations I and II who had more than a minor incapacitation for further military service as their length of service increased suggests that time alone, even in the Zone of the Interior, operated, up to a point, as a type of stress that contributed to the soldier's breakdown. If we disregard for the moment the men who should not have been in the Army in the first place and those who revealed special medical or administrative

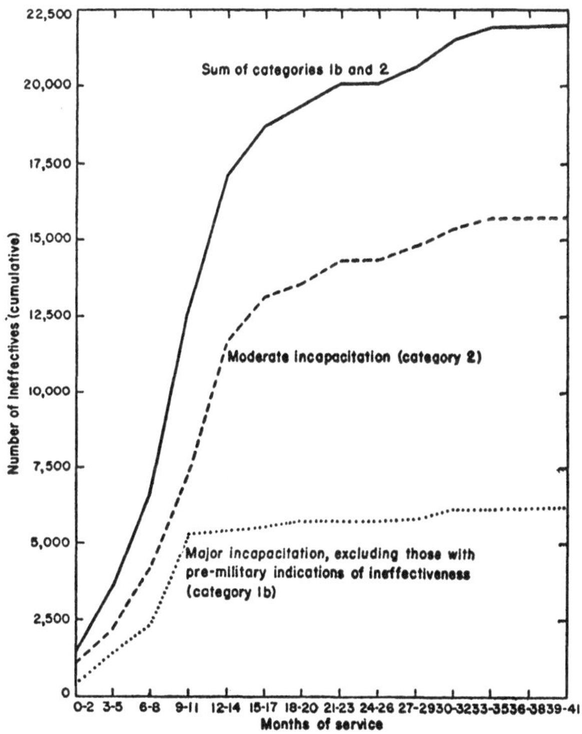

CUMULATIVE NUMBER OF INEFFECTIVES SERVING STATED NUMBER OF MONTHS OR LESS, ZONE OF INTERIOR DUTY ONLY (SITUATIONS I AND II), BY DEGREE OF INCAPACITATION

defects which necessitated their discharge, and consider only those whose ineffectiveness stemmed from moderate or serious psychiatric disabilities, we find a sharp rise in the number of soldiers who became ineffective as their length of service in the Army increased. The rate of increase, as shown in the accompanying figure, was very sharp up to 18 months, after which it became very modest.

A hypothesis that longer service alone constituted a heightened stress to which all soldiers reacted with increasingly severe incapacitation was not borne out by the data. Of the men who served only in the Zone of the Interior, virtually all who were properly screened and whom we classified as being severely incapacitated for further service broke down early and were discharged within their first year. The figure shows that there were two distinct reactions to length of service. Some men broke early. For the most part they showed severe incapacitation for further military service, reflecting serious defects within themselves or a heightened reaction to the new environment in which they found themselves. Most of the others were able to absorb the initial shocks of military life, but as time lengthened, they began to show wear and tear until they eventually broke down. But this group, in contrast to those who broke early, tended to be less severely incapacitated for further military service at the time of their breakdown.

A related question concerns the men who served overseas: did their total length of service or total length of overseas service contribute specifically to their breakdown? The data suggest such a relationship, but they must be interpreted with caution for they do not enable us to differentiate between the factor of time alone and the specific stresses that the men may have encountered. The following case records point to the difficulty of differentiating length of service from other factors in breakdown.

I.J., an Air Corps soldier, was shipped overseas early in November 1942, just two months after he enlisted. After serving about a year at Wheeler Field in Hawaii he was transferred to the South Pacific. His job was to drive a gasoline service truck. After about a year on Canton Island he began to grow increasingly nervous, suffered from frequent headaches and was unable to sleep. Not ill enough to be discharged, he was returned to Hawaii where he was again assigned to truck driving. He remained anxious (he had now been overseas nearly 2½ years) and was worried about his mother who was in poor health, and one day in his own words, "his nerves snapped" when a Hawaiian driver suddenly pulled in front of his truck. After this he began to have difficulty driving and soon could not drive at all. His anxiety symptoms grew worse and he was sent back to the United States where he was discharged with a diagnosis of psychoneurosis, anxiety reaction, severe.

J.K. spent 36 months in the Army, serving overseas as an infantryman. He participated in the Normandy invasion. He performed satisfactorily through 80 days of combat. Then he was injured by the blast concussion of an artillery shell. He regained consciousness two days later in a field hospital, but while in the hospital he developed a severe anxiety reaction, with persistent headaches, battle nightmares, and back pain. After he had been injured, which occurred after he had been overseas for a little more than a year, he was no longer able to perform effectively. He was returned to the United States and discharged for psychoneurosis.

K.L. was sent overseas as a cook in November 1943. En route in the Pacific his ship was torpedoed, and while in the water he saw a close friend washed away. He himself was rescued a day later but this experience, which in itself was traumatic, was intensified for him since he could not swim and had an intense fear of water. Although his military service had been satisfactory up to this point he was no longer able to function effectively; after two months hospitalization overseas he was returned to the States where further hospitalization failed to help him. He was therefore discharged for psychoneurosis.

While the length of time that I.J. had to spend overseas appears to have been connected with his breakdown, and while the number of days that J.K. had been in combat may have contributed to his acute response to the concussion which he suffered, K.L.'s case makes it clear that quite specific orders of stress independent of the time factor may be the crucial determinant in a soldier's breakdown.

Since less than 1 in 3 of all the cohort ineffectives served for 18 months or more the length of service criterion indicates that many in the ineffective group failed to remain in the Army long enough to have been useful. Of those who did, the length of time that they served, and particularly the length of their service overseas, is presumptive evidence that they represented a different group of soldiers—they were able to cope with their assignments for a considerable time before they broke down.

HIGHEST GRADE

As we pointed out earlier, the Army had to promote millions of men quickly to officer and noncommissioned officer ranks to meet its very large requirements. While the Army, like most large organizations, accepted the principle of seniority, it did within limits seek to select the more capable for promotion. Hence, one important index of a soldier's performance is the grade which he was able to achieve prior to separation.

The following table sets out the highest enlisted grades held by men in the cohort sample and in each of the four Situations.

HIGHEST ENLISTED GRADE HELD BY SITUATION, IN PERCENT

GRADE	TOTAL COHORT	SITUATION *I*	*II*	*III*	*IV*
Top Three NCO Grades	1.9	–	1.5	4.6	9.0
Sergeant and T/4	5.6	3.0	6.9	12.1	8.7
Corporal and T/5	9.6	4.7	13.9	19.4	13.7
Private first class	17.1	9.1	19.6	21.4	45.4
Private	65.8	83.2	58.1	42.5	23.2
	100.0	100.0	100.0	100.0	100.0

This distribution should be considered in light of similar data for the Army as a whole. As we stated in *The Lost Divisions*, during the period 1942-1945, approximately 60 percent of all enlisted men did not advance beyond private first class; 18 percent became corporals; almost 12 percent became sergeants or technicians fourth grade; and over 9 percent were in the top three grades. This means that a considerably smaller proportion of the cohort sample were promoted than of the Army as a whole. Nor is this surprising since such a high percentage of the cohort served for less than a year. It is worth noting, however, that even among the men in Situation I, more than one-sixth had been promoted at least once. On the other hand, the distribution of rank among the men in Situation IV is quite similar to that of the Army as a whole.

Although the importance of seniority in promotion is suggested by the grade distribution among the four Situations, it was not the only factor, for, as we have seen, the soldiers who served overseas had actually been screened several times. Yet the noticeably higher grade structure in Situation II as compared to Situation I reflects in large measure the heavy reliance that the Army placed on length of service as a key factor in promotion—at least in the lower ranks.

More than 2 out of every 3 men in Situation I whom the Army promoted to corporal or sergeant were found at the time of breakdown to be severely incapacitated for further service. However, none of their records contained pre-military indications which would have forewarned the Army of their psychological vulnerability. As the accompanying table indicates, in the other Situations a much smaller percentage of those who had been promoted to

INEFFECTIVE SOLDIERS PROMOTED TO CORPORAL OR HIGHER BY SITUATION

SITUATION	TOTAL	WITH MAJOR INCAPACITATION *Number*	*Percent*
I	2,947	2,117	72
II	4,051	1,573	39
III	2,931	1,488	51
IV	2,527	567	22

corporal or higher were severely incapacitated for further service.

These figures suggest that when commanding officers were able to observe their men for a longer time they were more likely to make successful selections for promotion. But another factor may help to explain the improvement in the selection process over time. The Army's repeated screening of those whom it sent overseas implies that they probably represented a more capable group from which to select men for promotion.

In the event that a soldier who was promoted could not handle his new responsibilities or if he was guilty of infractions of discipline, his officers did not hesitate to demote him. The following table shows the distribution of the entire cohort in terms of highest rank ever held and the rank held at separation.

HIGHEST AND LAST ENLISTED GRADES HELD, IN PERCENT

Grade	*Highest Held*	*At Separation*
Top Three NCO Grade	1.9	1.4
Sergeant and T/4	5.6	4.2
Corporal and T/5	9.6	6.3
Private, first class	17.1	14.5
Private	65.8	73.6
	100.0	100.0

Just under a third (31.7 percent) of the men who had been promoted to corporal or higher were reduced in rank at some time prior to their separation. Of the 12,500 who had been promoted to corporal or higher, the records of only about 1,000 gave pre-military indications of ineffectiveness. Of the 8,600 who still held a higher rank at separation, the records of only 200 had such pre-military indications. We saw in the preceding chapter that 16,800 of the cohort were not only severely incapacitated for further military service but also had pre-military indications of their ineffectiveness in their records. That only 200 of these men were separated with the grade of corporal or higher speaks well of the Army's screening for promotion during the war.

DECORATIONS AND AWARDS

One further indication of level of performance can be found in the decorations and awards earned by these soldiers. Of the 8,057 cohort ineffectives who served in combat, 4,500 or 56 percent were awarded the Bronze Star, Air Medal, Distinguished Flying Cross, or Silver Star. The following table shows the number of men in Situation IV who received at least one of each award:

Silver Star	29
Distinguished Flying Cross	174
Air Medal	558
Bronze Star	3,933

The total number of awards received by these "ineffective" soldiers exceeds the foregoing total since some men received the same award more than once for outstanding performance at different times. For example, of those who received the Air Medal more than two-thirds earned at least two Air Medals and a sixth earned at least five. Moreover, all who received DFC's were also awarded two or more Air Medals and about a third held two DFC's. Most of the men who were awarded or were eligible for the Bronze Star had also received the Combat Infantry or Medical Badge.

Although it is not directly related to their performance as individuals, it is interesting to observe that these men served where they were needed. Virtually all of these men received at least one Bronze Service Star attesting to their participation in a particular military campaign and two-thirds received at least two stars. Almost one-third of this group had been wounded in combat and had received the Purple Heart.

HOSPITALIZATION

The analysis up to this point has assumed that there is a connection between the length of time that a man spends in the Army and the value of his performance. But a distinction must be made between the total time that a soldier served and his days of effective duty. Among the most important deductions that must be made from total time served is the time that a soldier spent in the hospital. Not only was he of no use to his unit when hospitalized but the Army had to provide people to take care of him—instead of being an asset, he was a liability to the war effort.

The cohort ineffectives spent a total of 5,768,000 days in the hospital. The mean hospitalization for the 72,700 men in the cohort was 79 days. The mean length of service for the entire group was 15 months. This means that on the average about 18 percent of their total Army service was spent in the hospital. As one would expect, the longer a man served, the more were his days of hospitalization, especially if he participated in combat. The mean number of hospital days per man in each Situation were:

Situation	I	II	III	IV
Hospital days	42	65	162	207

In Situation I approximately 1 out of every 5 men was never hospitalized and in Situation II this was true for about 1 out of every 8 men. But almost all, 99.5 percent, of the men who served overseas had at least one period of hospitalization and the average number of admissions per man was nearly three.

There were striking differences also in the average length of the hospital stay of men who served only in the Zone of the Interior and those who went overseas. In Situations I and II the average stay was respectively 28 and 27 days while in Situation III it rose to 55 days, and in Situation IV to 75 days. The much longer hospitalization for the overseas group was primarily due to the fact that those who were not returned to duty overseas after being hospitalized remained in the hospital chain during their return to the United States and in most instances until they were separated from the service.

Of the men who were hospitalized, those who were adjudged to be moderately incapacitated for further duty had a noticeably higher average number of days of hospitalization than did those with either major or minor incapacitation:

Degree of incapacitation	Major	Moderate	Minor
Hospital days	88	112	70

Men with moderate incapacitation who were hospitalized were not hospitalized much more often than men with either major or minor incapacitation. The explanation for their longer hospital stay must be sought in the difficulties that the doctors found in deciding whether to return them to duty or to discharge them. Many of those with minor incapacitation were sent to the hospital only for processing in connection with their discharge. Those with major incapacitation usually presented no serious problems of diagnosis or evaluation. Men with moderate incapacitation, however, required more careful study. Frequently, they were put through a series of medical tests to discover, or to rule out, physical causes for their incapacitating symptoms. In many cases not only was an accurate diagnosis difficult but the medical officers needed time to reach a decision whether or not it was worthwhile to send such men back to duty.

The considerable length of time that men spent in hospitals requires that this factor be weighed in reaching an overall evaluation of a soldier's performance, and we did take it into account in developing our performance ratings.

MILITARY PERFORMANCE RATING UP TO BREAKDOWN

We assessed the military performance of all of the cohort ineffectives up to their "breakdown" in terms of the criteria set out in the Appendix. This was an objective evaluation based on clear-cut criteria. Because of the limitations in the original data, we determined upon a limited number of criteria and did not attempt refinements. The percentage distribution of the entire cohort sample according to our evaluation of their military performance prior to breakdown was:

Good	8.7
Acceptable	56.2
Poor	26.5
Not rated	8.6
	100.0

The not rated group consists only of certain men in Situation I. If a man's total military service was less than 3 months or if he was on a duty assignment prior to breakdown for less than 6 weeks, he was not rated. However, some indication of the quality of performance of the non-rated group is given by the fact that at the time of separation 3,600 of these 6,200 were considered to have major incapacitation and another 1,000 were moderately incapacitated for further service. Thus at least half, and probably three-quarters, of the non-rated were really poor soldiers. But all the non-rated were a net loss to the Army.

Taking the foregoing into account the table shows that up to the point of breakdown 2 out of every 3 men had performed acceptably or better; 1 out of 3 had not. The following table sets out the performance rating for men in each of the four Situations.

MILITARY PERFORMANCE RATING BY SITUATION, IN PERCENT

MILITARY PERFORMANCE RATING	SITUATIONS *I*	*II*	*III*	*IV*
Good	3.9	7.8	19.6	22.5
Acceptable	54.9	49.8	61.8	71.6
Poor	24.9	42.4	18.6	5.9
Not rated	16.3	–	–	–
	100.0	100.0	100.0	100.0

The fact that the highest proportion of men who were rated poor were in Situation II can be explained by the Army's policy to give men with certain behavior problems, such as alcoholism, several chances to reform before separating them. The fact that most of the men who served overseas were either acceptable or good reflects primarily their more careful selection. The fact that approximately 7 out of every 8 men in the cohort sample who served overseas performed in an acceptable or good manner is highly significant. It will be recalled that while the overseas group accounted for only 22 percent of our cohort ineffectives, 42 percent of the half million Army ineffectives had overseas service. This means that probably 185,000 men with overseas service in World War II who were prematurely separated for mental, emotional, or behavioral reasons had at least an acceptable, if not better, performance record up to the time of their breakdown.

INTERPRETATION

The figures which have been presented in this chapter covering the record of soldiers prior to their breakdown underscore the care that must be taken to distinguish among levels of performance and to avoid blanket judgments. While it is true that all of the soldiers in the cohort were ineffective in the sense that they were prematurely discharged (a term which applies alike to men who never did a day's effective duty and to men who served for three years and were awarded several decorations), this is of little value except as a point of departure.

Running through the figures which have been presented are three separate yet related aspects of performance: How long did these men serve? What was the level of their performance prior to breakdown? What was their potential for further service at the time of their breakdown? If all the men had served for less than a year and if they all had been adjudged at that time to be severely incapacitated for further service, then the conclusion would be inescapable that the entire group represented simply a net loss to the Army.

But we found that the problem was much more complicated. In the first place about half of the group served for more than a year and about 30 percent served for more than 18 months. A year and a half of military service is long enough to imply that a man was probably of some value to the Army.

Next, of all the men who served, only about 1 in every 3 performed poorly prior to breakdown. All of the others had either an acceptable or good performance record. The record of men who served overseas was particularly noteworthy since only 1 out of 8 was rated as poor.

What of their potential for further service? At the time of their breakdown less than half were severely incapacitated for further service. We found 2 out of 3 men with acceptable performance records and more than half of those with good records had only minor or moderate incapacitation. The Army could have secured more service from most of them but decided that it did not need them. A high proportion of those with poor performance ratings failed within the first 15 months of service—about 3 out of every 4. Concluding that many could never be turned into effective soldiers, the Army sought to cut its losses by discharging them before rather than after it had made a major investment in them. However, about half of those with a poor performance rating should never have been inducted into the Army since they were below prevailing standards for induction.

This chapter has presented several different ways of evaluating military performance. To further understand the factors which determine how various groups of soldiers performed, it will be necessary to study their background characteristics prior to induction and how the Army managed them after they came on active duty.

Chapter Six: BACKGROUND CHARACTERISTICS

ONE OF THE ARMY's basic policies during World War II was to reject all men considered to have defects that might interfere with their performing satisfactorily as soldiers. The War Department's Mobilization Regulations (MR 1-9) were specifically formulated to this end. The screening procedures kept out large numbers with varying orders of defects; nevertheless large numbers who were accepted later became ineffective. Various theories have been advanced to explain this unanticipated development.

A common explanation of why younger men failed to adjust to military service was their lack of experience in civilian life with the discipline of holding a job. Because of the unemployment of the 1930s many young people had never had a steady job and therefore had never learned how to integrate themselves into a group or how to follow directions.

Another explanation cited the home as the source of difficulty. Many recruits had never had to assume responsibilities before. Their parents had done everything for them and had made only minimal demands on them. When the members of this "new generation" were put into a demanding situation such as basic training, they were unable to meet it.

Another theory was that some soldiers failed because their approach to life was to sit by and do as little as possible. Blame was placed on the mores of urban life which bred the "city slicker." But when the Army discharged young men from rural areas, the explanation was offered that men brought up on the periphery of an industrial civilization could not adjust to the complexities of a modern technological system operating under pressure of time. Some of these men had never slept in a regular bed nor had used modern bath facilities; their diet had been restricted to a few staples; they had forgotten, if they ever knew, how to read or count.

While many apparently failed because of their educational and cultural deprivation, there were ineffective soldiers who seem to have had too much education. It was argued that such young men broke down because they had been overexposed to books and ideas and had been too sheltered from the world of reality. As a result they had lost their ability to adjust.

The ineffective performance of single men was explained by their having no family ties and therefore being unable to appreciate sufficiently the threat that the Nazis and the Japanese represented to our way of life. But when married men also proved ineffective, the contrary explanation was advanced, namely, that they were more worried about their wives and children than they were about the outcome of the war.

When Negroes proved ineffective, it was contended that World War I had proved conclusively that they could not fight. But considerable evidence accumulated during World War II to prove that a major cause for their ineffectiveness, especially among the better educated, was their resentment and frustration at not being permitted to join a combat unit and at being treated according to the color of their skin rather than in terms of their ability.

The foregoing explanations have been reviewed to remind the reader how widespread the practice has been both during and since the war to seek the cause of military ineffectiveness in the background of the soldiers who broke down in the service. But when ineffective performance is explained at once in terms of men being too young or too old, too poorly or too well educated, too dependent on or too independent of family ties, too urbanized or too rural, no reliance can be placed on the conclusions unless the specific factors can be given quantitative weights. The challenge which we face is to see whether we can uncover valid differences between effective and ineffective soldiers in terms of their characteristics and backgrounds.

In the companion volume, *The Lost Divisions*, a first attempt was made to weigh the role in military ineffectiveness of such specific factors as age, marital status, education, and race. We stated in the chapter on "Civilian Background and Military Performance," that we found that the older a man, the more likely it was that he would be ineffective; that the poorly educated and those with broken marriages accounted for a disproportionate number of ineffective soldiers; and that Negroes, in large part because of their poorer educational background, were heavily represented among the ineffectives. Yet these relationships remained in most instances ambiguous or blurred because we could not take into account in a gross statistical analysis the wide range in the degree of ineffectiveness and the complex factors which may have contributed to the breakdown of different soldiers. We are now in a position to explore these relationships with greater precision by analyzing the demographic characteristics of the soldiers in our cohort in terms of the Situation in which they broke down, the degree of their incapacitation for further service, and their performance in the Army up to the time of their breakdown.

Men suffering from physical defects are likely to account for the highest proportion of all ineffectives. Since physical defects uncomplicated by emotional or mental handicaps fall outside of this study, the next logical place to begin the consideration of individual factors in ineffectiveness is with age.

AGE

Draft legislation is always written in terms of age limits because the very young and the old are not suitable for military service. The Armed Forces generally prefer men between the ages of seventeen and twenty-six because they have more stamina, they are easier to train, and they are more willing to assume risks, but in a major war this group alone will not provide adequate manpower.

In World War II seventeen-year-olds could enlist but the lowest age at which men were drafted was eighteen, and it was not until late 1942 that men below twenty were inducted. The public has long felt that married men, and particularly fathers, should be drafted last, and therefore very few fathers were drafted until 1943, when manpower pressures required their service.

The following table provides a comparison between the age distribution of the cohort ineffectives and the age distribution of all men who came on active duty during the last four months of 1942.

AGE AT ENTRY, TOTAL COHORT INTAKE AND COHORT INEFFECTIVES, IN PERCENT

Age At Entry	*Total Cohort Intake*	*Cohort Ineffectives*
18 - 22	47.2	43.5
23 - 27	19.0	21.3
28 - 32	12.7	18.8
33 - 37	8.9	12.6
38 and older	12.2	3.8
	100.0	100.0

The table shows that just under 2 out of every 3 men who entered the Army during the cohort period fell within the prime age groups—eighteen to twenty-seven. Thus about 1 out of every 3 was somewhat handicapped if the Army was right in its belief that older men had more difficulties in adjusting to military life, and for the 1 out of every 5 who was thirty-three or older, age was more likely to be a significant barrier to adjustment. No special attention need be paid to the group who were thirty-eight or older because the Army had begun to discharge these men on grounds of age alone, which explains in large part why proportionately much fewer of this age group are found among the ineffectives. A residual group who had not been released through administrative channels and who proved ineffective were separated through medical channels and therefore fell within our sample. The proportion of ineffectives in the age group thirty-three to thirty-seven is undoubtedly understated. We know from other studies that as men get older they are more likely to suffer from physical conditions which are disabling. Many who were discharged on physical grounds would have probably otherwise been separated in the categories of ineffectiveness used in this study.

Even apart from the oldest group, the most significant fact is the higher proportion of ineffectives in the other older age groups. This is demonstrated in the following table which gives the rate of separation for ineffectiveness by age group.

RATES OF SEPARATION FOR INEFFECTIVENESS BY AGE, WITH A DISTRIBUTION OF INEFFECTIVES IN EACH AGE GROUP BY SITUATION, IN PERCENT

AGE AT ENTRY	RATE OF SEPARATION PER 1,000 ACCESSIONS, SEPT.-DEC. 1942	PERCENT DISTRIBUTION OF INEFFECTIVES WITHIN EACH AGE GROUP BY SITUATION				
		TOTAL	*I*	*II*	*III*	*IV*
18 - 22	37.9	100.0	45.2	25.2	14.0	15.6
23 - 27	46.2	100.0	52.0	26.9	12.3	8.8
28 - 32	61.4	100.0	53.2	29.3	7.7	9.8
33 - 37	58.3	100.0	70.7	19.8	5.0	4.5
38 and older	12.7	100.0	79.3	10.3	10.4	—
All ages	41.2	100.0	52.6	25.1	11.2	11.1

The separation rate increases steadily with age and is more than half again as great for men above twenty-eight as it is in the youngest age group. But it is the situational breakdown which allows us to get a clearer picture of the conditions under which age is most significant in performance. Aside from the fact that such a high proportion of the thirty-three to thirty-seven group was separated early, that is, within the first year, the table also shows that age was important only among those who never served overseas. Among those who served overseas, the youngest age group contributed the larger proportion of ineffectives. This does not mean necessarily that younger people are more strongly affected by the demands of overseas service, including combat. It more probably reflects the differential effect of the secondary screening of men who were sent overseas: proportionately fewer older men were sent overseas, particularly in combat units, and the older men who passed the screen were better equipped, physically and emotionally, than the ones who were left behind. The Army's preference for filling combat units with young men is demonstrated by the following table which shows the age distribution of our cases within each Situation.

AGE AT ENTRY BY SITUATION, IN PERCENT

	SITUATION			
AGE AT ENTRY	*I*	*II*	*III*	*IV*
18 - 22	37.4	43.6	54.4	61.2
23 - 27	21.0	22.8	23.5	17.0
28 - 32	19.0	22.0	13.0	16.6
33 - 37	16.9	10.0	5.6	5.2
38 and older	5.7	1.6	3.5	–
	100.0	100.0	100.0	100.0

Military ineffectiveness among overseas troops was concentrated among younger men—not only because they accounted for the vast majority of all troops assigned to overseas units but also because they had not been so carefully screened as the older men. It is questionable to assume on a priori grounds that older men in arduous assignments would have a lower rate of breakdown than younger men, and our data surely do not justify such a conclusion.

The question can be raised whether the higher separation rates among older men who served only in the Zone of the Interior was due to their more severe incapacitation for further military duty or whether it merely reflected the Army's conviction that older men would eventually prove ineffective and that it was therefore desirable to discharge them early. The table below gives the distribution by degree of incapacitation for each age group within Situation I, where the age factor loomed most significant.

DEGREE OF INCAPACITATION BY AGE AT ENTRY, SITUATION I, IN PERCENT

AGE AT ENTRY	TOTAL	DEGREE OF INCAPACITATION *Major*	*Moderate*	*Minor*
18 - 22	100.0	54.6	12.1	33.3
23 - 27	100.0	45.5	33.4	21.1
28 - 32	100.0	54.7	24.0	21.3
33 - 37	100.0	52.9	13.5	33.6
38 and older	100.0	88.1	11.9	–
All ages	100.0	54.3	19.1	26.6

Again disregarding those above thirty-eight, there is no increase in the number of men with major incapacitation from one age group to the next. The table does reveal that in the youngest and oldest age groups proportionately more men were discharged with minor incapacitation than in the intermediary age groups. The inference to be drawn from these figures is that the higher rate of discharge for older soldiers can be largely attributed to the Army's unwillingness to keep them even though they were only slightly incapacitated for further service.

Younger soldiers tended to perform better up to the time of breakdown than did older soldiers. The following table gives the distribution of military performance ratings for each age group.

MILITARY PERFORMANCE RATING BY AGE AT ENTRY, IN PERCENT

AGE AT ENTRY	TOTAL	MILITARY PERFORMANCE RATING *Good*	*Acceptable*	*Poor*	*Not Rated*
18 - 22	100.0	8.1	64.4	17.6	9.9
23 - 27	100.0	7.6	53.8	32.6	6.0
28 - 32	100.0	15.0	47.0	32.7	5.3
33 - 37	100.0	4.2	57.9	36.6	1.3
38 and older	100.0	4.9	16.7	29.2	49.2
All ages	100.0	8.7	56.2	26.5	8.6

The group eighteen to twenty-two years of age was the largest group of ineffectives and comprised 43 percent of the total. Approximately three-fourths, 72.5 percent, of this age group performed acceptably or better up to breakdown.

Nearly one-tenth of the eighteen- to twenty-two-year-old group and almost half of the oldest group were not rated—indicating that they had less than 90 days service or less than six weeks duty prior to breakdown. One group was composed of immature youngsters, away from home for the first time in their lives, who broke very early. The other were older men whose multiple deficiencies and inability to adapt to a new environment became apparent during their first weeks of basic training. Further evidence of the validity of the Army's insistence on young men for combat assignments is the finding that while a quarter of the older men over thirty-two exposed to combat had a poor military performance rating only about 5 percent of the younger men were rated "poor."

The foregoing analysis generally confirms the findings in *The Lost Divisions* that age is definitely a factor which contributes to ineffectiveness. However, as noted earlier in this chapter, it was not so in the case of men who served overseas. This means that if older people are selected carefully so as to eliminate those with hidden defects, their performance, even under the stress of combat, is likely to be as good as that of younger people. But in the absence of careful rescreening the rate of ineffectiveness will increase markedly with age.

EDUCATION

As we indicated earlier, our analysis in *The Lost Divisions* of the total number of ineffectives in World War II revealed that the rate of ineffectiveness among men with a grammar school education or less was over two and a half times the rate among the better educated. The poorly educated were disproportionately represented, even among soldiers separated because of psychoneuroses and psychoses. We noted in that context that 122,000 were separated on the ground that they were inapt, which often meant that their inadequate educational background made it impossible for them to meet the tasks that the Army set them.

We can now analyze with greater precision the relationship between education and ineffectiveness, and can consider individuals without any or with only minimal schooling as well as those with varying amounts of education.

The distribution of the cohort ineffectives and of all the men entering the Army in the cohort period according to their educational background is presented below.

EDUCATIONAL LEVEL ACHIEVED, TOTAL COHORT INTAKE AND COHORT INEFFECTIVES, IN PERCENT

Educational Level Achieved	*Total Cohort Intake*	*Cohort Ineffectives*
Grammar school or less	37.3	59.9
Some high school	25.8	21.5
High school graduation	23.9	14.2
Some college	13.0	4.4
	100.0	100.0

This table indicates that the ineffective group was composed of a much higher percentage of soldiers with only a grammar school education or less and that it contained a noticeably smaller proportion than the total cohort of high school graduates and men with at least some college education.

These same facts can be expressed even more clearly in the form of rates of separation for ineffectiveness per 1,000 accessions. The following table gives these rates for men of each major educational level and shows the percent distribution of ineffectives in each educational group by Situation.

RATES OF SEPARATION FOR INEFFECTIVENESS BY EDUCATIONAL LEVEL ACHIEVED, WITH A DISTRIBUTION IN EACH EDUCATION GROUP BY SITUATION, IN PERCENT

EDUCATIONAL LEVEL ACHIEVED	RATE OF SEPARATION PER 1,000 ACCESSIONS, SEPT.-DEC. 1942	PERCENT DISTRIBUTION OF INEFFECTIVES WITHIN EACH EDUCATION GROUP BY SITUATION				
		TOTAL	*I*	*II*	*III*	*IV*
Grammar school or less	66.2	100.0	55.8	27.1	9.6	7.5
More than grammar school	26.3	100.0	48.1	22.0	13.5	16.4
Some high school	34.2	100.0	41.7	27.2	14.9	16.2
High school graduation	24.5	100.0	50.1	17.3	12.4	20.2
Some college	14.0	100.0	72.0	12.3	10.4	5.3
Total Cohort	41.2	100.0	52.6	25.1	11.2	11.1

Soldiers who had attended only grammar school had separation rates more than two and a half times as high as those with more education (66 : 26), and compared to those with at least some college education their separation rate was almost five times as high (66 : 14). These data understate the relationship between education and performance. Not only did the better educated group produce proportionately fewer ineffectives than the poorly educated—they also were the group from which most officers were selected. Although being commissioned does not automatically make a soldier "effective," there is no question that most officers proved effective and performed at higher levels of responsibility. Consequently, the better educated group definitely out-performed the poorly educated soldiers—on one hand producing fewer ineffectives and on the other producing more leaders.

The preceding table provides further understanding of the relation between a man's educational background and his failure in the Army. The data indicate that a disproportionately high number of soldiers in two educational groups were separated in the first year: almost three-quarters of those with some college education and more than half of those with only grammar school. A relatively high proportion of men in the two intermediary educational groups did not become ineffective until they had served overseas or had been in combat. Moreover, the mean level of education of men who were separated in Situations I or II was just over 7 years, while the comparable figure for the overseas ineffectives was over 9 years. These data indicate that among the ineffective soldiers, men who served only in the Zone of the Interior had significantly less education than did those who served overseas. Just as with age, the Army's secondary screening resulted in retaining in the United States a much higher proportion of the less qualified.

The strikingly high proportion of ineffectives with some college education who failed in Situation I reflects the fact that this group included many severely emotionally disturbed individuals, a high proportion of whom were suffering from a psychosis. This is substantiated by the finding in the following table that 89 percent of those with some college education who were discharged during the first year were judged to be severely incapacitated for further

DEGREE OF INCAPACITATION BY YEARS OF SCHOOL COMPLETED, SITUATION I, IN PERCENT, WITH PERCENTAGE SHOWING PRE-MILITARY INDICATIONS OF INEFFECTIVENESS

YEARS OF SCHOOL COMPLETED	TOTAL	DEGREE OF INCAPACITATION *Major*	*Moderate*	*Minor*	PERCENT OF TOTAL WITH PRE-MILITARY INDICATIONS
0-3	100.0	64.0	12.4	23.6	41.8
4-7	100.0	53.6	11.2	35.2	32.6
8	100.0	49.1	19.5	31.4	16.9
Some high school	100.0	49.5	18.9	31.6	24.8
High school graduation	100.0	38.9	50.8	10.3	19.2
Some college	100.0	88.8	11.2	—	24.8
Total Situation I	100.0	54.3	19.1	26.6	28.8

service. This table also shows that the men with the least education had the highest proportion with pre-military indications of ineffectiveness.

The following table indicates the extent to which this relationship persisted throughout all four Situations. In each Situation those with the least educational achievement among those having major incapacitation for further military service were much more likely to reveal pre-military indications of a disqualifying condition than were those who were better educated.

PRE-MILITARY INDICATIONS OF INEFFECTIVENESS AMONG THOSE WITH MAJOR INCAPACITATION BY SITUATION AND BY EDUCATIONAL LEVEL

SITUATION	PERCENT OF THOSE WITH MAJOR INCAPACITATION WHO HAD PRE-MILITARY INDICATIONS OF INEFFECTIVENESS: *Ineffectives with Less Than an 8th Grade Education*	*Ineffectives with at Least an 8th Grade Education*
I	62.6	41.5
II	80.5	51.8
III	39.2	17.5
IV	12.8	6.6
Total Cohort	61.7	36.1

The extent to which those with the least education (less than fourth-grade education) were particularly handicapped is revealed by the following figures which indicate that as of the time of breakdown more than half of this group were assessed to have major incapacitation for further military service.

MAJOR INCAPACITATION FOR SERVICE BY SITUATION, ALL INEFFECTIVES AND THOSE WITH LESS THAN FOURTH GRADE EDUCATION, IN PERCENT

Situation	*All Ineffectives*	*Ineffectives with Less than 4th Grade Education*
I	54.3	64.0
II	35.9	42.9
III	51.4	57.6
IV	32.2	50.4
Total Cohort	46.9	55.4

The relationship here is consistent. The highest proportion of the poorly educated in each Situation who had to be separated were found to have major incapacitation.

Not only did the less educated perform more poorly in general—as shown by their higher separation rates—but men with little education did not perform as well up to their breakdown as did those with more education. The following table gives the distribution of military performance ratings of ineffective soldiers at each educational level.

MILITARY PERFORMANCE RATING BY YEARS OF SCHOOL COMPLETED, IN PERCENT

YEARS OF SCHOOL COMPLETED	TOTAL	MILITARY PERFORMANCE RATING			
		Good	*Acceptable*	*Poor*	*Not Rated*
0 - 3	100.0	1.4	38.2	50.9	9.5
4 - 7	100.0	2.4	58.2	31.8	7.6
8	100.0	17.1	62.9	18.7	1.3
Some high school	100.0	14.3	59.8	21.6	4.3
High school graduation	100.0	11.9	65.3	4.2	18.6
Some college	100.0	23.1	49.8	7.7	19.4
Total Cohort	100.0	8.7	56.2	26.5	8.6

Men with the least education were, as the earlier data have indicated, most likely to break down and to be most severely incapacitated for further military service after their breakdown. Moreover, they were of least value to the Army prior to their breakdown. Of those with less than four years of education more than half were rated as poor soldiers and another tenth were discharged so quickly that they were not even rated. Nearly one-third, 31.8 percent, of those who completed only 4 to 7 years of school also performed poorly as soldiers. On the other hand, the better educated groups included not only far fewer performers but significantly higher proportions of men with good military records.

While relatively few of the ineffectives had graduated from high school or had attended college, the foregoing table makes clear that a relatively high proportion—about one-fifth—of the best educated served for only a few weeks and were therefore not rated. Apparently the superior educational background of these men had led the examiners at induction stations to overlook the presence of indications of ineffectiveness based on serious emotional or behavior defects.

The foregoing analysis gives substantial support to the validity of the Army's original unwillingness to accept men with very little or no education and further helps to illuminate why the Army, after it was forced to accept illiterates, made a major effort to establish Special Training Units at Reception Centers to train them. The poorly educated were surely severely handicapped in their military assignments, even if we make the same allowance for preconceptions and prejudice here as in the case of age. It is probable that some of the poorly educated were given short shrift because some officers did not want to train men who required special attention because they were found to be illiterate or semi-illiterate.

PRE-MILITARY OCCUPATION

A man's ability to hold a job is an important indication of his overall adjustment, particularly if attention is given to the level of work which he performs and the income he earns. Therefore we sought information about the pre-military occupation of the cohort ineffectives. Since more than two-fifths of these men were twenty-two years of age or younger, their occupational experience was at best limited. And because of the widespread unemployment of the 1930s those just coming of working age were even less likely to have had much experience. Because of this, our occupational data on these men before they entered military service are rather limited.

Moreover, it is difficult to assess fully the economic position of those who came from farm families. In some instances the soldier may have been the main wage earner, as when, for example, he had taken over the farm after his father had died. Others helped their fathers run the farm but had jobs been available elsewhere they might have left. As it was, they remained at home and tried to do enough to earn their room and board plus a little spending money. Still others combined farm work with off-farm employment on a regular or intermittent basis.

After the depression of the 1930s came a turn for the better, and 1941 to 1942 was a period of rapid economic expansion with many defense jobs opening up at good rates of pay. A large number of men made an occupational change at this time, often shortly before they were inducted into the Army. For the following analysis, a man who had left the farm only a few months previously or had transferred recently from an unskilled laboring job to a machine operator's job in a new munitions plant was classified in terms of his earlier occupational status. But if he had made the shift a year or more before induction, he was classified according to his most recent occupation.

The following table presents the distribution of the cohort ineffectives according to their major occupational background before the war.

OCCUPATION OF COHORT INEFFECTIVES BEFORE THE WAR

Type of Occupation	*Percent*
Farm	37.9
Unskilled and service	24.9
Semi-skilled and skilled	22.5
White collar	13.7
Miscellaneous or not stated	1.0
	100.0

The ineffective group contained a substantially higher proportion of soldiers with a farm background than one would have expected on the basis of the number of farmers in the total population. In 1940 the residence of about one quarter of the young males of military age was classified as rural-farm by the U. S. Census. A good part of the explanation for the disproportionate number of men with a farm background among the ineffectives lies in their lower educational achievement. We have noted earlier that the poorly educated had much higher separation rates for ineffectiveness. Sixty-nine percent of the men with less than 4 years of schooling and 45 percent of the group with between 4 and 7 years of school was composed of men with a farm background.

The close relationships between education and occupation can also be indicated by pointing out that 32 percent of the ineffectives who had been farmers had completed no more than 3 years of school and 69 percent, no more than 7 years; while only 9 and 36 percent respectively of the rest had had only this little education. Many of the poorly educated farm laborers were separated as inapt rather than as emotionally disturbed. They rarely presented a behavior problem. Nonetheless they were incapable of adapting to the demands of a large organization.

Somewhat more farmers proportionately than non-farmers were deemed to have major incapacitation for further service (50 vs. 45 percent); and among those with major incapacitation, farmers also had a higher proportion of ineffectives with pre-military indications (52 vs. 47 percent). Farmers did not, however, tend to be discharged earlier than non-farmers—51 percent of the farmers as compared to 53 percent of the non-farmers were discharged in Situation I.

The unskilled and service group also contained a high proportion of men who had made only a marginal adjustment in civilian life. Those with more ability had moved into semi-skilled, skilled, or white collar occupations, depending on the opportunities available to them, which in many instances were determined by the level of education which they had acquired. Fifty-six percent of the ineffectives with an unskilled or service occupational background had completed less than 8 years of school; one-sixth had completed 3 years or less. Their civilian work records contained considerable evidence of their limited capabilities—they moved from one marginal job to another. Their records contain more clear-cut evidence of pre-military ineffectiveness than the farm group whose immobility helped to mask their limitations.

Both the farm and unskilled groups had a somewhat higher proportion of ineffectives classified as being severely incapacitated for further service at the time of breakdown than was the case with semi-skilled and skilled and white collar occupational groups (50 and 47 percent vs. 42 and 43 percent). Moreover, the proportion of ineffectives whose records revealed pre-military indications of ineffectiveness was much higher for the farm and unskilled groups (26 and 27 percent vs. 17 and 17 percent).

Both the farmers and the unskilled and service workers who were eventually discharged as ineffective tended to perform up to their breakdown much more poorly than soldiers with a semi-skilled, skilled, or white collar background. The following table shows the distribution of military performance ratings for ineffective soldiers according to their occupational backgrounds before the war.

While about one-third of the farmers and unskilled and service workers were rated as poor soldiers, it should be noted that a considerable percentage of the unskilled were discharged without having been rated. But in both groups well over half had performed in at least an acceptable manner prior to breakdown. Despite this relatively good record, the contrast with the performance level of the other occupational groups is striking. Three out of every four of the semi-skilled and skilled group and seven out of every eight of the white collar group had an acceptable or good performance record prior to breakdown.

MILITARY PERFORMANCE RATING BY TYPE OF PRE-MILITARY OCCUPATION IN PERCENT

TYPE OF OCCUPATION	TOTAL	MILITARY PERFORMANCE RATING *Good*	*Acceptable*	*Poor*	*Not Rated*
Farm	100.0	6.2	52.1	34.3	7.4
Unskilled and service	100.0	6.0	47.5	32.7	13.8
Semi-skilled and skilled	100.0	9.2	66.0	19.2	5.6
White collar	100.0	20.4	67.5	4.9	7.2
Total Cohort	100.0	8.7	56.2	26.5	8.6

These differentials hold true for each Situation, and widen as length of service in the Zone of the Interior increased. Even in overseas and combat duty, where the performance record of most men prior to breakdown was generally high, significant occupational differences were found: white collar workers were the best, followed in turn by semi-skilled and skilled, unskilled and service, and farmers.

MARITAL STATUS

In our society marriage is considered to be a sign of personal maturity and social integration. It is generally assumed that in marriage each partner will support and gain support from the other and will therefore be in a better position to cope with life's problems.

If an individual marries at a much younger or much older age than is typical for members of his group, it may indicate some order of instability. Individuals who have been divorced or separated may be considered to be unstable to the extent that the presumption is accepted that both partners share responsibility for the failure of the marriage. And the widowed, even though no responsibility attaches to them, have also been scarred.

Induction for a married man or continued duty for a man who married while in the service usually implied separation and as such represented a deprivation and strain. In *Breakdown and Recovery* several cases are presented which show the strain which separation from home and family can create. In *The Lost Divisions* we sought to determine whether marital status independent of age was associated with ineffectiveness in the Army and concluded that the clearest finding related to soldiers with "broken marriages." This group had a considerably higher rate of ineffectiveness than either single or married men. We are now in a position to analyze this and other relationships between marital status and military ineffectiveness in greater detail.

The following table sets out in percentage terms the marital status of the cohort ineffectives when they entered military service and when they were discharged.

MARITAL STATUS OF COHORT INEFFECTIVES AT INDUCTION AND AT DISCHARGE, IN PERCENT

Marital Status	*At Induction*	*At Discharge*
Single	55.5	48.2
Married	35.2	40.2
Broken marriage	9.3	11.6
	100.0	100.0

Almost 1 out of every 14 men who entered the Army single was married at the time of his separation. This is noteworthy since more than half failed to serve for a year. The other interesting finding is that such a relatively high percentage of the group—almost 1 out of every 10—had a broken marriage at induction, reflecting in large measure the Army's deliberate policy of selecting older men who did not have dependents.

The following table presents the marital status by age group for the cohort ineffectives at the time of their induction.

MARITAL STATUS BY AGE, IN PERCENT

AGE AT ENTRY	TOTAL	MARITAL STATUS AT ENTRY		
		Single	*Married*	*Broken Marriage*
18-22	100.0	75.2	22.8	2.0
23-27	100.0	46.1	45.6	8.3
28-32	100.0	41.9	46.7	11.4
33-37	100.0	22.8	48.7	28.5
38 and older	100.0	57.9	17.5	24.6
All ages	100.0	55.5	35.2	9.3

These figures reveal that while about 3 out of every 4 men in the youngest age group were single at induction, more than half the twenty-three to twenty-seven-year-old group were, or had been, married. As we would expect, the proportion of married men increases with each age group except for those thirty-eight years of age and older. The explanation for the high proportion of single men in the oldest age group must be sought in the Army's induction and separation policies. The Army tended to induct older men who did not have family responsibilities, and in late 1942 and 1943 it speeded the discharge of older men.

One way to estimate the relationship between marital status and military ineffectiveness is to assess the degree of incapacitation among the various marital groups at the time of breakdown. The following table presents the relevant data.

DEGREE OF INCAPACITATION BY MARITAL STATUS AT BREAKDOWN, IN PERCENT

MARITAL STATUS	TOTAL	DEGREE OF INCAPACITATION		
		Major	*Moderate*	*Minor*
Single throughout service	100.0	53.6	22.5	23.9
Married at induction	100.0	36.7	44.9	18.4
Married while in service	100.0	31.5	30.1	38.4
Total married at discharge	100.0	35.8	42.5	21.7
Broken marriage	100.0	62.5	15.7	21.8

These data indicate that the married men were more heavily

concentrated in the group with moderate incapacitation for further service. Both the single and broken-marriage groups contained proportionately many more with major incapacitation; our detailed data also revealed that these two groups contained higher proportions of men with pre-military indications of ineffectiveness. This last was especially true for those with broken marriages: of the 62.5 percent with major incapacitation (as shown in the above table) virtually all had pre-military indications of ineffectiveness. Apparently, men with broken marriages who failed in military service were basically unstable. The fact that their marriage had foundered was only one aspect of a more generalized weakness in their adjustment potential. As might be expected, these men were considerably older than either the single or married men who became ineffective in military service.

The following distribution shows the group which was married at induction in terms of age and degree of incapacitation for further military service.

DEGREE OF INCAPACITATION BY AGE, COHORT INEFFECTIVES WHO WERE MARRIED AT INDUCTION, IN PERCENT

AGE AT ENTRY	TOTAL	DEGREE OF INCAPACITATION *Major*	*Moderate*	*Minor*
18-22	100.0	25.2	59.4	15.4
23-27	100.0	39.5	43.0	17.5
28-32	100.0	40.0	39.0	21.0
33-37	100.0	41.4	36.0	22.6
38 and older	100.0	82.5	17.5	—
All ages	100.0	36.7	44.9	18.4

One interesting finding can be extracted from the foregoing. Since only a minority of the youngest age group were married at induction, it is noteworthy that of all age groups they had the largest proportion of men with moderate incapacitation for further service. A possible interpretation would be that the minority who married early had special needs that they sought to meet through marriage. Military service forced them to leave their wives, on whom they were emotionally dependent, and they found this enforced separation very upsetting.

There was little difference in the military performance prior to breakdown among men who were married throughout their period of service, were married after induction, or who remained single. Those whose marriages were broken at induction or which broke during their military service tended to be poor soldiers. The following table gives the distribution of military performance ratings for soldiers with different marital status.

MILITARY PERFORMANCE RATING BY MARITAL STATUS, IN PERCENT

		MILITARY PERFORMANCE RATING			
MARITAL STATUS	TOTAL	*Good*	*Acceptable*	*Poor*	*Not Rated*
Single throughout	100.0	7.3	60.3	20.0	12.4
Married after induction	100.0	9.6	66.5	23.9	–
Stable marriage throughout	100.0	12.0	59.5	22.0	6.5
Broken marriage at induction	100.0	2.4	25.8	67.1	4.7
Marriage broken in service	100.0	12.4	15.9	71.7	–

Nearly half of the ineffective soldiers were single throughout their military service. Two thirds of them performed acceptably or better prior to their breakdown, as did the other large group, those with a stable marriage.

The proportion of poor soldiers among those whose marriage was broken either at entry or while in service is indeed striking. Since more than two thirds of these men performed poorly, their failure in marriage and failure in service, as has already been suggested, reflect basic weaknesses in their personalities. It is possible, however, that for those whose marriage was broken while in service, worry and anxiety about what was happening at home contributed to their poor military performance.

RACE

The last demographic factor to be reviewed in connection with military ineffectiveness is that of race. The Army deliberately limited its intake of Negroes to the percentage they represented in the population—roughly 1 in 10. However, during the cohort period the Army began to accept on a controlled basis large numbers of Negroes who had originally been rejected for military service because of illiteracy. This means that the number of poorly educated Negroes in the cohort sample is unduly large and is undoubtedly one of the factors which can explain the startling disparity in the separation rates of Negroes and non-Negroes. The separation rate for Negroes—84.2 per 1,000 accessions—was more than double the rate for whites—36.2 per 1,000 accessions. Thus, while 1 out of every 10 accessions was a Negro, just over 1 out of every 5 separatees was one.

That education played a major role in the higher separation rate for Negroes is apparent from the educational achievement of Negroes entering the Army during the latter part of 1942. The following table compares the educational level of Negro and white soldiers who entered active duty during the cohort period.

EDUCATIONAL LEVEL ACHIEVED BY RACE, TOTAL ARMY INDUCTIONS, SEPT.-DEC. 1942, IN PERCENT

		LEVEL OF EDUCATION ACHIEVED			
RACE	TOTAL	*Grammar School or Less*	*Some High School*	*High School Graduation*	*Some College*
Negro	100.0	67.1	21.0	6.9	5.0
White	100.0	33.8	26.4	25.9	13.9
All races	100.0	37.3	25.8	23.9	13.0

Twice as many Negroes as whites, proportionately, fell into the lowest educational achievement level. There is no doubt that even within this group Negroes had completed substantially fewer grades of school than did the whites and usually in inferior schools. The lower quality of education available to Negroes is reflected in the higher separation rates for those in the groups with less than high-school graduation. The inversion of the rate for high-school graduates probably reflected the Army's disinclination to lose men who might be capable of becoming noncommissioned officers in Negro units. These conclusions are demonstrated by the data in the following table.

RATES OF SEPARATION FOR INEFFECTIVENESS BY RACE AND EDUCATIONAL LEVEL ACHIEVED

EDUCATIONAL LEVEL ACHIEVED	SEPARATION RATES PER 1,000 ACCESSIONS SEPT.-DEC. 1942 *Negro*	*White*
Grammar school or less	103.1	57.7
Some high school	62.7	31.6
High school graduation or better	15.1	21.0

The Negro soldier who proved ineffective was poorly educated, even more so than the white ineffective soldier: 82 percent of Negro ineffectives had no more than a grammar school education as compared to 54 percent of the white soldiers.

There were noticeable differences, however, as to the proportion of separations of Negroes in the four Situations as shown in the following table.

RATES OF SEPARATION FOR INEFFECTIVENESS BY RACE, WITH A DISTRIBUTION OF INEFFECTIVES OF EACH RACE BY SITUATION, IN PERCENT

RACE	RATE OF SEPARATION PER 1,000 ACCESSIONS, SEPT.-DEC. 1942	TOTAL	SITUATION *I*	*II*	*III*	*IV*
Negro	84.2	100.0	47.6	31.8	16.4	4.2
White	36.2	100.0	54.0	23.3	9.8	12.9
All races	41.2	100.0	52.6	25.1	11.2	11.1

Proportionately just about as many Negro as white ineffectives served overseas. Among those whose duty was solely within the Zone of the Interior, Negroes tended to be discharged later. Many officers found it difficult to assess correctly the behavior of poorly educated Negroes, even those who were emotionally disturbed. Moreover, with Negroes serving in segregated units standards were lowered to take account of the more limited background of the majority of men.

The proportionately greater number of Negroes found in Situation III reflects Army assignment policies. By and large Negroes tended to be assigned to such Service units as the Transportation Corps, Quartermaster Corps, and Corps of Engineers. But a certain number were also assigned to combat units; the number in our sample, however, who fell in Situation IV (combat) was too small to generalize from these data.

The extent to which the Army was unduly burdened by accepting Negroes whom it should have rejected at induction is suggested by the following: nearly one-third, 32.5 percent, of the Negro ineffectives not only had major incapacitation for further service but had pre-military indications of ineffectiveness in their records. The figure for the whites was much lower—one-fifth.

One of the reasons why so many slipped through is that once the Army began to process illiterates, even on a quota basis, it found difficulty in differentiating among them. Many examiners threw up their hands at the effort of distinguishing between those with little and those with greater promise of performing effectively in military service. The data surely support the Army's fear of being inundated with too many poorly educated Negroes whom they could not train quickly enough to make into effective soldiers.

There was less difference in the military performance prior to breakdown of Negroes and whites than one might have expected in view of the higher separation rate of Negro soldiers for ineffectiveness and their much lower educational achievement. The following table gives the distribution of military performance ratings for Negro and white ineffective soldiers in the cohort prior to breakdown.

MILITARY PERFORMANCE RATING BY RACE, IN PERCENT

RACE	TOTAL	MILITARY PERFORMANCE RATING *Good*	*Acceptable*	*Poor*	*Not Rated*
Negro	100.0	6.1	56.3	31.7	5.9
White	100.0	9.4	56.2	25.1	9.3
All races	100.0	8.7	56.2	26.5	8.6

Although proportionately more Negroes were discharged for ineffectiveness than were white soldiers, those who were separated did not have a significantly poorer record of military performance. At least a partial explanation of this otherwise incongruous finding probably lies in the practice already alluded to of the Army's adjusting downwards the standards it applied in disciplining, promoting, and rating the effectiveness of men in Negro units—factors which we included in our evaluation of military performance.

SUMMARY

The foregoing analysis shows how misleading over-simplified generalizations about the men who broke down in World War II can be. In point of fact, included among the ineffective soldiers were:

Men of all ages
Men of all levels of education
Men of all types of occupations
Men of every marital status
Men of all races

It is true, however, that among these demographic groupings were sub-groups which had different probabilities of breaking down in the Army and different potentials for further military service. This is suggested by such findings as the following:

Age

Men above twenty-eight were one and a half times as likely to be ineffective as men below twenty-two.

Younger soldiers were more likely to perform satisfactorily prior to breakdown than the older soldiers.

Education

Men who had only a grammar school education or less were about five times as likely to become ineffective as men who had had some college education.

While about 3 out of every 5 of the least educated had performed poorly prior to breakdown, this was true for only 1 out of every 4 or 5 with a high school education.

The least educated were more than one and a half times as likely to be of no further use to the Army after breakdown as the high school graduate.

Pre-Military Occupation

Farmers accounted for a disproportionate number of the ineffective soldiers.

About 2 out of every 5 farmers and unskilled workers had a poor military performance record prior to breakdown while this was so for only 1 out of every 8 white collar workers and 1 out of every 4 semi-skilled and skilled workers.

Marital Status

Men with broken marriages—whether broken before or after entry into service—were more than twice as likely to have been poor soldiers than either single men or married men whose marriages remained intact.

Three out of every 5 men with broken marriages were of no further use to the Army after breakdown while this was true for only about a third of those whose marriages remained intact.

Race

Negroes were more than twice as likely to prove ineffective as were white soldiers.

There was no significant difference in the rated performance of Negro and white soldiers prior to their breakdown.

A simplified assessment of the foregoing would lead to the conclusion that the most likely group to break down in military service were Negroes in their thirties, with less than a fourth-grade education, of farm background, whose marriages had been broken. Least likely to break were white, single men below twenty-two with some college education, who had had a clerical job. But the analytical data which have been presented can lead to a deeper understanding of the relationships between these major demographic factors and military performance and breakdown.

With regard to age, the analysis revealed that when the Army was able to screen older men with care those who passed performed quite well. The poorer performance of older men frequently reflected some specific disadvantage that had gone unrecognized. The Army, like many other organizations with some prejudice against older men, had tended to discharge them just as soon as they showed signs of becoming ineffective.

While the analysis in terms of occupational background suggested that farmers had particular difficulties in adjusting satisfactorily to military life, closer study revealed that it was largely because of limitations in their educational background that they had so high a rate of ineffectiveness. The importance of the educational factor in the adjustment to military service of different occupational groups was borne out by the high ineffectiveness that was also found to exist among the unskilled and service group.

The analysis of the relation between marital status and military performance indicated that the men with broken marriages had apparently basically unstable personalities. The substantial majority in this group were found at the time of breakdown to have major incapacitation for further service and almost all of them had premilitary indications of ineffectiveness. The other suggestive finding was the difficulty that married men in the youngest group experienced when they were separated from their wives to whom they looked for special support.

The findings appeared to confirm the widespread belief that Negroes made poor soldiers, but a careful review of the data made clear that a key factor responsible was the inadequate educational background of most Negroes. It was not the color of his skin or his disposition that made him a poorer risk to the Army than a white man but rather his severe educational deprivation.

The conclusion is inescapable that while age and marital status could help to differentiate to a slight degree the performance of men in the Army, the major determinant among the demographic factors which we have reviewed was education. We had repeated evidence of the importance of the educational factor not only when we studied it separately but also while assessing occupational and racial determinants in performance.

While an illiterate or poorly educated person could meet the demands that the Army made on him, especially if he were in good health, had good native intelligence, and received an appropriate assignment, he was much more vulnerable than one who had had better education. It was much easier for the latter to cope with the complexities of military life and to make the speedy adjustments that were required. The uneducated man was likely to encounter great difficulties in keeping the pace and as he began to fall behind he was likely to become emotionally upset. Others became disciplinary problems simply because they did not understand what was required of them, or at best had only a dim perception of the rules and regulations.

Of all the factors that we have reviewed, an adequate education emerges as the overriding prerequisite for effective performance in military service.

Chapter Seven: MANAGEMENT POLICIES AND PROCEDURES

WE HAVE SEEN that there were many soldiers who had such severe defects before induction or else developed them while in the service that the Army could not have taken any action which would have enabled them to serve effectively after their breakdown. But there were many others who were only moderately or slightly incapacitated at the time of breakdown and whose further military effectiveness depended to a large degree on how the Army handled them.

In this chapter we will consider a number of the Army's management practices in order to evaluate their impact on the effectiveness with which soldiers performed during World War II. In such a review of management practices one should start at the beginning of a soldier's career in the Army and consider the effect on him of various policies and practices from his induction right up to the day of his discharge. Such an effort would require an assessment of the personnel procedures followed at reception centers where recruits were initially classified and assigned; the adequacy of the training to which he was later exposed; the quality of leadership given by both commissioned and noncommissioned officers; the extent to which the Army maintained a reasonable balance between helping the soldier who encountered difficulties, either initially or later, and its judicious use of discipline to discourage the shirker and the slacker and thereby contributed to unit morale.

It would be desirable to review all of these and still additional facets of Army management policies and practices in order to assess their impact on soldiers' performance. In *The Lost Divisions* we were able to consider a number of these important relationships between management and performance. Here we can bring into focus some additional materials. Specifically, we will deal with the classification and assignment system, including reassignment, and with training, medical care, and the command structure. Our reference points are two: first, to identify wherever possible the manner in which Army policies affected the performance of soldiers prior to breakdown and, second, to appraise the Army's decisions to rehabilitate or discharge them after they broke down.

CLASSIFICATION AND ASSIGNMENT

The assignment of a recruit to a branch of service represents only one facet of the assignment system. Yet during the war it represented the most important initial decision about the soldier and it carried farflung implications for his future service. If assigned to one of the Arms, he was likely to undergo rather rigorous training in units which were under pressure to meet an early readiness date, and each week of training brought him closer to combat. If assigned to one of the Services, the likelihood of his being eventually exposed to combat was much less. And if assigned to the Air Corps, he was frequently sent for prolonged technical training, usually to school, before being sent overseas as a member of a unit or as an individual replacement.

The series of tables which follow will enable us to analyze various characteristics of the cohort ineffectives in terms of the branch of service to which they were assigned initially or from which they were eventually discharged. Differences among the branches may reflect differences in the quality of the men assigned to them, differences in the stress to which these men were exposed, or differences in discharge policies followed by the several branches—or a combination of two or more of these factors.

The following table shows the distribution of all cohort ineffectives by major branch of service at the time of their discharge

BRANCH OF ASSIGNMENT, COHORT INEFFECTIVES AND TOTAL ARMY

BRANCH OF ASSIGNMENT	COHORT INEFFECTIVES Number	COHORT INEFFECTIVES Percent	MEAN STRENGTH, 1943-45, TOTAL ARMY Percent
Arms	32,052	44.1	34
Services	26,083	35.9	38
Air Corps	11,088	15.2	24
No branch assignment	3,477	4.8	4
Total	72,700	100.0	100.0

together with an estimated distribution of the total Army strength. These data indicate that the Arms tended to separate a proportionately higher number than either the Services or the Air Corps. This conclusion is reinforced by a review of the respective separation rates. Estimated rates of separation for ineffectiveness for the major branches during 1943-45 are given in the following table.

RATES OF SEPARATION FOR INEFFECTIVENESS BY BRANCH OF ASSIGNMENT

BRANCH OF ASSIGNMENT AT DISCHARGE	ESTIMATED RATE OF SEPARATION PER 1,000 MEAN STRENGTH 1943	1944	1945
Arms	9.1	2.8	2.7
Services	5.5	3.0	2.3
Air Corps	3.1	1.7	2.1

The Arms had the highest separation rates in 1943, although the differences among the branches had largely disappeared by the end of the war. The heavy separations from the Arms early in the war was primarily a reflection of two factors: the relatively lower quality of personnel assigned to the Arms and the excessive pressure of time under which units in the Arms were seeking to complete their training cycle. The fact that there was little difference in the rates among the branches late in the war in large part reflects the continuous rescreening of personnel. The extent to which men with different qualities were initially assigned to the several branches was reduced through time. The difference in separation rates that remained reflected primarily various orders of stress faced by the troops and different separation policies pursued by the major branches.

In *The Lost Divisions* we reviewed the policy followed by the War Department in deliberately allocating the best educated men to the Air Corps, the next best to the Services, and the least educated to the Arms. We also noted that various other policies, such as the method of selecting enlisted men for Officer Candidate Schools and the Army Specialized Training Program, further reduced the quality of ground force personnel. The following table demonstrates the substantial differences among the branches in the educational level of the cohort ineffectives.

EDUCATIONAL LEVEL OF INEFFECTIVES BY BRANCH OF ASSIGNMENT, IN PERCENT

BRANCH OF ASSIGNMENT AT DISCHARGE	TOTAL	LEVEL OF EDUCATION ACHIEVED *Grammar School*	*Some High School*	*At Least High School Graduation*
Arms .	100.0	67.4	16.9	15.7
Services	100.0	62.8	22.1	15.1
Air Corps	100.0	37.6	32.8	29.6
No branch assignment	100.0	40.2	22.8	37.0
Total	100.0	59.9	21.5	18.6

While the Services had slightly better educated men than did the Arms, the Air Corps separatees were by far the best educated, so much so that they appear to be a distinct group. The consistently lower rate of separation of Air Corps personnel throughout each of the three years must be explained in large part by the initial allocation of better educated men to this branch.

Further insight into the importance of the educational factor can be gained by studying the military performance ratings of soldiers in each branch who became ineffective, together with the degree of their incapacitation for further military service after breakdown.

MILITARY PERFORMANCE RATING BY BRANCH OF ASSIGNMENT, IN PERCENT

BRANCH OF ASSIGNMENT AT DISCHARGE	TOTAL	MILITARY PERFORMANCE RATING *Good*	*Acceptable*	*Poor*	*Not Rated*
Arms	100.0	7.6	61.2	20.1	11.1
Services	100.0	6.2	55.1	35.2	3.5
Services	100.0	19.1	46.8	24.5	9.6
Air Corps					
No branch assignment	100.0	4.4	48.6	26.5	20.5
Total Cohort	100.0	8.7	56.2	26.5	8.6

The strikingly higher proportion of Air Corps personnel who had a good performance rating prior to breakdown reinforces the earlier finding that the Air Corps initially received a much higher percentage of well-qualified men. The separation of a much higher percentage of soldiers with a prior record of good performance than either the Arms or the Services may also reflect that the Air Corps personnel were exposed to higher orders of stress or that, with large numbers of well-educated men, the Air Corps pursued a much easier discharge policy. Some indication of the importance of these factors can be gleaned from a consideration of the degree of incapacitation for further service of men discharged by the three branches. This is set out in the table below.

DEGREE OF INCAPACITATION BY BRANCH OF ASSIGNMENT IN PERCENT

BRANCH OF ASSIGNMENT AT DISCHARGE	TOTAL	DEGREE OF INCAPACITATION *Major*	*Moderate*	*Minor*
Arms	100.0	45.6	27.8	26.6
Services	100.0	44.9	33.9	21.2
Air Corps	100.0	48.0	29.3	22.7
No branch assignment	100.0	70.5	29.5	–
Total Cohort	100.0	46.9	30.3	22.8

In each branch, the highest proportion of those separated consisted of the most seriously incapacitated. The Air Corps actually separated the highest proportion in this category, except for the men with no branch assignment. Moreover the Arms, rather than the Air Corps, tended to separate the largest proportion with only minor incapacitation. It seems clear then, that the Air Corps was not pursuing an easier discharge policy than the other branches—in point of fact, theirs was a little stricter. Thus, in spite of the Air Corps' better cut of manpower, a somewhat higher proportion of the men it discharged had major incapacitation for further service. While it is possible that these men were exposed to greater orders of stress, a review of their pre-military background sheds some additional light on the issue.

PRE-MILITARY INDICATIONS OF INEFFECTIVENESS BY BRANCH OF ASSIGNMENT

BRANCH OF ASSIGNMENT AT DISCHARGE	PERCENT WHO HAD PRE-MILITARY INDICATIONS	
	Among All Ineffectives	*Among Ineffectives with Major Incapacitation for Service*
Arms	18.4	40.3
Services	24.6	54.8
Air Corps	29.6	61.8
No branch assignment	34.2	48.5
Total Cohort	23.1	49.2

It is not easy to understand why of those with major incapacitation for further service, the Air Corps group should include the highest proportion with pre-military indications of ineffectiveness. A likely explanation is that the examining physicians failed to discern at induction emotional disorders among these better educated men.

Of the ineffective soldiers with a good performance record whom the Air Corps separated only about a quarter were severely incapacitated; the Services had twice and the Arms three times that proportion. This means that service in the Air Corps did not result in severe incapacitation of soldiers whose records prior to breakdown had been good.

An interesting aspect of the personnel policies pursued by the different branches is the speed with which they acted to discharge men whom they regarded as ineffective. The following figure depicts the number of months served by the men discharged from the different branches.

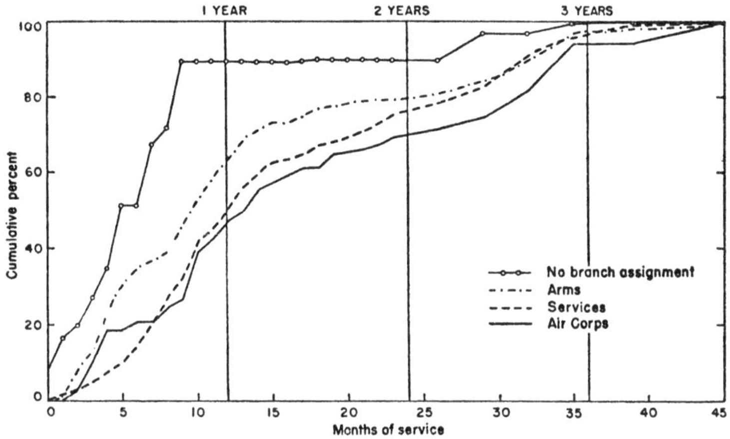

CUMULATIVE PERCENTAGE OF INEFFECTIVES SERVING STATED NUMBER OF MONTHS OR LESS, BY BRANCH OF SERVICE FROM WHICH DISCHARGED

The figure shows that of all branches the Arms moved fastest to separate the ineffectives and that, except for those who broke down during their first few months of service, the Air Corps moved slowest. As we might have anticipated, men without a branch assignment were discharged most rapidly; the fact of their not having an assignment indicates that many of them had been identified as ineffectives immediately after coming on to active duty.

The Arms moved much faster than the other branches to separate its ineffective soldiers in every Situation except combat. In Situation I the Arms had separated at the end of 5 months about 53 percent of all who went out during their first year of service; the comparable figures were 23 percent for the Services and 44 percent for the Air Corps. In Situation II the Arms had half of that group separated at 13 months but the Services had separated only a third and the Air Corps a fifth by that time.

The most likely explanation for this consistently speedier action by the Arms to separate its ineffective soldiers lies in, as we have noted, the special pressures under which it operated in the Zone of the Interior to ready its units for overseas shipment. In contrast, the Air Corps, once it decided to invest in training a man, tended to hold on to him until time proved that he could no longer perform effectively.

In Situation III ineffective soldiers assigned to the Arms were separated much earlier than men assigned to the Services or to the Air Corps. This, however, merely reflects the fact that they broke down relatively soon after their arrival overseas and before they had a chance to enter combat. Those who were in combat—and three-fourths of the ineffectives who served overseas and who were discharged from the Arms did see combat—served much longer.

This cursory review of assignment policies demonstrates that the branch to which a soldier was initially assigned played some part in influencing his ability to perform effectively. He had a better chance, other things being equal, if he were assigned to the Services rather than to the Arms, for the latter were under the greatest pressure to complete their training and so had the least patience with the slower learner. But we also found that the separation rates for ineffectiveness in the several branches were also influenced by the quality of manpower originally assigned to them.

REASSIGNMENT

A man's failure in one branch did not necessarily mean that he was of no further use to the Army. Many who failed as aircraft crew members were able to serve satisfactorily on the ground. Others who did not have the stamina for the infantry did quite well in a service unit. An important aspect of the relation between assignment and performance can be illuminated by considering whether the men who failed in one area were given a second chance.

Of the 72,700 cohort ineffectives, 13,927 served in a branch other than the one from which they were ultimately discharged. This represents a minimum reassignment rate of just under 20 percent. Even though this figure does not take into account reassignments to different units within the same branch, it appears surprisingly high.

The following table provides a summary of the numbers of men who had more than one branch assignment.

ADDITIONAL BRANCH ASSIGNMENTS OF COHORT INEFFECTIVES WHO WERE TRANSFERRED*

BRANCH OF ASSIGNMENT AT DISCHARGE	INEFFECTIVES TRANSFERRED	ADDITIONAL BRANCH ASSIGNMENT		
		Arms	*Services*	*Air Corps*
Arms	1,825	1,388	401	255
Services	10,122	6,636	3,783	1,284
Air Corps	1,607	286	1,458	677†
No branch assignment	373	289	220	–
Total	13,927	8,559	5,862	2,216

* Distribution does not necessarily add up to totals since some men served in more than one additional assignment.

† Assignment to an Arm or Service intervened between Air Corps assignments.

This table indicates that the Arms and to a lesser extent the Air Corps sloughed off a considerable number of men to the Services and that there was considerable reassignment within the Services. It also shows that to a limited degree there was reassignment of men within the Arms, back to the Air Corps after an intervening assignment with an Arm or Service, and from the Services to the Air Corps.

Of the transferred ineffectives nearly 88 percent had served in one of the Services, 65 percent in one of the Arms, and 23 percent with the Air Corps prior to their discharge. Moreover, of men discharged as ineffective from the Services, 43 percent were transferees; the percent for the Arms and the Air Corps was much less—23 and 25 percent respectively.

The educational level of the Arms was slightly improved through such transfers. Three-fourths of the ineffectives transferred out of the Arms had no more than an eighth-grade education while only a small proportion, 4 percent, were high-school graduates or better. The incoming men, on the other hand, were better educated. The Services had the opposite experience; they lost many of the better educated and gained many of the poorly educated. Nearly one-quarter of the soldiers transferred out were high-school graduates or better compared to under 3 percent of those who came in. More than three-fourths of the ineffectives transferred to the Services had no more than an eighth-grade education. Despite this unequal exchange the distribution of ineffectives ultimately discharged from the Services showed a somewhat higher educational level than obtained for the Arms. Air Force ineffectives consistently had the highest educational level. Most of the men (83 percent) whom the Air Corps had transferred to another branch before they were eventually discharged for ineffectiveness had no more than a grammar-school education; whereas a fair number of those the Air Corps received by transfer from other branches were high-school graduates or college men.

The extent to which reassignments were made among the Situations is brought out in the following data:

Situation	*Percent Reassigned*
I	4.8
II	36.2
III	40.4
IV	27.5
Total Cohort	19.2

These figures show that only 1 man in 20 in Situation I was reassigned prior to being discharged. It appears that if a soldier failed in his first assignment, he was separated. In contrast, between one-fourth and two-fifths of all men in the other three Situations were reassigned at least once. In large measure this reflected the effort of the Army to salvage those in whom it had made a substantial investment. A better understanding of the effect of the reassignment process requires that we assess the degree of incapacitation for further military service of the soldiers who were transferred from one branch to another.

Chapter Four showed that a high proportion of men in Situation I were characterized after breakdown as being severely incapaci-

DEGREE OF INCAPACITATION OF TRANSFERRED INEFFECTIVES BY SITUATION, IN PERCENT

SITUATION	TOTAL	DEGREE OF INCAPACITATION *Major*	*Moderate*	*Minor*
I	100.0	58.1	–	41.9
II	100.0	14.4	56.4	29.2
III	100.0	52.3	33.9	13.8
IV	100.0	40.3	53.4	6.3
Total transferred ineffectives	100.0	33.2	43.2	23.6

tated for further service. The foregoing table points up the fact that some of these men had been transferred prior to breakdown. It is likely that they were transferred because their commanding officer wanted to be rid of them. It would have been better had they been discharged immediately. But the table also shows that among those discharged in Situation I were men who had been transferred who showed only minor incapacitation for further service. It is possible that the unit to which they were reassigned never gave them a chance to show whether they were capable of performing satisfactorily. The fact that they had been transferred by another branch might have been taken as presumptive evidence that they were incapable of serving effectively. It is clear, however, that very few (under 5 percent) of the men discharged in Situation I were given a second chance by transfer to another branch; and of these few who were, better than half (58 percent) probably should not have been since they soon revealed major incapacitation for further service. The small percentage of transfers reflects inherent limitations in making use of the reassignment process as well as a disinclination to make use of it when it might have proved useful.

An interesting question to consider is the percentage of men who were discharged with only minor incapacitation who had a second chance through reassignment. The data showed that relatively few had such a chance—20 percent for the cohort as a whole. In Situation I, 7.5 percent of those with minor incapacitation for further service were afforded the chance of serving in more than one branch; in Situation II, 58.9 percent; in Situation III, 28.0 percent; and in Situation IV, 9.5 percent. The higher proportion in Situation II probably reflects the leaving behind of men culled from units that were on their way overseas. Many of these soldiers were assigned to service units while awaiting their discharge from the Army.

DUTY ASSIGNMENTS AT BREAKDOWN

An important clue as to how Army personnel policies influenced performance can be found in a review of the soldiers' duty assignments at the time of their breakdown.

DUTY ASSIGNMENT AT BREAKDOWN

		Percent
Training		32.1
School	2.4	
Training Centers	13.1	
Units	16.6	
Duty		63.2
Zone of Interior (never overseas)	43.3	
Zone of Interior (returned from overseas)	4.6	
Overseas–Non-combat	12.9	
Overseas–Combat	2.4	
Casual		4.7
Total Cohort		100.0

In light of our earlier finding that more than half of all ineffectives were separated during their first year of service, it is not surprising to learn from the above table that approximately 1 out of every 3 soldiers was still in training just prior to his breakdown. In point of fact this figure is an understatement, for about 12,000 of those classified "Duty-Zone of Interior" were in the Arms and had not been overseas and, as has been pointed out previously, these men were for all practical purposes in training. The same holds true for a smaller proportion of the 18,000 Service and Air Corps personnel who had never been overseas and who were on duty status in the Zone of the Interior at the time of their discharge.

Another interesting point is that approximately 3,500 men, or just under 5 percent of the total group, were in special training units either at replacement centers or elsewhere. These were the illiterate and poorly educated men who were receiving instruction in basic reading and writing.

The finding that the majority of men who broke in training were assigned to units is important. Since the quality of training was generally much better at replacement training centers, because of superior instructors and training equipment, men who had been sent to units directly for their training were at a disadvantage. As we noted earlier, most units also had less flexibility to make adjustments because of the severe time pressures under which they operated.

Differences in the incapacitation of soldiers for further military duty according to their assignment when they broke down are indicated in the following table.

DEGREE OF INCAPACITATION BY DUTY ASSIGNMENT AT BREAKDOWN, IN PERCENT

		DEGREE OF INCAPACITATION		
DUTY ASSIGNMENT	TOTAL	*Major*	*Moderate*	*Minor*
Training	100.0	63.2	11.0	25.8
Duty: Z. I., never overseas	100.0	37.7	39.1	23.2
Duty: Z. I., returned from overseas	100.0	37.5	31.3	31.2
Duty: Overseas, non-combat	100.0	50.9	32.3	16.8
Duty: Overseas, combat	100.0	16.3	72.4	11.3
Casual	100.0	34.0	54.2	11.8

The table points up striking differences among men in different duty assignments at the time of breakdown in terms of their potential for further service. Among those who broke down in training, the predominant group had major incapacitation. Those in a Zone of Interior duty assignment were less seriously handicapped for further service, especially those who broke down on ZI duty after returning from overseas. In the overseas groups, those who broke down while serving under non-combat conditions were more severely incapacitated for further service than those who actually broke in combat. Not only did relatively few soldiers break in combat but very few of those who did were severely incapacitated for further military duty.

More than 2 out of every 5 men who became ineffective in training had pre-military indications of ineffectiveness, while this was true for only 1 out of 6 of those who had never been overseas and were on duty assignments at the time they broke down and but 1 out of 60 of those who had returned from overseas and were assigned to domestic duty. Moreover, the ratio was 1 out of 9 for soldiers overseas who broke under non-combat conditions and only 1 out 47 for those who broke in combat. This bears out our earlier remarks concerning the more careful screening of men sent overseas, especially in combat units. Very few of the group who broke in combat and even fewer of those who had successfully served overseas only to break down on their return to the United States had revealed obvious signs prior to their military service that they might become ineffective.

While the vast majority of the men who became ineffective in Situation I were in training or in a duty assignment which in many instances involved on-the-job training, many more in Situation II were performing regular duty, especially those in the Services and the Air Corps. An additional finding of considerable interest is that of the 16,178 cohort ineffectives who served overseas, 72.7 percent actually broke overseas while 27.3 percent broke after they had returned to the Zone of the Interior. More men from Situation IV (combat) than from Situation III (non-combat) broke after their return—36.4 percent vs. 18.4 percent. Although some of these men still faced the possibility of further service in another theater, for most the chance of being reassigned to combat was remote.

A few points stand out from this review of the soldiers' assignments at breakdown. A high proportion never finished basic training. A considerable number, however, were in duty assignments in the Zone of the Interior when they broke. Others had been able to serve overseas in combat or non-combat positions. While the majority of those with overseas service became ineffective while abroad, a significant minority did not break until they had been returned to the United States. The highest proportion of those with major incapacitation were soldiers who broke in training; the smallest, those who had been in combat.

MEDICAL CARE

Among the conspicuous differences between the American Army and other armies in World War II was the outstandingly high level of medical care that was available to our soldiers. The Russian soldier had access to a military hospital if he were in need of surgery; otherwise he had to rely primarily on such medical resources as were available in the civilian community in which he found himself. The United States called onto active duty almost 40 percent of the practicing physicians of the country to care for about 8 percent of the nation's manpower—the 12 million in uniform.

In the preceding chapter we noted that about 18 percent of the entire time that the cohort ineffectives were on active duty was spent in the hospital. The ineffective soldier was hospitalized, on the average, for a total of just under 80 days; for those who had been in combat the average was much higher—over 200 days. In addition to the time that they spent in the hospital, many soldiers made extensive use of the dispensary. Our data, however, are based on individual medical records rather than on unit records and so do not reflect the full use made of outpatient facilities by the men in our sample. While the Army was very careful to preserve all the individual medical records pertaining to a soldier's hospitalizations and make them a part of his permanent file at the Personnel Records Center, this was not always the case with individual records pertaining to outpatient treatments.

In the Army the hospital served a double purpose. It was the only place to send a man who was not fit to perform duty, so that many who were admitted suffered from only minor disabilities. The hospital was also used for evaluating soldiers who gave some evidence of disability to determine whether they should be returned to active duty or discharged to civilian life. The hospital system became, therefore, a major discharge channel and much of the time of medical officers was devoted to evaluating and processing marginal performers.

An indication of the heavy processing load carried by the hospitals is the large proportion of individuals with major incapacitation for further military service who were discharged during the early months of their service. Of the more than 46,000 men in Situations I and II who were hospitalized, just under half were adjudged to have major incapacitation for further service. And a little over half (53 percent) of this group had pre-military indications of ineffectiveness. Thus deficiencies in initial screening added greatly to the demands placed upon the Army's medical service.

As might be expected, men with longer service in the Zone of the Interior (Situation II) were hospitalized longer on the average than men discharged earlier (Situation I). Soldiers who had served overseas had considerably more hospitalization than those who served only in the Zone of the Interior; those who had been in combat (Situation IV) spent the greatest number of days in the hospital. The mean days of hospitalization for men in each of the Situations by the degree of their incapacitation for further military service is shown in the following table.

MEAN DAYS OF HOSPITALIZATION BY DEGREE OF INCAPACITATION AND BY SITUATION

SITUATION	DEGREE OF INCAPACITATION		
	Major	*Moderate*	*Minor*
I	53.5	63.2	41.6
II	67.6	89.1	41.5
III	163.5	179.2	141.5
IV	225.7	199.9	193.3

Men with moderate incapacitation for further service had a somewhat higher number of hospitalizations and their average stay was slightly longer because the diagnoses of their conditions were not as clear-cut as for men with either major or minor incapacitation. When a man with a major disability entered the hospital, the medical officers had less difficulty in arriving at a diagnosis and disposition; and among those with only minor incapacitation were many whose admission to the hospital was solely for a medical evaluation, not treatment.

It was common belief in the Army that many "rode the sick book" in order to avoid duty and to build up a record which would lead the Army to discharge them. Our data are too incomplete to warrant a definitive statement on this point. We know from a previous sample study that only some dispensary visits were noted and retained as part of the soldier's individual medical record. If we assume that the incomplete data are free of bias, our data show that in Situations II and IV soldiers with major incapacitation for further service tended to use outpatient facilities somewhat more frequently than those who were less severely disturbed.

Differences among the ineffective soldiers who made use of the hospital are brought out in the following table which presents the data by the clinical categories under which the Army discharged these men:

Reason for Separation	*Mean Number of Hospitalizations*	*Mean Days of Hospitalization*
Psychoneurosis	2.5	104.3
Psychosis	1.9	115.7
Undesirability	2.3	59.0
Inapt	1.1	22.6

The low figures for the inapt group reflects the fact that these men served for the shortest period of time and that they were less likely to require treatment for emotional disorders than did the others. The undesirable group had a relatively high rate of hospitalization—almost as high as the psychoneurotics, who had the highest rate. Moreover, they made the greatest use of the dispensary. Many of these men made extensive use of the medical facilities because of venereal disease or alcoholism.

These few figures underscore the extent to which the Army's

medical installations were used not only to treat the sick and injured but to assess and process men who gave evidence of ineffectiveness. The important role of the medical officer in the Army's personnel system will become even clearer as we review how ineffective soldiers were identified.

HOW INEFFECTIVENESS WAS MANIFESTED

The following table shows how the soldiers' ineffectiveness was initially evidenced:

	Percent
Poor performance	22.7
Disciplinary problem	5.7
Symptomatic behavior	19.6
Somatic complaints	52.0
	100.0

When alleged "poor performance" in the duty to which he was assigned was observed and noted by his superiors, we classified a soldier in this category. We did not make an independent evaluation of his actual performance since we were interested here only in ascertaining how he came to be initially identified as ineffective. Included in this group are a few cases where lack of intellectual capacity, although not specifically reflected in low performance, was given as the cause of ineffectiveness.

The classification disciplinary problems needs no elaboration. Men with records showing persistent misbehavior, chronic alcoholism, repeated AWOL, or insubordination were included in this category.

Under symptomatic behavior we have included soldiers with fainting spells, enuresis, bizarre behavior, suicide attempts, etc. Somatic complaints included soldiers who had ill-defined aches and pains in the head, back, stomach, legs. For the most part such men took the initiative and sought help while most of the group with symptomatic behavior were identified by others.

The extent to which men with these different manifestations of ineffectiveness were handicapped for further military service is shown by the following table.

DEGREE OF INCAPACITATION BY INITIAL MANIFESTATION OF INEFFECTIVENESS, IN PERCENT

INITIAL MANIFESTATION OF INEFFECTIVENESS	TOTAL	DEGREE OF INCAPACITATION *Major*	*Moderate*	*Minor*
Poor performance	100.0	46.1	19.7	34.2
Disciplinary problem	100.0	79.3	10.8	9.9
Symptomatic behavior	100.0	72.4	19.6	8.0
Somatic complaints	100.0	34.1	41.1	24.8
Total Cohort	100.0	46.9	30.3	22.8

These figures indicate that men who were disciplinary problems were seriously disturbed and had major incapacitation for further service. The same is true, but this was more to be expected, of men who developed symptomatic behavior. Those with somatic complaints tended to have a moderate degree of incapacitation and in fact constituted the greatest proportion (70.6 percent) of this group.

The extent to which the records of these several groups gave evidence of pre-military ineffectiveness is brought out in the following which indicates the proportions with prior warning signs among those who at the time of breakdown had major incapacitation for further service:

	Percent
Poor performance	83.4
Disciplinary problem	87.6
Symptomatic behavior	38.4
Somatic complaints	27.9

Two facts stand out: one, that soldiers with disciplinary problems had a high rate of pre-military indications; the other, that soldiers who were identified because of symptomatic behavior had a relatively low rate. While the first suggests that the Army failed to take cognizance of these indicators at screening, particularly evidence concerning the selectee's heavy use of alcohol, the second shows that many who developed symptomatic difficulties in service probably could not have been identified at induction.

The ways in which soldiers' ineffectiveness was manifested in the different Situations are outlined below.

SITUATIONAL DISTRIBUTION OF COHORT INEFFECTIVES BY INITIAL MANIFESTATION OF INEFFECTIVENESS, IN PERCENT

INITIAL MANIFESTATION OF INEFFECTIVENESS	TOTAL	SITUATION I	II	III	IV
Poor performance	100.0	56.8	38.9	3.0	1.3
Disciplinary problem	100.0	39.3	43.8	12.6	4.3
Symptomatic behavior	100.0	43.3	16.9	19.5	20.3
Somatic complaints	100.0	55.8	20.1	11.5	12.6
Total Cohort	100.0	52.6	25.1	11.2	11.1

The poor performers were discharged early; many of those with symptomatic behavior quite late; the largest proportion of the disciplinary problems were separated in Situation II. It is not surprising that soldiers who were unable to meet the Army's performance demands failed early. The fact that men who became disciplinary problems were separated primarily in Situation II reflected the Army's policy not to move too quickly against these men, especially those who were alcoholics. Many performed well when sober and the Army hoped that they might reform. Men with symptomatic behavior were prominently represented among the two overseas groups; they were capable of absorbing the minor stresses of military life but could not cope effectively with the major deprivations of overseas service.

One out of 9 ineffectives was identified in a hospital to which he had been admitted for purely physical reasons. Some, for example, developed severe anxiety symptoms while hospitalized for a wound incurred in combat; but others who had entered the hospital because of relatively minor conditions such as a sore throat appeared to the medical officer to be somewhat nervous and were tagged as "psychoneurotic" and consequently discharged. Surprisingly few men, 4.7 percent only, broke while in casual or transient status, that is, while in reception centers, replacement depots, redistribution stations, or en route as an individual replacement. Although only 2.4 percent were actually in the stockade when the first action was taken to start them on the road to discharge, many of those who were, were later discharged after medical treatment and hospitalization for psychosis. Often their infractions of discipline were rooted in severe emotional disturbances which had been overlooked until they were carefully examined by a competent medical officer.

Two of every 5 ineffective soldiers were initially identified by a line officer and the remainder were picked up by medical officers except for a very few who were spotted by others, usually chaplains. As the table below shows, the line officer identified more of the seriously disturbed, those with major incapacitation for further service. Medical officers started more of those with only minor incapacitation on the way out.

INITIAL IDENTIFICATION OF INEFFECTIVENESS BY DEGREE OF INCAPACITATION, IN PERCENT

INITIAL IDENTIFICATION OF INEFFECTIVENESS	DEGREE OF INCAPACITATION *Major*	*Moderate*	*Minor*
Line officers	52.8	26.5	40.8
Medical officers	44.8	73.5	59.2
Others	2.4	–	–
	100.0	100.0	100.0

Apparently men who could no longer be useful to the Army were so conspicuous that the line officers, even without long experience or medical competence, were able to identify many of them. Also included in this group with major incapacitation were many whose deficiency consisted primarily of a lack of educational background and this came directly to the attention of line officers.

As we might expect, the medical officers primarily identified those who came to the hospital or dispensary with somatic complaints. The line officers picked up almost 3 out of 4 with symptomatic behavior and, we may add here, 2 out of every 3 men who were eventually discharged because of a psychosis. While the initial identification was made by the line, such cases were of course examined by medical personnel who made the actual diagnoses. The behavior of these soldiers, however, was so eccentric that even a layman could spot it.

The relative security and comfort of the hospital stood in sharp contrast to the dangers and deprivations of combat. For this reason we undertook a special analysis of the impact of hospitalization on soldiers who had been in combat. In total 8,057 served in combat, almost all of whom (95.9 percent) were eventually discharged from a hospital. Approximately half of the total, 3,921, were admitted to the hospital directly from combat. Of this number, 1,707 had developed a psychiatric disability; the remainder, 2,214, had been wounded in action or had become ill to the point where they required hospitalization. Only later did they develop clear-cut psychiatric symptoms. Another 1,140 men, who had been wounded in combat but had been returned to duty from the hospital, later reentered the hospital chain and were eventually discharged for a psychiatric disability which they had developed in the interim. These figures suggest the "holding power" of the hospital. It was not easy for men to return to combat or to remain effective once they had been exposed to the security and comfort of the hospital.

SUMMARY

The materials presented in this chapter substantiate what has been suggested earlier—that many of the soldiers whom the Army discharged as ineffective were never qualified to perform in the Army in a satisfactory manner. The materials also indicate that the performance of many others was influenced by the way in which the Army managed them.

We noted that many recruits underwent training in ground force units that were racing against time to meet an early readiness date for overseas shipment. Their commanders had little patience with soldiers who fell behind and moved quickly to discharge them.

Among the most striking findings was the limited effort that the Army made to transfer men who demonstrated early in their military service that they were not doing well in their assignment. Only 1 man in 20 who was discharged within the first year of service had been reassigned. The Army preferred to take its chances with a replacement rather than to run the risk of spending additional time and effort in facilitating the adjustment of a man who had already demonstrated some inability.

But the transfer data also revealed that when the Army had made a considerable investment in a man, it was much more likely to try to salvage him through reassignment. In total about 1 in 5 of the cohort ineffectives had been transferred prior to separation. However, 4 out of every 5 men who were discharged with only minor incapacitation for further military service had never been given a second chance.

The analysis also revealed the important role played by medical officers and the hospital system in evaluating and discharging ineffective soldiers. About 1 out of every 2 soldiers who were eventally discharged for ineffectiveness had developed somatic complaints and sought medical help. Some of them entered a hospital for a physical condition and while there came to the attention of the staff as disturbed or nervous and were therefore separated. A considerable proportion of combat soldiers who were wounded developed secondary emotional difficulties while in the hospital, which led to their eventual discharge. Nineteen out of every 20 of the cohort ineffectives who had been in combat were discharged from a hospital.

Some soldiers developed such bizarre behavior that it was relatively easy for a line officer to recognize that they were seriously ill. But the authorities had more difficulty in spotting serious emotional disorders among those who had been apprehended because of disciplinary problems. However, later evaluation by a medical officer led to the realization that a high percentage of them were seriously disturbed.

Had the Army had more time, it would have been worthwhile to take more care in making initial assignments; in reassigning many who failed to perform effectively in their first assignment;

in training medical officers to avoid treating the soldiers as if they were civilian patients; and in providing more orientation for line officers about the importance of obtaining medical consultation when handling the soldiers who became serious disciplinary problems. But the Army did not have time. Many things that it did or left undone reflect this fact. But whatever the reason, the way in which the Army managed its men had much to do with the way in which they performed.

Chapter Eight: REDUCING INEFFECTIVENESS

THE ARMY had been forewarned by its experience in World War I that sudden large-scale mobilization would flood it with a considerable number of men who would sooner or later prove ineffective. The large number of ineffective soldiers in the American Expeditionary Forces in World War I about whom General Pershing complained in his cables to the War Department served as a warning to the military planners as they formulated their mobilization plans prior to World War II. Much of the Army's planning during the years between the wars was directed towards devising methods which would reduce, if not eliminate, the intake of large numbers of unsuitable men. With the onset of mobilization in 1940 the Army looked to the screening process to prevent the induction of men with actual or potential disabling defects; the planners anticipated that by spotting and rejecting these men before induction, the Army would be spared the expense of discharging them prematurely after they broke down in training or in combat.

The length to which the Army went in its attempt to control ineffectiveness through screening prior to induction is illustrated by the fact that approximately 2 million men were rejected because they appeared to have a mental, emotional, or behavioral defect. As we have shown in *The Lost Divisions*, the rejection rates in World War II were about 11 times as great as in World War I for men with emotional defects and 4½ times as great for men with mental defects. But the materials presented in the companion volumes as well as the preceding chapters make it clear that the Army's effort to control ineffectiveness by relying so heavily on the screening mechanism proved inadequate.

It may be that the Army's theory was correct and that the difficulty lay in implementation. It is possible that if the screening had been carried out more efficiently, the number of ineffective soldiers would have been greatly reduced. It is also possible that the theory of relying on initial screening had inherent limitations and that only a part of the ineffectiveness which plagued the Army in World War II could have been controlled by better screening alone.

We considered this problem at length in *The Lost Divisions* and sought to make clear that the selection criteria which an organization uses can never be established without regard to its manpower requirements and the size and qualities of the pool from which it must draw its personnel. One of the long-term major advantages of the Navy over the Army has been its smaller size, which has made it much easier for the Navy to pursue a more selective personnel policy.

Relatively early in World War II the Army was forced to lower its standards for induction, particularly its educational requirements. The Army soon realized that it could build up rapidly to a peak force of more than 8 million only by reducing its selection criteria. But the fact that the Army was unable to maintain its high selection standards does not diminish the value of assessing the efficiency of the screening mechanism both in terms of what it aimed to do and what it actually was able to do.

Even if the manpower requirements had been much smaller and the Army had been able to maintain the higher standards of selection, it is doubtful that the problem of ineffectiveness could have been controlled by screening alone. It would have been reduced, but not eliminated. The materials previously analyzed have shown that the way in which the Army managed its men exercised a significant influence on their performance. The aim of this chapter is to set out, on the basis of the data which we have reviewed, recommendations about selection and management policies that might contribute to a reduction of ineffectiveness in the Armed

Forces. Our second objective is to consider to what extent the lessons of military experience may be applicable to the management of men in other types of large organizations.

SELECTION

One way to review the Army's experience with selection is to distinguish between initial selection and later screening in depth, especially during the early months of a recruit's active service. Actually the process of evaluation continues throughout the whole of a man's service for there is constant need for re-assessment in connection with promotion and, in combat and other strenuous assignments, with the state of the soldier's physical and emotional reserves. But a critical assessment of his strengths and weaknesses is most important during the early period of a soldier's service.

As far as initial selection was concerned, the Army's experience in World War II brings the following into sharp focus. Since policy changes always create problems, especially in an organization which is forced to rely on relatively inexperienced personnel, the Army would have been in a better position had it had a clearer understanding earlier of both its requirements and the characteristics of the manpower pool. Such knowledge would have enabled it to avoid many of the sudden shifts in selection policy which did so much to confuse the examiners and to lower their effectiveness. That the frequent policy changes made it exceedingly difficult for the examiners to do their job well is made clear in the comments which we received from a group of leading psychiatrists who had participated in the screening at induction stations, and which were published in *Psychiatry and Military Manpower Policy: A Reappraisal of the Experience in World War II.*

The Army insisted during most of the war that the major criterion of acceptability for military service was ability to serve as a combat soldier. However, probably no more than 1 in 3 soldiers ever engaged the enemy in combat. The establishment of such a high standard meant that the selection process was less effective than it should have been since it screened out many who could have served well in non-combatant assignments.

While we have seen in the preceding chapters that there was much evidence to support the Army's substantial reliance on the educational screen to avoid inducting illiterates and poorly educated men, much less support was found for its faith in the psychiatric screen through which it sought to reject men with emotional defects. There is no basis in theory for assuming that clinical diagnoses are good predictors of future work performance, especially when the psychiatric symptoms do not reflect severe pathology. The error of equating the two grows out of a failure to understand that a man's ability to perform in the Army or in civilian life depends not only on his emotional stability, but also on his intellectual-educational background, his skills, his motivation, and the duty to which he is assigned. Moreover, a man's psychological condition is not static, but is subject to change depending on alterations in the external environment and his emotional response to these changing conditions.

The Army was right in wanting to reject men who were likely to become psychiatric casualties but it erred, except for those with clear-cut evidence of severe pathology, in believing that it could identify potential ineffectiveness through a short psychiatric examination. Had the Army concentrated on rejecting only the seriously disturbed, it would have rejected fewer men who could have served and probably would have accepted fewer of those who eventually failed. Almost 1 out of every 4 men in the cohort sample slipped through the screen although their records contained clear indications of ineffectiveness that would have justified their rejection. But the analysis also disclosed that about 1 out of every 2 men who at the time of breakdown were severely incapacitated for further service in the Army could not have been identified at induction on the basis of their pre-military records.

A more modest screening objective would probably pay big dividends. It would be desirable, for example, if instead of having to divide their limited time among all selectees, the examiners were able to concentrate on the marginal group. Towards the end of the war such an experiment was in fact instituted by the adoption of a Neuropsychiatric Screening Adjunct which was given to all men who were being processed. Only those who received a critical score on this easily administered test were supposed to be assessed by the psychiatrist.

On the basis of the findings in the preceding chapters, it is clear that among the groups who should be singled out for more careful assessment are, first, all men with less than an eighth-grade education. Since in many schools, children are automatically promoted to the next higher grade even when they have not mastered the earlier work, it is desirable to assess with special care all who have not graduated from elementary school to be sure that they are in fact literate. Next it is desirable to review carefully the records of all men who cannot account for significant periods of time in their late adolescence or adulthood. Inquiry may disclose that they have spent time in a mental or penal institution or had extended periods of idleness, in which case a further and more careful evaluation would be called for. Among the cohort ineffectives many could have been identified at induction if the examiners had been able to spend more time with them.

The high proportion of men with broken marriages who proved ineffective would justify paying particular attention to this group. Likewise a large proportion of those who marry very young had a sufficiently poor record to justify more careful evaluation, as well as those with a history of law-breaking in civilian life. Because physical and other disabilities increase with age, the older group also warrants special attention.

While the foregoing groups add up to a sizable number, it is still manageable if most of the available examining talent is devoted to them. There is no question that such a redirection of screening resources would add considerably to the overall effectiveness of the screen. But it must be added that even improved screening would not keep out all who will prove ineffective. This points to the need for a secondary screening after the men come on active duty.

SECONDARY SCREENING

More than half of the ineffective soldiers in the cohort group were separated during their first twelve months of service, 23 percent before six months. But this does not mean that the Army had established a formal secondary screening procedure to assess the quality of a soldier's performance during his first months on active duty. Actually, the procedure was quite different. Once a man was inducted, he was presumed qualified to serve. If he was unable to keep up with the training schedule or failed in his assignment, he was discharged; he received a medical discharge for any condition that was presumed to have arisen after induction or to have been aggravated by service.

The Army never developed special procedures to sort out marginal recruits. At best it improvised. In the process it initiated a large number of constructive actions but it never had a full-scale program aimed at controlling ineffectiveness by discharging during the early months of service men who demonstrated serious difficulties in adjustment.

Our data revealed that a high percentage of those who failed during the first year did so while they were still in training—more than 1 out of every 2. Most of these men were trained not at Basic or Replacement Training Centers but directly in units. The fact that so many men were not able to take their basic training at Training Centers but often had to fit themselves into a group that was already advanced in its schedule only added to the pressures with which they had to contend. Moreover, it was unlikely that they had access to the important supportive facilities that were more characteristically found at the large training centers—particularly the mental hygiene units and the special training units for slow learners.

Actually even the large training centers were not adequately provided with these important facilities. Not until the second half of 1943 was the training program completely revamped and Special Training Units organized at Reception Centers to give men the special training they needed before they were assigned for regular training. By the time this reform was instituted many of the cohort sample had already been discharged for ineffectiveness. But the point is relevant that such facilities are easier to set up and operate at large reception or training centers where they can be available to the many who encounter initial difficulties in adjusting to the Army because their intellectual skills are inadequate or because they have become emotionally disturbed by the shift from civilian to military life. If soldiers can receive support during this trying period it may make the difference between their succeeding or failing in the Army.

Training recruits at large centers has the additional advantage of enabling the Army to select and indoctrinate supervisory personnel who can become more skilled in dealing with the newly inducted. If all recruits receive their basic training at the same type of installation under specially trained personnel, men with major incapacitation for further service can be quickly identified and discharged and there is less likelihood that others with minor symptoms of maladjustment who with a little support could function effectively will be let out.

The need for the careful indoctrination of line officers in the handling of recruits is underscored by our finding that they played such a prominent role in identifying the ineffective soldier. It is important that all officers gain more understanding about inapt and unstable soldiers in order to deal more competently with them. Many recruits were helped over an initial hurdle by an understanding sergeant or lieutenant.

Another advantage which can accrue from concentrating the basic training of recruits is that their assignments can be postponed until the Army has more opportunity to test them and more time to find suitable assignments. The British went so far in World War

II as to put all inductees through a combined center so as to be able to assign them more appropriately among the three major forces—Army, Air, and Navy.

The earlier analysis of assignment and reassignment pointed to the relatively haphazard manner in which it was carried out. Because of the great pressure of time, the Reception Centers had to be emptied every four days or so and men were therefore posted to whatever divisions or units were at the moment in need of manpower; little consideration could be given to whether they had the qualities that would enable them to perform satisfactorily in these assignments. If a combat unit required several thousand men, most if not all who were at the time in the Reception Center, irrespective of their age or physical stamina, might be forwarded. If a Signal unit needed men, all who were available might be forwarded, even those who had never reached the fourth grade in school.

The Army's inability to make maximum use of the assignment and reassignment system was undoubtedly costly. It need only be recalled in this connection that only about 1 man in 20 in the cohort who failed during his first year of service was ever reassigned. Most of the men had one chance, that was all. Yet there were many who could have succeeded in the Infantry who could not possibly master the more theoretical training required of soldiers in a Signal unit. In turn, there were many older men with good educational backgrounds who could have functioned quite well in communications work who simply could not qualify as riflemen.

Of course, the Army tried to take these differences into account in making its assignments, but it was greatly handicapped by limitations of time and facilities in utilizing the full potentialities of assignment and reassignment to control ineffectiveness. It is difficult enough in the midst of a war to do what must be done. But it is impossible to do it well if the gains and costs of following a particular procedure have not been clearly assessed. The Army set out to train divisions as rapidly as possible. It paid little attention to the possibility of conserving manpower by making more effective use of its assignment and reassignment procedures.

PERSONNEL POLICIES

We have outlined some of the gains which would accrue from using the initial selection procedures and screening in depth to cut down the number of ineffective soldiers. As more seriously handicapped men are rejected at induction and more marginal soldiers are helped to surmount the difficulties of initial adjustment, the outcome will be improved. A valuable by-product of making special efforts to help recruits would be the readier identification of those who cannot make the grade even with special assistance. By separating them quickly, the Army would avoid further unprofitable investment in them.

There are a series of broad policy considerations which transcend the specific problems of selection and screening in depth—though many have pertinence to these areas—that can also contribute towards the reduction of ineffectiveness.

While the Army, no matter what policies it might have adopted, could not have prevented certain soldiers from breaking down, for others the presence or absence of support may well have determined whether they could continue or had to be discharged. We have called attention to the valuable contributions that the special training units and the mental hygiene units made by helping new recruits to increase their skills or reduce their anxiety and thereby to meet the demands that they faced. But the value of such services was by no means limited to helping men during the crucial initial months of their service.

We found that in every Situation a considerable number of men were discharged with only minor or moderate incapacitation for further service. This means that had the Army wanted and been able to offer them one or another kind of support they could probably have been returned to duty and continued to serve effectively.

But the Army was handicapped by a serious shortage of the kind of qualified personnel who would have been best able to offer support to soldiers who began to experience difficulty.

This was part of the problem. Part lay elsewhere. Many line and medical officers believed that when a man showed evidence of instability he would eventually prove to be of no further use to the Army and therefore, it would be wise to discharge him as quickly as possible. This is why many of them made little effort to help such soldiers. Many of the soldiers did not necessarily require the specialized services of a psychiatrist; all that they needed was a helping hand from someone in authority who had some understanding of their problem and for whom they had respect.

The essential difference between an experienced officer and a novice was in the extent to which they were able to maintain the morale and effectiveness of their troops. The immediate referral to the dispensary or the hospital of all soldiers who showed even minor degrees of incapacitation was an abrogation of command responsibility which could be explained but not justified by the immaturity of many officers and by the prevailing view that all ineffective soldiers were "psychiatric cases." Much more could have been done to give the line a clearer understanding of the range of emotional problems that were likely to crop up and suggestions as to how to deal with them. Moreover, it would have been especially desirable to indoctrinate the noncommissioned officers since they had so much more direct contact with the men and were therefore in the best position to help them.

Underlying the assignment and reassignment procedure was the basic doctrine of exchangeability. The Army went though most of the war committed to the belief that any soldier should be able to do any assignment for which he had been trained—that is, he should be potentially fully exchangeable with any other soldier. This explains why it used the criterion of fitness for combat in initial screening and why it hesitated to make room within its personnel system for "limited service" men. Late in the war the Army introduced the PULHES System which modified its inflexible personnel procedures and required its officers to take into account in making assignments and reassignments the soldier's physical and emotional strengths. But, as we observed in *The Lost Divisions*, the reform came too late to have been really effective. The unwillingness of the Army to complicate further what was already because of size and dispersion a very complicated assignment system is readily understandable.

The fact that so many units followed the practice of passing on their ineffective men, including serious disciplinary problems, rather than dealing with them forthrightly compounded the suspicion that most transferees would fail to perform effectively. Only in overseas theaters where replacements were less readily available were officers more willing to give men a second chance.

The major aim of the Army's personnel policy was to induct and train men who would perform effectively in combat, for victory depended primarily on the perseverance and skill of the combat soldier. The Army did well in culling over troops in varying stages of training and in selecting for combat assignments those who gave promise of performing effectively. While the innate qualities of a soldier had much to do with the level of his performance in combat, other factors were important, including the way in which the Army treated him. Men might resent the fact that they were forced to live and fight under very adverse conditions while so many others held safe jobs in the rear. They would accept bad luck but not gross inequity.

It is worth recalling in this connection that many in the cohort sample with combat experience broke down not in combat but only after they had been reassigned to a non-combat unit overseas or had returned to the United States. At that point if they were treated in a cavalier fashion, as many were because the units which they joined had no need of additional manpower or could not make use of their special skills, they decided that they had no further obligations to perform effectively. They felt that having done their best and risked life and limb for their country they were entitled to more consideration. If they thought that the Army was treating them unfairly, they became recalcitrant and frequently became disciplinary problems. There were many others, of course, who were so relieved to be out of danger that they did not give a second thought to whether they were being treated equitably. And there were still others who once they stopped fighting were overwhelmed to the point of becoming ineffective by the fears which they had been able to contain as long as they had been in actual danger.

Although the Army frequently failed to give adequate consideration to combat veterans, especially in their reassignment to appropriate duties after they had completed their tour at the front, it also erred in the opposite direction by being oversolicitous. A major source of this difficulty was the hospital. Most medical officers were inclined to handle all patients as if they were suffering from a physical ailment which justified the use of all available diagnostic and therapeutic measures. While this approach insured that the sick and injured would be well treated, it had unforeseen consequences for the large number of men with vague and unspecific complaints which were primarily emotional or motivational in origin. It must be recalled in this connection that many line officers sent troublesome soldiers into the hospital and that many men who sought escape took themselves to the dispensary so often that they were sooner or later admitted to the hospital.

Once in the hospital all patients were systematically examined and tested, even those who had no organic difficulties. This helps to explain the large number of days that the ineffective soldier spent in the hospital each time that he was admitted. Army hospitals were staffed largely with civilians in uniforms, many of whom had not been properly indoctrinated about the role of the Medical Department in the conservation of military manpower so that they frequently failed to understand the impact of their policies and procedures on the effective strength of the Army. Moreover, many medical officers believed that if they had a personnel function, it was to relieve the line of soldiers who became ineffective but could not be readily discharged through administrative channels.

Closer coordination between the medical and line officers usually obtained in the combat zone where the pressure to conserve manpower was much greater. But even here the hospital system frequently contributed to personnel losses. There was such a great discrepancy between the conditions under which men fought and those under which they were hospitalized that, once men had slept in clean sheets, eaten hot food, and experienced the relaxation in discipline, only the strongly motivated would cooperate with the doctors to speed their recovery and return to combat with its deprivations and dangers.

All of the factors in the situation—other than a man's ties to his buddies—conspired to bind him to the hospital. It is not surprising therefore that a high percentage of all those in the cohort who had combat experience became ineffective after they were hospitalized. Many who were admitted because of a wound were discharged many months later because of a psychoneurosis which became manifest only during their stay in the hospital.

While it was desirable for the Army to provide the best medical care for all soldiers, and particularly for those wounded in combat, it was not necessary to prolong the hospital stay of so many men and to keep them in such a favorable environment that it sapped their will to soldier. The frequent friction between the line and the medical officer during World War II was not the responsibility of either but grew out of a lack of a comprehensive policy that would have enabled medical installations to keep effective the maximum number of troops. By early 1945 a definitive approach had been worked out but the war was almost over.

Without broadening the context of the present study, passing reference should be made to the fact that during the Korean hostilities the Army applied many of the lessons which it had learned during World War II. It recognized that many soldiers who began to perform ineffectively should not be admitted to the hospital for psychiatric treatment but rather should be given guidance and support by their commanders. By strengthening individual and group morale, the Army saved many men from breaking down. The Army also recognized the importance of simple supports, especially for combat soldiers—warm food, occasional periods of rest, a stated maximum period of service in the combat zone. There was also much closer liaison between line and medical officers. Great care was taken not to send to the rear a man who had an emotional breakdown in combat until he had been evaluated and treated near the front with the aim of returning him to his unit as soon as possible. And only a very few were evacuated to the United States. The conditions under which we fought in Korea, as in every war, were special and distinctive; nevertheless many lessons learned in World War II were put to constructive use.

The point has been made earlier that the Army during World War II would have gained from a larger investment in the indoctrination and training of its officer personnel, both commissioned and noncommissioned. It is true that such an effort would have taken time and made additional demands on the already overextended group of experienced officers. And yet, since the Army had to rely primarily on civilians who had little or no military background or experience, a greater investment in leadership development would have been profitable.

Among the ways that the Army might be able to help itself in the face of an acute shortage of experienced personnel is to leave officers in their assignments a little longer so that they could transfer more of their knowledge and experience to others who take over from them. In World War II the theory that a man was equally capable of doing a large number of different jobs was applied as uncritically to officers as to enlisted men.

Another way in which the Army's supervisory functions could be improved is by a more constructive use of specialist personnel. There is little point in sending incompetent soldiers to the hospital in such droves that their mere processing and evaluation swamps the psychiatric staffs. A third or a half of the psychiatric staff could be assigned to help junior line officers and their noncommissioned personnel deal directly with poor performers. This was done at a few posts and proved most effective overseas where some division commanders had their psychiatrists serve primarily in an advisory capacity to their line officers.

Another illustration of how specially qualified officer and noncommissioned officer personnel could be better utilized was contained in the earlier recommendation to put all recruits through replacement training centers. A skilled and experienced cadre which handles tens of thousands of recruits could develop sharper diagnostic and stronger supportive skills. Moreover, if during World War II the Army had been able to assign to command positions more individuals who had a special understanding of, or interest in, certain groups such as Negro soldiers, it could have cut its manpower losses. While the major reason for the differentially high separation rates for Negroes was, as we have pointed out in *The Negro Potential*, the meagerness of their educational background, a further contributing factor was the lack of effective leadership to which many were exposed.

Aside from the specific policies that have been briefly reviewed, the utilization of military manpower was also greatly influenced by what might be designated as the Army's personnel stance. Attention was called earlier to the difficulties that flowed from sudden changes in Army policies, particularly those affecting selection and separation. A sudden shift in direction left the officers in the field confused and baffled. The more frequent the change, the greater was the confusion, and the less effectively could they carry out their assignments to screen men for service or to evaluate whether certain soldiers should be separated. It would be difficult to think of a more costly practice from the viewpoint of manpower utilization than the sudden and repeated shifts in personnel policy.

In addition to confusing those charged with making the crucial decisions about inducting or discharging a man, these policy shifts had the further disadvantage of opening or closing avenues of intake or outflow with such frequency that the personnel system could not operate efficiently. The outstanding example of this was seen first in the radical lowering of induction standards in the latter half of 1942 when our cohort was coming on active duty, the introduction of the easy discharge policy shortly thereafter, and the sudden tightening of separation criteria in November 1943.

Such radical shifts in policy were also disturbing to the troops and helped to undermine the motivation of many of them. When the Army was following an extremely conservative separation policy whereby only men who were clearly of no further use were discharged, many soldiers who were only slightly incapacitated had an incentive to keep trying. They knew that their disabilities would not lead to a discharge. But when the Army suddenly adopted a policy that directed the discharge because of minor disabilities of men who were performing satisfactorily, many no longer were motivated to keep going. Since the Army apparently wanted them out they were glad to give up.

If we evaluate the Army's management of its manpower during World War II in perspective, most of its difficulties can be traced to its lack of experience in handling such large numbers of men under the exigencies of modern war. Its major failure occurred before the war commenced—there had been inadequate planning. This being so, it was inevitable that the Army would have to improvise, and improvisation in always expensive.

We must never lose sight of the fact, however, that the Army's improvisation, no matter how costly it appears in retrospect, proved successful. The Army learned as it went along and succeeded in correcting its mistakes, at least most of them. The summary recommendations that have been distilled from the Army's experience and that are directed toward the improved utilization of manpower —a more carefully focused selection system, the greater availability of supports, the better use of the assignment system, greater consideration for the combat veteran, the closer integration of the medical and personnel systems, more indoctrination and training of its leadership, and greater stability in personnel policy—are the fruits of research. They should not be read as criticisms of those who did their best in the emergency. They are offered as guidelines to those who must plan for tomorrow, so that the nation can profit from its past.

BROADER IMPLICATIONS

The major findings that have been extracted from this study of ineffectiveness during World War II which have pertinence to both military and civilian organizations can be summarized in the following broad generalizations:

1. As the number of men who must be screened to meet an organization's needs increases, less should be expected of the selection mechanism. Pressures of time and an inexperienced examining group, the impossibility of expanding rapidly if large numbers are rejected, and the inherent limitations of selection devices to differentiate validly as to the performance potential of men with differing backgrounds underwrite this conclusion.
2. As the assignments for which men are being selected become broader and less specific, the selection process will be less reliable. All that can be accomplished by such screening is to eliminate men who will presumably fail to perform effectively at even the simplest assignment. If the criteria are set higher, many who could perform effectively at simple assignments are needlessly rejected.
3. Initial selection can be effective to the extent that those charged with responsibility have a clear understanding of the characteristics of the manpower pool and of the real—not ideal—requirements of the organization. The objective of an organization to add only men who are free of all significant handicaps can never be fully realized and in a period of rapid expansion can not even be approximated.
4. Heavy reliance on a man's educational achievement as a criterion for assessing his potential performance is justified up to a point because individuals without a specified minimum will be unable to cope with most assignments. Moreover, the amount of

education that a man has secured is a rough indication not only of what he has been able to accomplish during the early years of his life but also of his motivation to achieve. But it is an error to read too much into a man's educational background. Some have had their way smoothed for them by their parents; others have had to surmount great hardships in obtaining schooling. Some are natively intelligent; others are not. Educational achievement is a useful index of potential performance but it must be evaluated critically and must not be relied upon exclusively.

5. The increasingly widespread practice of many organizations to rely on psychiatric assessments to evaluate a man's potential performance appears to be misguided. A man's emotional stability is only indirectly related to his ability to perform effectively. The latter depends on many things, particularly his intellectual ability and his motivation. Psychiatric appraisal is called for when individuals give clear evidence that they are seriously disturbed or when there is a question about their emotional stability.

6. Since the performance of large groups is always dependent to a marked degree on the quality of leadership, it is a good investment for an organization, especially one that is expanding rapidly, to devote considerable resources to the indoctrination and training of its supervisory personnel.

7. One of the specific advantages which accrue to large organizations from their size is the opportunity to exploit the great range of their job opportunities. Since many men can do well in some jobs but not in others, the adept use of assignments and reassignments can contribute markedly to the more effective utilization of manpower.

8. Since a man's performance is so greatly affected by his motivation, management must seek to avoid establishing or perpetuating conditions which will weaken the motivation of individuals to work effectively. It must weigh the impact even of supporting services such as medical care to be sure that they are not so organized as to detract from effective performance.

9. No organization can elicit a high level of performance unless

its personnel policies are attuned to the basic concepts of equity. If men see that management deals arbitrarily or unfairly with those who have done their best, they will fail to put forth their best efforts and will dissipate their energy fretting about their own future treatment.

10. The key to effective manpower utilization is in sound personnel planning. Nothing is more costly to a large organization than a failure to recognize in advance some of the major challenges which it will confront. Trained people can never be secured on a moment's notice. They must be developed. And effective team work can never be commandeered; it results from shared experiences. Long-range planning is prerequisite to effective manpower utilization.

Part III: CIVILIAN READJUSTMENT

Chapter Nine: THE PROCESS OF READJUSTMENT

A MAJOR QUESTION to which we directed our attention was what happened to the soldiers who broke down while in the Army after their return to civilian life. There were several reasons why the answers to this question were expected to prove illuminating. Knowledge of the postwar adjustment of these men would add another dimension to the understanding of performance. Since most men remained in the Army for less than 60 to 90 days after their breakdown, their military records alone did not give more than a first indication of the severity of their condition and a preliminary prognosis. Hence follow-up materials would provide important supplementary information which could throw new light on patterns of ineffective performance, especially on its duration, and on the ways in which individual, organizational, and situational factors contributed to a man's recovery or failure to recover.

In our companion volume, *Breakdown and Recovery*, we dealt at length with certain aspects of readjustment by presenting and evaluating case records of soldiers who succeeded in making a satisfactory recovery in civilian life from their breakdown. In this connection we singled out the records of men whose readjustment appeared to be directly connected with one of the following strategic factors: their innate qualities, physical, mental, emotional; the help which they received from their parents or their wives; their occupational experience; the benefits which they received from the Veterans Administration; the wider options and greater freedom of the civilian society; and, finally, the buoyancy of the economy which made it relatively easy even for those who were upset by their Army experience to find some kind of paid employment. We chose those cases specifically to highlight the role of one or another of these factors in helping the veteran to readjust. In the design of that book no provision was made for the study of soldiers who failed to readjust.

In this volume our treatment is at once more comprehensive and more analytical. We will deal with the entire cohort of ineffective soldiers and will include those who failed to adjust as well as those who succeeded. Further we will seek to delineate more sharply than was possible in the companion volume the stages of readjustment, differentiating in particular those who made an early readjustment from those whose adjustment was delayed; and further differentiating these two groups from the men who failed to become effective performers in civilian life. Instead of organizing the materials to call attention to the significance of a particular factor in the readjustment process, which was the principle underlying the analysis in the companion volume, we will seek to evaluate the complex of factors which contributed to the rehabilitation of large numbers of veterans as well as those which prevented the successful recovery of others.

In short we will move away from a predominantly qualitative analysis to one in which we will seek to cast our findings in statistically significant categories. Thus the studies of the readjustment of the ineffective soldier to civilian life in these two volumes complement each other.

SOME CLUES TO READJUSTMENT

The detailed analysis of the data about men who broke down while on military service provided some clues to the orders of difficulty that they were likely to face on their return to civilian life. Over 34,100 of the 72,700 cohort ineffectives represented by our sample, or 47 percent of the total, were assessed at the time of their breakdown to be severely incapacitated for further service in the Army. Of this number 16,800, or 23 percent of the cohort, were found to have had indications in their pre-military records of ineffectiveness that should have led to their rejection. Clearly many of these men were likely to find it very difficult to adjust successfully after discharge.

Other signs of potential difficulty could be seen in the fact that included among those with major incapacitation for further military service were 6,600 ineffectives, or 9 percent of the cohort, who were separated for a psychosis. While some individuals recover from a psychosis, many do not; at best they have periods when their illness is in remission. Another group with a relatively poor prognosis were the 5,300 men, 7 percent, who were separated for reasons of undesirability, which meant that they were discharged without honor. In turn, such a discharge meant for the majority of cases that they were barred from benefiting from most of the services of the Veterans Administration and that they had to overcome the reluctance of employers to hire them.

The fact that 8,300 men, 11 percent, had a poor performance record prior to coming into the Army and that as many as 19,300, 26 percent, had a poor military performance record prior to breakdown were yet further indications that many would probably find it very hard to make a satisfactory adjustment to civilian life.

These data about the pre-military and military performance of the cohort ineffectives only serve to remind the reader that to the extent that there is some underlying continuity to a man's performance from one period of his life to another, and from one environment to another, we would have reason to anticipate that a sizable proportion of the men who proved ineffective while in the Army would have major, and some would have insurmountable, difficulties in adjusting satisfactorily to civilian life.

THE VETERANS ADMINISTRATION PROGRAM

Before setting out the framework within which we undertook to study the postwar adjustment of the ineffective soldiers, it is both necessary and desirable to review the comprehensive benefits which were available to most of them under the several programs of the Veterans Administration and to determine what use they made of them. The American public assumed an obligation even before the end of World War II to assist veterans in a great variety of ways to speed their readjustment to civilian life. An understanding of these efforts is important in its own right and as a background for evaluating the specific experiences of the ineffective soldiers after their discharge as they sought to take up again the threads of civilian existence. At the time of discharge the vast majority of servicemen had a home to which they could return and relatives who could lend them a helping hand to ease their readjustment to civilian life. The law saw to it that those who had enlisted or had been drafted were normally entitled to return to their former jobs. Moreover, there were a large number of social agencies that stood ready, especially in the larger urban communities, to help the veteran who was in need of one or another type of specialized assistance. The extent to which veterans were helped by relatives, friends, and established social agencies is impossible to reconstruct, but we are in a position to appraise the numbers who made use of the extensive services offered by the Veterans Administration.

Congress specified July 25, 1947 as the official termination of World War II for purposes of computing the rights of veterans to various programs of the Veterans Administration. To qualify for most programs a veteran had to have served for at least 90 days on active duty and must have been separated under conditions that were not dishonorable. During World War II approximately 1 percent of all servicemen were discharged without honor and many of these, but by no means all, were disqualified for veterans' rights. A rough estimate suggests that 16 million veterans of World War II were eligible for benefits. In 1950 about 15.4 million veterans of World War II were in civilian life—they comprised approximately 10 percent of the total population and 3 out of every 10 males who were twenty years of age and over.

The G.I. Bill (Public Law 346) contained three major benefits:

a readjustment allowance of $20 dollars a week for a period not to exceed 52 weeks for unemployed veterans or those who were only partially employed; education and training benefits; and guaranteed and insured loans.

A veteran could make use of the readjustment allowance during the two-year period following his discharge. Thus by 1952 the allowance had expired for the vast majority. From the start of the program in September 1944, until June 30, 1952, 8,998,776 unemployed veterans and 700,866 self-employed veterans filed new claims. In total these veterans claimed over 164 million weeks of unemployment, or an average of 18 weeks per veteran, and 6.5 million months of partial self-employment. The total cost was in excess of $3.8 billion—$359 per unemployed veteran; $844 per self-employed. About 3 out of every 5 veterans received a modest amount of money for a period of months which enabled them to take some time to consider the job market and decide what they wanted to do.

Public Law 346 also made it possible for any eligible veteran to pursue a course of his own choice in any approved school or training establishment which would admit him. Only limited information is available about the extent of the training undertaken. More is known about how many veterans entered training than is known about how many completed the courses they started or how well they did in them. By July 1953, about 7,800,000 veterans—approximately 1 out of every 2 who were eligible—had either terminated training or were still in the program. Of this number 958,000—6 percent of all who were eligible—had exhausted their right to this benefit which varied, depending on their military service, from 15 months to a maximum of 4 years.

The following quotation from an Information Bulletin (IB 7-58, Oct. 12, 1953) of the Veterans Administration points up the numbers who pursued different types of training:

Of the 7,807,000 veterans who entered this training, over 2 million pursued courses in schools of higher learning, 3½ million in schools below the college level, 1½ million in job-training establishments, and almost ¾ million in farm training involving on-farm and related school training.

At the peak of the program in December 1947, 2½ million were enrolled. The special research study of the Veterans Administration which was reported in this bulletin indicated that about 1.7 million studied for the professions or in the humanities; 2.6 million were trained as craftsmen; 700,000 pursued courses in management and business administration; 434,000 trained for clerical and sales jobs; 750,000 enrolled in institutional on-farm training, a combination of classroom study and practical training on the farm; and 300,000 attended high school or grade school. Many of this last group of veterans later went on to specialized training. Veterans pursued training in other fields, but these include the ones in which most veterans trained.

Through June 1954, the government had expended more than $14 billion on this program, mostly for subsistence to veterans, as follows:

Purpose	*Amount*
Subsistence Allowance	$9,995,041,000
Tuition	3,891,730,000
Supplies and Equipment	486,334,000
	$14,373,105,000

The third major benefit in the G.I. Bill made it possible for eligible veterans to secure a government guarantee for home, farm, or business loans secured from private lending institutions. In the first ten years of the program nearly 4 million veterans took advantage of this provision—the vast majority, more than 9 out of 10, for home loans.

In addition to the educational and training benefits offered under Public Law 346, a disabled veteran was eligible under Public Law 16 to receive vocational counseling and training to assist in his rehabilitation. While the number of months of training which might be pursued was not written into the law, the Veterans Administration sought to complete the rehabilitation of these veterans within a four-year period. The Veterans Administration kept close reins on this program. A veteran did not have free occupational choice. His course had to be approved by his counselor and his program was carefully monitored. Some disabled veterans, denied the type of training they wanted under Public Law 16, enrolled under Public Law 346. Up to mid-1953 about 1.2 million had applied for training under Public Law 16; 1,087,000 had been approved, but only 600,000 had actually entered training. Of these, 350,000, or about 3 out of 5, were declared rehabilitated, and 30,000 were still in the program. The remaining 220,000 had transferred to training under Public Law 346 or had dropped out completely.

The following table summarizes the occupational objectives pursued by disabled veterans under Public Law 16 as of the end of 1952.

OCCUPATIONAL OBJECTIVES OF VETERANS ENTERING TRAINING UNDER PL 16

Occupational Objective	*Number of Veterans*	*Percent*
Professional	122,000	20.5
Semi-professional	41,000	6.9
Managerial and official	43,000	7.2
Clerical and sales	68,000	11.4
Services	14,000	2.4
Agriculture	80,000	13.4
Trades and industrial	227,000	38.2
	595,000	100.0

Veterans Administration studies indicate that 9 out of 10 disabled veterans who had completed their training were able to make use of their skills in their postwar employment. Of those who failed to complete their courses, only about 6 out of 10 were making use of such training as they had been able to acquire.

The following table summarizes the number of veterans who entered different types of training under Public Laws 346 or 16. Since some pursued training in more than one area, the figures are not additive:

Type of Training	*Number of Veterans*
Institutions of higher learning	2,700,000
Schools below college level	3,850,000
Job training	1,870,000
Institutional on-farm training	770,000

The following figure shows the trend for each level of training during the postwar period. Job training and college programs reached a peak in the immediate postwar years, while schools below the college level and institutional on-farm training had their largest enrollments in 1950. But by the end of 1954 the major educational and training effort was nearing its end.

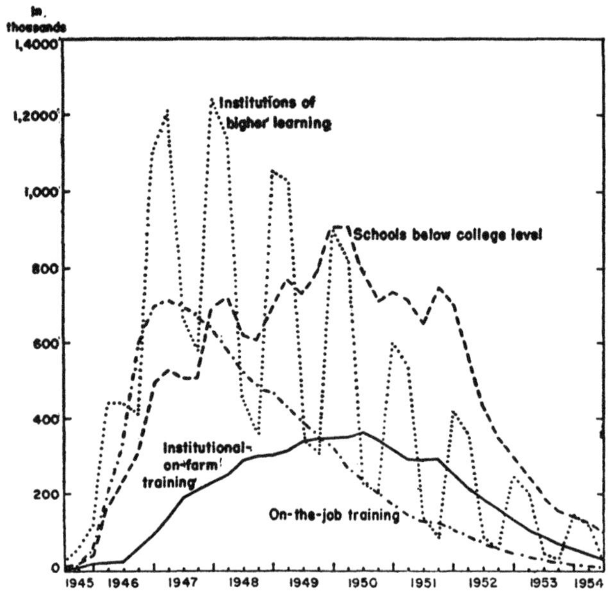

WORLD WAR II VETERANS IN TRAINING UNDER PUBLIC LAWS 16 AND 346, END OF QUARTER, 1945-1954

Source: *Annual Reports,* Administrator of Veterans Affairs. (Some quarterly figures estimated.)

The Veterans Administration also provided a wide range of medical and related benefits for eligible veterans. We are primarily interested in outpatient medical care and hospitalization. If an eligible veteran did not live in a community which contained or was close to a Veterans Administration outpatient clinic, he was entitled to be treated by a local physician whose fee would be paid by the Veterans Administration. During 1950 about 100,000 physicians participated in the "home town" medical care plan. An interesting sidelight on this plan is the following reply from the Veterans Administration to a participating physician who was taking care of a veteran with a psychiatric disability. He had written for advice as to how to treat the patient since he himself was not a psychiatrist.

> L.M. [the veteran] is felt to be a chronic schizophrenic reaction, moderate degree, paranoic type, manifested by suspiciousness, vague delusions of persecution. He has many fears about his self-assertiveness and feelings of inferiority. He avoids close relationships with others and has many sexual conflicts. He is regarded as competent.
>
> About the most that can be done to help this veteran is to accept him as an individual and to be interested in him and sympathetic with his problem. Probably T______ is not a large enough town to have an occupational therapy workshop. If one were available encourage him to participate in such a program. He could do work in leather making, woodwork, weaving, or leather work. This would be of great value.
>
> Medication for mental condition is seldom indicated and when it is usually consists of symptomatic medication such as mild sedatives or stimulants given as needed but not at regular lengths.
>
> These cases are discouraging but sometimes with acceptance and understanding they either maintain their level of adjustment or show some improvement over a long period of time, etc., etc.

The foregoing indicates the special efforts which were made to help veterans who because of their residence could not make use of Veterans Administrative installations. Extensive hospitalizations, including shock therapy, had failed to improve L.M.'s condition. His unreasonable fear of hospitals and of travel, together with his mother's desire to keep him with her, led the Veterans Administration to do what it could to maintain the veteran at home.

The magnitude of the medical services provided by the Veterans Administration is underscored by the scale of its outpatient and inpatient services. In 1950 total outpatient medical treatments (excluding examinations) totaled about 5.4 million, of which 875,000, or 16 percent, were for neuropsychiatric illness. The vast majority of this case load represented veterans of World War II. The Veterans Administration has estimated that in the early 1950s about 60 percent of all veterans eligible for and requesting outpatient treatments had a psychiatric disability.

During 1953 the Veterans Administration provided nearly 40 million patient days of care. It operated about 114,000 beds of which over 50,000 were designated as psychiatric. By the end of 1953 close to half of the nearly 58,000 psychiatric patients were World War II veterans. The average length of stay of World War II veterans in that year was 52 days; for those treated for psychosis the average was 235 days, and for other psychiatric disorders, 39 days. There were a total of 11,700 admissions for psychosis from among World War II veterans in 1953 and 19,100 for other psychiatric reasons.

The very crowded conditions in most state hospitals and the high costs of private hospitalization for psychiatric illness helped to swell the proportion of mentally ill veterans who sought admission to the Veterans Administration hospitals. The fact that the quality of care in most of these hospitals had been noticeably improved in the postwar years acted as an additional magnet to the psychiatrically ill veteran.

No firm data exist as to the total number of veterans who made use of the Veterans Administration hospitals but a reasonable estimate can be ventured. From the latter part of 1942 through 1953—the period covered by our case materials—there were approximately 2,850,000 admissions of World War II veterans to Veterans Administration hospitals or to other hospitals where the Veterans Administration paid the bill. About 15 percent of these admissions were for psychiatric or neurological conditions. Since some patients were admitted more than once during this period, these figures establish the maximum use made of Veterans Administration hospitals by veterans of World War II: for all causes, 2,850,000 out of a total veteran group of 16 million, or 18 percent; for neuropsychiatric reasons, 414,000, or 2.6 percent.

Through a special study undertaken in 1948 the Veterans Administration found that about one-third of all psychiatric patients discharged within a two-year period were readmitted; a few veterans were in and out no fewer than 15 times during the two-year period. Using these percentages as a guide it is probable that no more than 270,000 veterans were admitted to Veterans Administration hospitals for psychiatric illness during the period 1942 to 1953—or only 1.7 percent of the total veteran population of World War II.

An eligible veteran who was discharged from military service with a disability that had arisen in or was aggravated by service and that interfered with his ability to earn his livelihood was entitled to compensation. The amount of the compensation varied with the degree of impairment created by the disability—from 10 percent to 100 percent. A relatively small number of World War II veterans (65,000 by June 1957) received disability pensions even though their condition was not service-connected. The law provided that if a veteran became permanently and totally disabled, he was entitled under certain conditions to a pension even though his disability was not connected with his military service.

The postwar peak in service-connected disability compensation payments occurred in 1947 when 1,728,516 veterans of World War II were receiving compensation, 475,397 for neuropsychiatric disabilities. A decade later the numbers had declined somewhat and stood at 1,591,217 and 354,710 respectively.

In determining its rating of disabilities the Veterans Administration paid particular attention to the "average impairment in earning capacity resulting from such diseases and injuries and their residual conditions in civil occupations." Total disability is defined as "any impairment of mind or body which is sufficient to render it impossible for the average person to follow a substantially gainful occupation." The degree of disability was to be determined in general "by the extent of the social and industrial inadaptability . . . which produces impairment of earning capacity." *The Schedule for Rating Disabilities* also stresses that "war psychosis or psychoneurosis . . . having its onset as an incident of battle or enemy action . . . requires special attention from the standpoint of military pensions."

As with hospitalization there are no firm figures as to the total number of veterans who received disability compensation, but a reasonable estimate can be made. On June 30, 1954, 1,628,952 World War II veterans were receiving compensation and during the preceding eleven years, 804,720 awards had been terminated. This provides a maximum of 2,433,672 veterans who had received such awards—just about 15 percent of the total eligible group.

The three accompanying figures depict the changes which occurred over a decade—1943-1953—in the proportions of World War II veterans receiving disability compensation for service-connected disabilities at 10, 20-40, 50-90, and 100 percent levels for all causes, for psychoses, and for psychoneuroses, respectively. The first figure indicates that by 1953 only a relatively few veterans (less than 5 percent) continued to be considered totally disabled, and in point of fact less than 1 in 5 of those receiving compensation was considered seriously disabled (50 percent or more disability). More than 2 out of 5 received only 10 percent disability compensation, which amounted to $15 monthly in 1953.

As one would anticipate, veterans suffering from a psychosis were more seriously disabled, which is reflected in the fact that of those receiving compensation about 6 out of 10 received 50 percent or more compensation and 3 out of 10 received 100 percent. The opposite is true of those disabled by psychoneurosis. Only 1 in 10 received 50 percent or more compensation. More than half received only 10 percent.

An inspection of the second figure shows that up to 1949 there were radical declines in the proportion of veterans receiving 100 percent disability for psychosis. Early in the war the Army sent almost all patients discharged because of a psychosis directly to a Veterans Administration hospital thereby indicating that they were totally disabled. Later many soldiers separated because of a psychosis were discharged to the care of their families. This led the Veterans Administration to weigh more carefully the degree of

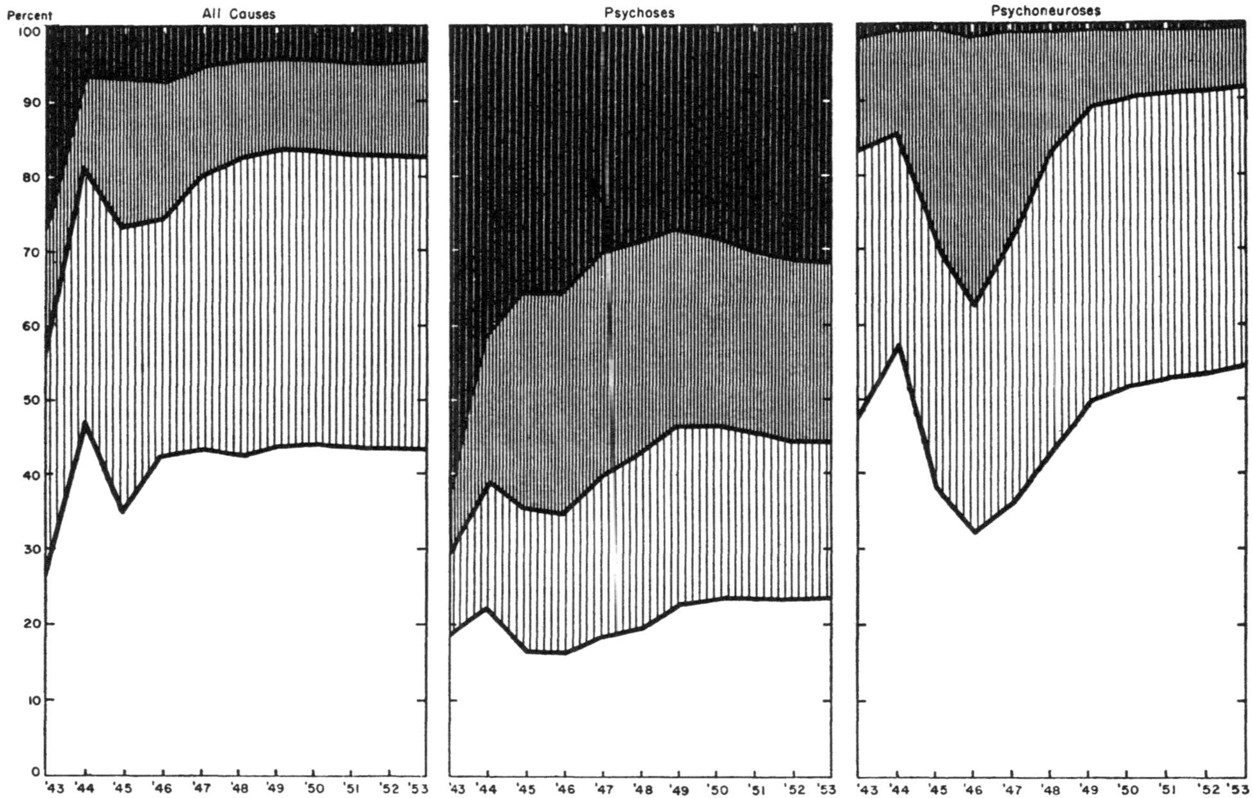

PERCENT DISTRIBUTION OF WORLD WAR II VETERANS RECEIVING COMPENSATION FOR SERVICE-CONNECTED DISABILITIES, BY DEGREE OF IMPAIRMENT, FOR ALL CAUSES, FOR PSYCHOSES, AND FOR PSYCHONEUROSES, ANNUALLY AS OF June 30, 1943-1953

Source: *Annual Reports*, Administrator of Veterans Affairs: unpublished tabulations prepared by the Veterans Administration.

their disability. Since 1949 there has been a slow, steady increase in the numbers of veterans who are receiving 100 percent disability compensation because of psychosis. On June 30, 1957, a third of all veterans disabled because of psychosis were receiving 100 percent compensation.

The third figure indicates that in 1946 the Veterans Administration started to reduce the proportion of veterans receiving more than 10 percent disability for psychoneurosis, especially those receiving 50 percent or more. In the immediate postwar years the Veterans Administration had followed a liberal policy with respect to the combat group. Since many of them improved rapidly, the Veterans Administration was able to revise their compensation payments downward or to eliminate them completely.

Through June 30, 1957, the Veterans Administration had expended a total of $15 billion on disability compensation, including pensions and benefits to dependents of deceased veterans of World War II. Compensation payments to living veterans with service-connected disabilities accounted for $11.2 billion of the total. During the past five years compensation payments to living veterans of World War II have remained at just over a billion dollars a year.

Not only did the federal government make many billions of dollars available to help veterans readjust, but it pursued an active policy of publicizing the benefits which were available to them. The following extract is from a letter, written in April 1947, from a Veterans Administration office in the South to one of the veterans included in our cohort sample:

> This letter is written as an invitation to you to call on the undersigned at ______ for a personal interview to determine if you are fully and correctly informed of your veteran's rights and entitlement to benefits under existing legislation. At the time of the interview, we will determine whether you are receiving all the benefits you desire, and if the contact division may be of any further service to you in securing outpatient treatment, hospitalization, medical and dental care, reinstatement or conversion of your GI insurance, vocational rehabilitation, education and training, etc.

The letter went on to give the office hours, and asked the veteran, if he could not come in personally, to write them if they could help him. This same type of letter, sometimes more extensive, sometimes less, sometimes as a form, sometimes as a personal letter, was found in many of the claims folders which we reviewed.

USE OF VETERANS' BENEFITS BY COHORT INEFFECTIVENESS

This brief review of the range of benefits available to the veterans of World War II will enable us to determine to what extent the cohort ineffectives paralleled or differed from the average veteran in their readjustment at least with regard to their use of these benefits. In making these comparisons it is important to recall that 4,616 of the cohort sample served for less than 90 days and that 5,268 were discharged under other than honorable conditions. Most of the former and about two-thirds of the latter were ineligible for many benefits, including education or training under the G.I. Bill.

A total of 27,593 in the cohort took advantage of the educational or training benefits under Public Law 346 or Public Law 16, representing 38 percent of the entire group and 42.7 percent of the estimated eligibles. Somewhat more than half of all World War II veterans made use of these benefits in contrast to slightly more than two-fifths of the eligibles in the cohort.

The following table provides information about the number and percentage in the cohort and in the total World War II veteran group that participated in the several programs. Again the figures are not additive since some veterans participated in more than one program.

TYPE OF TRAINING PURSUED, COHORT INEFFECTIVES AND ALL VETERANS

TYPE OF TRAINING	COHORT INEFFECTIVES			WORLD WAR II VETERANS	
	Number Pursuing	*Percent of Total*	*Percent of Eligible*	*Number Pursuing*	*Percent of Total*
Institutions of higher learning	3,443	4.7	5.3	2,700,000	16.9
Schools below college level	14,640	20.1	22.7	3,850,000	24.1
Job training	6,312	8.7	9.8	1,870,000	11.7
Institutional on-farm training	9,833	13.5	15.2	770,000	4.8

As this table demonstrates, the cohort ineffectives differed substantially from all veterans in that they made much heavier use of farm training and undertook much less college education. This difference reflects the fact that the cohort group was more heavily drawn from the farm and also was less well educated than the average veteran of World War II. With regard to the use made of trade schools and other schools below college level, there was little difference between the two groups.

As to hospitalization, 16,110 of the cohort sample were hospitalized in Veterans Administration hospitals or in hospitals where the Veterans Administration assumed financial responsibility for their care. This represented 22.2 percent of the entire group or 23.3 of those who were eligible. We noted earlier that the maximum percentage of all World War II veterans who made use of the hospital could not have exceeded 18 percent. Considering the fact that approximately 2 out of every 3 members of the cohort were discharged from the Army on medical grounds, their use of hospitals in the postwar period was strikingly small.

The 72,700 cohort ineffectives accounted for 28,896 admissions, of which 13,602, or 47.1 percent, were for psychiatric illness. Thus, there were 40 hospitalizations per 100 cohort ineffectives, 19 of which were for psychiatric reasons. The nearly 16 million veterans of World War II had a total of 2,850,000 admissions to the end of 1953, 414,000, or 14.5 percent, for psychiatric illness. Thus on the average there were 18 hospitalizations per 100 World War II veterans, less than 3 of which were for psychiatric illness.

The cohort ineffectives utilized the Veterans Administration facilities at more than twice the average rate and seven times more frequently for psychiatric illness. Back of these striking differences between the two groups lies the fact that approximately two-thirds of all ineffectives were discharged medically, specifically with a psychiatric diagnosis, while the demobilized veterans—who constitute the bulk of the veteran population—had no medical disability at the time of their return to civilian life.

A total of 30,779 cohort ineffectives received disability compensation; this represented 42.3 percent of the entire group and 44.5 percent of those who were eligible. We earlier estimated that not more than 2,430,000 veterans of World War II, or 15 percent of the total, could have received disability compensation up to June 1953. At the very least, proportionately three times as many cohort ineffectives received compensation as did World War II veterans as a group. The following table compares the percent of the cohort ineffectives initially awarded disability compensation with the percent of all living World War II veterans receiving compensation a year after demobilization was instituted:

	Percent
Cohort (initial rating)	42.3
Living World War II veterans, June 30, 1946	
All causes	12.0
Neuropsychiatric illness	3.6

The foregoing becomes more revealing when one takes note of the fact that while 65 percent of the cohort sample were discharged on medical grounds, only 42 percent were receiving compensation a year or so after their return to civilian life. In contrast, while about 10 percent of all veterans of World War II were discharged on medical grounds, 12 percent were in receipt of compensation at that time. This points to the speed with which many of the cohort group were apparently able to readjust.

The following table summarizes the initial level of impairment of both groups shortly after their discharge from military service.

LEVEL OF IMPAIRMENT, COHORT INEFFECTIVES AND ALL VETERANS RECEIVING COMPENSATION, INITIAL PERIOD

	LEVEL OF IMPAIRMENT, IN PERCENT			
	10%	*20-40%*	*50-90%*	*100%*
Cohort (initial rating)	33.1	26.0	27.4	13.5
Living World War II veterans, June 30, 1946				
All causes	42.6	32.0	18.2	7.2
Neuropsychiatric illness	26.4	29.7	33.6	10.3

The table demonstrates that while the cohort ineffectives had a generally higher level of impairment than the average World War

II veteran who received disability compensation, there were no important differences between the two groups when the comparison is restricted to veterans with neuropsychiatric disabilities.

At the time of our questionnaire, in the winter of 1953-54, 16,948 cohort ineffectives, or 25.3 percent of those eligible, were drawing disability compensation. In June 1953, 10.6 percent of all living World War II veterans were drawing compensation, but only 2.4 percent for psychiatric reasons. The following table compares the percent of the cohort ineffectives receiving disability compensation at last report with the percent of the total veteran population receiving compensation in 1953:

	Percent
Cohort (final rating)	23.3
Living World War II veterans, June 30, 1953	
All causes	10.6
Neuropsychiatric illness	2.4

The foregoing reinforces the earlier finding about the relatively greater ease with which the cohort group was apparently able to get along without compensation in the postwar period. Between the initial and the final period there was a decline of 45 percent among the cohort group who continued to receive compensation, but the corresponding decline for all World War II veterans with a neuropsychiatric disability was only 33 percent.

The following table summarizes the level of impairment of both groups in 1953, eight years after the end of hostilities.

LEVEL OF IMPAIRMENT, COHORT INEFFECTIVES AND ALL VETERANS RECEIVING COMPENSATION, FINAL PERIOD

	LEVEL OF IMPAIRMENT, IN PERCENT			
	10%	*20-40%*	*50-90%*	*100%*
Cohort (final rating)	45.8	26.3	16.4	11.5
Living World War II veterans, June 30, 1953				
All causes	43.3	39.3	12.7	4.7
Neuropsychiatric illness	40.3	34.9	16.0	8.8

Of those receiving disability compensation, the cohort ineffectives were more severely disabled than World War II veterans with a psychiatric disability, as indicated by the higher proportion among the cohort who were totally disabled (100 percent). But the high percentage, 45.8 percent, of that part of the cohort sample in receipt of disability compensation who were receiving only 10 percent compensation, together with the 76.7 percent of the entire cohort not receiving any compensation, suggests that by 1953 a sizable group was no longer handicapped by their service-connected disabilities in adjusting to civilian life.

These are truly striking figures. Despite the fact that 2 out of every 3 soldiers in the cohort group were discharged from the Army on medical grounds, 3 out of every 4 were by the early 1950s no longer receiving any compensation, and of the 1 in 4 who still drew compensation almost half were receiving only a minimal amount—10 percent. The full significance of these findings will become clear as the analysis of the readjustment process continues.

THE READJUSTMENT OF THE COHORT INEFFECTIVES

We have described at some length the use that the cohort ineffectives made of the wide range of benefits available to them because of our belief that both in intent and in actuality the assistance made available by the Veterans Administration played a significant role in the readjustment of many in the cohort group.

As when we evaluated their military performance, so in evaluating their readjustment to civilian life we adopted a series of objective criteria giving heavy weight to their occupational adjustment, although we included certain social indices such as significant conflict with the law. A man was adjudged to have made a good adjustment if he held a steady job, except for short periods when he was seeking to better his position; if the level of his work and his earnings were clearly above his prewar employment; if there was no record of poor work performance such as excessive absenteeism; and if he had never been dismissed from his job for cause. Moreover, if he made use of educational and training benefits, these must have been meaningfully related to his occupational goals and his performance as a student must have been satisfactory as evidenced by attendance, mastery of work, and completion.

We considered that a veteran had made a poor readjustment if he was unable to hold a steady job, if he had a record of excessive absenteeism, ran into serious difficulties with the law, and gave other objective evidence of failing to meet the obligations of a responsible member of society. An intermediate group of men who showed little signs of advancing beyond the jobs which they had held prior to induction, but who met none of the criteria which characterized poor readjustment, we considered to have made an acceptable adjustment. The details which guided our evaluation are set forth in the Appendix.

The fact that we placed such heavy weight on a man's occupational readjustment makes it necessary to stress that his work adjustment did not necessarily parallel his recovery in a clinical sense. While many men could not get or hold a job because they were so seriously disturbed, others found in work a way of circumventing some of their psychological difficulties. The following cases, which we classified as having at least an acceptable postwar adjustment, illustrate this.

M.N., a combat veteran, was discharged from the Army with a diagnosis of schizophrenia, paranoid type. For several years after his return to civilian life he had great difficulties, because of his illness, in making a satisfactory occupational adjustment. In 1948 he became so ill that he had to be hospitalized as incompetent. In 1953 he was doing quite well in a job as shoe salesman in which he had been steadily employed for nearly three years, despite the fact that in the opinion of the doctors his psychosis was only in partial remission.

N.O. had been discharged from the Army as moderately incapacitated for further military duty after serving only in the Zone of the Interior. He went to college on the GI Bill and while a student was rated as 30 to 50 percent disabled due to chronic, moderate anxiety reaction. He was irritable, excitable, suffered from insomnia and nightmares. Nevertheless N.O. was able to secure his Bachelor of Science degree and has been working steadily for a farm equipment company. He has received several promotions. His complaints persist but he has not lost any time from work.

O.P., a Negro veteran who was discharged from the Army after having developed a psychosis while serving overseas, continued to have many serious complaints but not so serious as to require hospitalization. He appeared shy and reclusive, cried easily, and on occasion was depressed or hysterical. His stomach was upset frequently and he became fatigued easily. Yet he went on to college, secured his degree in biology, and has been steadily employed as a biologist in a cancer research institute for the past several years.

These brief abstracts should indicate that our rating of the veteran's readjustment refers primarily to his work life, not to the state of his feelings or emotions.

In order to understand better the process of readjustment we made not one, but three, evaluations of each veteran. The initial assessment was within the first two years after his discharge from the Army. The final assessment was within the two years prior to the last contact with the veteran. The intermediate rating was for the period between these two and pertained to at least one year.

A fourfold rating scheme—good, acceptable, poor, and not rated—used at three points in time would result in sixty-four possible patterns of postwar adjustment. This was clearly too many to analyze and it would not be meaningful because of the inherent complexities of so elaborate a scheme and because of the small number of cases in many of these minor patterns. Careful inspection revealed that the materials could be better analyzed in terms of three major patterns—early, delayed, and unsuccessful readjustment. The method used to combine the different patterns is set out in the Appendix. Here we shall describe these three patterns briefly.

Men were classified as having made an "early" recovery if at the time of their initial or intermediate assessment they were considered to have made either a good or acceptable adjustment and if they also received a rating of either good or acceptable when they were evaluated for the last time. This means that we paid no attention to the minor fluctuations between good and acceptable which took place from one rating to another. The following case is of a soldier who made a strikingly quick recovery after his return to civilian life.

In his early thirties P.Q. served as a truck driver with an armored infantry unit in Europe. Twice rendered unconscious by blast concussions, he was evacuated for exhaustion. He complained of recurring headaches and was bothered by hearing voices. His auditory hallucinations continued and he developed numerous somatic complaints while he was in the hospital, but by the time he received his medical discharge for psychosis, schizophrenia, acute reaction type, he no longer was hearing voices.

Two months after his discharge from the Army he began work as a mechanic's helper with an auto sales and service company in his home town. While with the company he entered on-the-job training as an auto mechanic under Public Law 16. Completing this course satisfactorily in four years, he has remained with the firm and is now employed as a full-fledged automobile mechanic. He is considered by his employer to be a very good worker.

Psychiatric examinations made in 1946 and 1947 revealed few residuals of his acute psychotic episode, although he tired somewhat easily and required more sleep than previously. His initial disability rating of 50 percent was reduced to 10 percent and finally was terminated when he was adjudged to have no impairment of earning capacity.

Those whom we classified as having made a "delayed" readjustment were men who at the time of their initial or intermediate rating were assessed as having made a poor adjustment but who at the time of their final rating were considered to have made either a good or acceptable adjustment. Again we disregarded whether a man at the time of his final rating was acceptable or good—if his earlier ratings had been poor and his final rating was at least acceptable, he was classified as having made a "delayed" readjustment. Some men made little effort to find a job until they had exhausted their savings and benefit rights.

Q.R. served as a crewman with a barrage balloon battery in North Africa until he broke down rather suddenly with a psychosis. His manic-depressive reaction cleared in the military hospital and he was discharged to his own custody in November 1943. For the first year and a half after discharge he did not work at all because of various somatic complaints—headache, backache, etc. According to the veteran's own statement in his reply to our questionnaire he stayed around home until his money ran out and then he had to go to work. In 1945 he got a job driving a gasoline truck, which he held for five years, at which time he obtained a better paying job, which he has held ever since, as a gasoline station operator.

Those who were placed in the "unsuccessful" category comprised all whose final rating was poor. Most of this group had also had an initial and intermediate rating of poor, but some men who had started out to make a good or acceptable adjustment failed along the way. They were included among the "unsuccessful" readjustment group because what counted most was their status at the time furthest removed from their breakdown in the Army. R.S. is an example of such a case.

R.S. was twenty-three when he was discharged from the Army in 1945 after breaking down in a noncombatant position overseas. He was suffering from psychoneurosis which was diagnosed as a severe obsessive-compulsive state. In the first two years after discharge he held at least eight different jobs; he had been discharged from several because of conflicts with his supervisors and had voluntarily resigned from several others because he could not tolerate working indoors. In 1950 he was still complaining of nervous tension and nightmares and his work record had remained very poor. His condition was considered to be chronic.

Forty-four percent of the cohort, or 32,000 out of the 72,700 represented by our sample, were adjudged to have made an early adjustment. The single largest sub-group, approximately 20,500, was composed of men who at two of their three ratings were considered to have made an acceptable adjustment, and at the third were acceptable or not rated. The adjustment of another 8,600 was rated as having improved from acceptable to good. The third significant sub-group was about 2,000, for whom two out of three ratings were good, with the third being good or not rated.

The "delayed" category consisted of approximately 8,000 men, or 11.1 percent of the cohort. Three out of every 4 of these men were rated poor initially but were rated acceptable at the time of their final assessment; another 1,700 had improved from poor to good between their initial and final ratings.

The "unsuccessful" numbered 14,000, or 19.3 percent of the cohort. The predominant sub-group consisted of men whose postwar ratings were consistently poor—11,800. The remainder were men who were initially rated good or acceptable but whose final rating was poor, or who were rated poor initially and finally but who were rated acceptable at the time of their second evaluation.

The group whose adjustment pattern remained unknown totaled over 18,600, or 25.6 percent of the entire cohort sample.

The following table provides a quantitative summary of the major postwar patterns of adjustment:

Readjustment Pattern	*Number*	*Percent*
Early	31,978	44.0
Delayed	8,075	11.1
Unsuccessful	14,002	19.3
Unknown	18,645	25.6
	72,700	100.0

For one-third of the 18,645 rated as unknown, information pertaining to their readjustment is available, but it is limited to a single period. About 2,000 had a first rating of good or acceptable, and another 1,750 had a last rating of acceptable. There are about 1,000 whose first rating was poor and another 1,500 whose last and only rating was poor.

We cannot, however, distribute the unknown group among the three patterns in the same proportion as men about whom complete information is available. In view of the very considerable information that we have available about this group prior to discharge from the Army, they appear to be more handicapped than the average man who made an early or even a delayed readjustment. It is reasonable to assume that about 2 out of every 3 would have made a successful readjustment sooner or later, while 1 out of 3 probably would not. If the unknown group is distributed in this ratio, it would bring the total number who had an unsuccessful readjustment to just under 20,000 or 27.4 percent of the total. This would mean that over 52,000 men—or approximately 7 out of every 10—made a satisfactory readjustment. Despite their failure in the Army, about half the cohort sample made an early readjustment to civilian life.

SUMMARY

The materials presented in this chapter have outlined the very sizable benefits that the American public made available to all men who had served for at least 90 days in World War II and who had not been discharged under dishonorable conditions. While there is no single figure that clearly reflects in dollars or other terms the value of these benefits to the veterans of World War II, sufficient information exists to put the total in the many tens of billions of dollars even by the early 1950s—readjustment allowances of about $4 billion; G.I. education and training, over $14 billion; disability compensation, over $10 billion; and hospital and outpatient expenditures that within the first postwar decade were at least $4 billion.

These figures do not include the advantages which veterans received from special low cost insurance, government guaranteed loans at preferred rates of interest, and still other benefits. Moreover, disability compensation and hospital and outpatient care continue at the rate of at least $1.5 billion annually for veterans of World War II alone.

The data which have been presented pointed to significant differences among the veterans of World War II in the benefits of which they availed themselves and of the help which they received from them. While it is true that the average readjustment allowance came to less than $400 per man, it is noteworthy that 3 out of every 5 veterans made use of this particular benefit, suggesting that a large number of men found this modest amount of extra cash helpful to them during the initial period of readjustment. A much larger amount, about $2,000 on the average, was received by the 1 out of every 2 veterans who took advantage of their educational training benefits. Not more than 1 in 6 received any disability compensation, but the average total amount up to 1957 has come to $6,000. However, the largest group receives under $250 annually. While some men who are seriously disabled receive relatively large amounts, the majority receive very little. Up to 1954 only 1 in 6 made any use of their hospital benefits, which reflects the fact that most veterans are in an age group which makes relatively little use of the hospital and that among those who required hospitalization, there were many who preferred or had no option but to make use of other facilities.

As far as the cohort ineffectives were concerned we found that they made somewhat less use than the average veteran of their education and training benefits—2 out of 5 as against 1 out of 2. In sharp contrast, however, was the much higher percentage of the cohort group that received disability compensation—42 percent as compared to less than 15 percent of all World War II veterans. The cohort group was also found to have made somewhat greater use of their hospital benefits—22 percent as compared to under 18 percent of all veterans of World War II—and had a much higher rate of hospitalization for psychiatric illness.

In the following chapter an effort will be made to assess the role of these and other factors in the readjustment of the cohort ineffectives. At this time it is important to recall only that of the 72,700 in the group over 52,000 made a satisfactory readjustment—approximately 7 out of every 10.

Chapter Ten: SUCCESSFUL AND UNSUCCESSFUL READJUSTMENT

IT IS DIFFICULT to exaggerate the importance of mere discharge from the Army in the later adjustment of many soldiers. Many had broken down only after they had used their reserves in coping with the demands that military life made on them. While the hospital offered a respite to many who broke—others were overwhelmed by the prospect, as their symptoms receded and they began to feel better, that they might be sent back to duty. Freedom from the pressures and dangers of military life was not possible as long as a man was in uniform. Not until he was discharged could a soldier really feel safe.

Many soldiers improved greatly between the time that they broke down and their discharge. Some were helped by therapy; others by time alone; many were buoyed up simply by the prospect of returning to civilian life. Since so many who had broken down had succumbed to pressures in the military situation, they started to recover as soon as they had passed through the separation center and received their discharge.

But leaving a burdensome and traumatic situation was only half the story. Many soldiers soon discovered that civilian life was also full of problems and pressures, many of which would tax them to the utmost. Some came back to family situations that had greatly deteriorated during their absence and found that their hopes and plans for the future which had helped to sustain them during many difficult periods while they were in the service would have to be radically revised. For example, one found that since his mother had died he could not continue to live under the same roof with his father and share the working of the farm. Another was shocked to discover that his wife, to whom he was deeply attached, had waited until his return home to inform him of her plans to get a divorce. A third was forced to realize that his old job no longer gave him any real satisfaction—although he had liked the work before he had been drafted. A considerable number who had looked forward to returning to school and preparing for a better job found that they could neither sit in class nor study at home.

We see, then, that the readjustment of the cohort ineffectives to civilian life was influenced not only by the experiences which the men had undergone in the Army but also by the problems which they encountered after their return to civilian life. However, their readjustment was facilitated by the various types of help they were able to obtain, particularly by their use of the wide range of benefits provided by the Veterans Administration.

In studying the postwar recovery of the cohort sample we shall make use of the three major patterns of recovery previously described—the early, the delayed, and the unsuccessful. We will first explore the relations between the range of military experiences of these men and their postwar adjustment. Next, we will analyze their recovery patterns in light of the nature and severity of their breakdown. Then we will evaluate their readjustment in terms of their individual qualities and characteristics. Finally we will seek to assess the influence of benefits made available through the Veterans Administration on the rapidity and completeness of their readjustment.

MILITARY EXPERIENCE AND POSTWAR ADJUSTMENT

Whether the length of time that a man served in the Army and the strenuousness of his assignment influenced the pattern of his recovery after his discharge can be explored by reviewing the readjustment patterns of the cohort ineffectives in terms of the four Situations which characterized the nature of their military service. The following table presents the pertinent data.

READJUSTMENT PATTERN BY SITUATION, IN PERCENT

SITUATION	TOTAL KNOWN	READJUSTMENT PATTERN *Early*	*Delayed*	*Unsuccessful*	PERCENT WITH KNOWN PATTERN
I	100.0	63.0	13.3	23.7	73.0
II	100.0	61.0	12.1	26.9	68.5
III	100.0	41.6	19.4	39.0	76.4
IV	100.0	56.1	22.2	21.7	92.0

From this table we see that the combat group, Situation IV, contained the lowest proportion of men who failed to recover; the overseas non-combat group, Situation III, the highest. These two groups, which included all the men who served overseas, contained many whose postwar adjustment was delayed. Furthermore, it was the overseas non-combat group that had the lowest percentage of men who made an early readjustment. The combat group's record of early readjustment, however, was almost as good as those who had never been sent overseas.

Since the situational analysis is only roughly correlated with length of service, it cannot provide a clear indication of whether the length of time spent in the Army had an effect on civilian readjustment. A tabulation of months of service in relation to the readjustment patterns comes closer to assessing the influence of the time factor. The following table presents the pertinent data.

READJUSTMENT PATTERN BY LENGTH OF SERVICE, IN PERCENT

MONTHS COMPLETED	TOTAL KNOWN	READJUSTMENT PATTERN *Early*	*Delayed*	*Unsuccessful*	PERCENT WITH KNOWN PATTERN
0-5	100.0	58.7	10.0	31.3	67.0
6-11	100.0	65.4	15.7	18.9	77.3
12-17	100.0	59.7	9.4	30.9	66.9
18-23	100.0	40.7	26.7	32.6	71.7
24-29	100.0	58.1	16.1	25.8	79.8
30-35	100.0	56.5	17.0	26.5	89.5
36 and over	100.0	51.0	28.7	20.3	70.5

This table substantiates the earlier finding that a high proportion of men who served less than one year made an early recovery. Included in this group were many who were discharged at the first sign of faltering. But the table also shows that prolonged service does not appear to have been a counter-indication to early recovery. However, it does appear to have had some effect on delaying the recovery of a considerable number of men. With regard to those who were unable to make an adjustment their length of service in the Army seems to have been of no particular significance. Thus, it would appear that the strain of military service cannot be assessed solely in terms of the time factor alone.

We have seen that most of the cohort ineffectives did not serve overseas. But for those who did the following table presents the relationships between the time that they had served overseas and their postwar adjustment.

READJUSTMENT PATTERN BY LENGTH OF OVERSEAS SERVICE, IN PERCENT

MONTHS COMPLETED	TOTAL KNOWN	READJUSTMENT PATTERN *Early*	*Delayed*	*Unsuccessful*	PERCENT WITH KNOWN PATTERN
5 or less	100.0	51.4	19.2	29.4	83.4
6-11	100.0	56.6	20.7	22.7	81.7
12-17	100.0	48.0	21.2	30.8	87.7
18-23	100.0	30.2	26.0	43.8	80.1
24 and over	100.0	55.6	11.2	33.2	95.8

Except for soldiers who spent more than 18 months but less than 2 years overseas (the last group, 24 months and over, contains too few cases to be significant), length of foreign service did not have a bearing on the proportions who readjusted early. But apparently after a year and a half abroad, there was some additional diminution in a man's reserves which affected the rate of his recovery. This is brought out in the somewhat higher proportion of this group found to have a delayed readjustment. Finally, the greatest proportion of men who failed to readjust were also found among the group that spent at least a year and a half overseas. Of course, here too it is impossible to distinguish clearly between the factor of time alone and the special stresses, such as combat, that might have been associated with longer service overseas. But it does appear that after a year of overseas service, men found it more difficult to readjust to civilian life.

Since we have been unable so far to discover whether soldiers with longer service were affected by specific stresses, the following table has been prepared to assess the relation between different orders of stress and patterns of readjustment.

READJUSTMENT PATTERN BY SEVERITY OF SERVICE, IN PERCENT

SEVERITY OF SERVICE	TOTAL KNOWN	READJUSTMENT PATTERN			PERCENT WITH KNOWN PATTERN
		Early	*Delayed*	*Unsuccessful*	
Combat, wounded	100.0	52.5	27.0	20.5	94.9
Combat, not wounded	100.0	58.0	19.6	22.4	90.5
Overseas, non-combat	100.0	41.6	19.4	39.0	76.4
Zone of Interior	100.0	62.4	12.9	24.7	71.6

Among the combat groups there was a higher proportion who were able to make an early recovery than there was among others who served overseas. And the combat groups also had the smallest proportions of men who were unable to readjust. This finding, together with the previous finding that prolonged overseas service was correlated with unsuccessful civilian readjustment, places the emphasis on the time factor rather than on specific orders of stress such as combat or injury. Apparently either prolonged Army service, especially overseas, took its toll or else there was a significant difference in the quality of the men who served in combat and non-combat assignments which would explain these differences in postwar adjustment.

In the case of those who made a delayed recovery, the figures indicate a positive correlation with the severity of stress, that is, the more severe the stress the greater the proportion who fall into this pattern. But here, too, we cannot be sure whether differences between the early and the delayed recovery patterns reflect primarily differences in the degree of stress to which men were exposed, or differences in response, or differences in the type of men involved—this last, a hypothesis which we have already found necessary for explaining those with an unsuccessful readjustment pattern.

Additional evidence bearing on this question can be gleaned from the following table which correlates the military performance ratings of these soldiers prior to their breakdown with their postwar readjustment patterns.

MILITARY PERFORMANCE RATING BY READJUSTMENT PATTERN, IN PERCENT

MILITARY PERFORMANCE RATING	TOTAL COHORT	READJUSTMENT PATTERN *Early*	*Delayed*	*Unsuccessful*	*Unknown*
Good	8.7	12.2	9.1	6.2	4.3
Acceptable	56.2	66.0	71.4	42.6	43.3
Poor	26.5	12.7	14.3	45.4	41.2
Not Rated	8.6	9.1	5.2	5.8	11.2
	100.0	100.0	100.0	100.0	100.0

There were no significant differences in the military performance records between the men who readjusted early and those who adjusted after some delay. But those who failed to readjust contained a strikingly high proportion of men who had performed poorly in the Army. Making allowance for those about whom we have no postwar information, we estimate that at least half of those who performed poorly in the Army also proved unsuccessful in their efforts to readjust on their return to civilian life. This suggests that contained in the unsuccessful group were many men who perhaps had never been able to perform satisfactorily, a point that we will explore further in the following chapters.

Those with a delayed recovery pattern may well contain a high proportion of men with less potentialities than those who made an early recovery but still with more potentialities than those who failed to readjust. Whether they do in fact comprise an intermediary group can be determined only after additional information has been reviewed about their performance and background.

A key index of the quality of a man's performance in the Army was the grade which he was able to achieve. It is therefore worth reviewing whether this factor is significantly related to the soldier's readjustment pattern. The following table shows the readjustment pattern of the men according to the highest enlisted grades they held.

READJUSTMENT PATTERN BY HIGHEST ENLISTED GRADE HELD, IN PERCENT

GRADE	TOTAL KNOWN	READJUSTMENT PATTERN *Early*	*Delayed*	*Unsuccessful*	PERCENT WITH KNOWN PATTERN
Top three NCO grades	100.0	78.5	6.5	15.0	96.9
Sergeant or T/4	100.0	77.3	9.6	13.1	84.8
Corporal or T/5	100.0	56.7	13.7	29.6	80.6
Private first class	100.0	54.8	20.9	24.3	88.5
Private	100.0	58.3	14.1	27.6	68.2

The higher a man's grade in the Army, the more likely he was to make an early adjustment to civilian life. But 1 out of 7 ineffectives who became sergeants failed to adjust in civilian life. However, the proportion of men who failed to readjust among those who were not promoted to sergeant was almost twice as great.

A related index of military performance is the disciplinary action taken against a man measured in terms of the number and kinds of courts-martial which he received. Because 87 percent of the entire cohort sample were free of disciplinary action, the following table combines all courts-martial irrespective of the charges.

READJUSTMENT PATTERN BY COURT-MARTIAL ACTION, IN PERCENT

NUMBER OF COURTS-MARTIAL	TOTAL KNOWN	READJUSTMENT PATTERN *Early*	*Delayed*	*Unsuccessful*	PERCENT WITH KNOWN PATTERN
None	100.0	63.4	14.7	21.9	77.1
One or more	100.0	20.3	17.0	62.7	56.0

As one would have expected, men who became disciplinary problems in the Army had more difficulty in readjusting to civilian life. The detailed data also revealed that soldiers with several courts-martial, especially those of a more serious nature, were much more likely to be unsuccessful in their postwar readjustment than men who had committed only minor infractions of Army regulations.

We reviewed the data to see whether the length of time a soldier spent in Army hospitals had any influence on his readjustment pattern. We found that men who had never been hospitalized, most of whom had received administrative discharges for inaptitude, tended to readjust early; there were relatively few among this group whose readjustment was unsuccessful. For those who were hospitalized, the length of time they spent in the hospital did not appear in general to have had any particular relevance for their later readjustment. Men with longer periods of hospitalization were just as likely to make an early adjustment as men with shorter ones. Those who had been patients for inordinately long periods—over 300 days—were, however, more likely to have a delayed recovery pattern. Soldiers wounded in combat comprised a large part of this latter group. Neither did the length of military hospitalization differentiate men who failed to readjust. This is not surprising when one recalls that soldiers who were seriously ill at discharge were frequently transferred quickly to a Veterans Administration hospital. In contrast the combat wounded, who as noted earlier had a good readjustment record, were frequently hospitalized in the Army for long periods.

A few broad generalizations can be precipitated from this review of the relations between a soldier's military performance record and his postwar adjustment.

The first is a negative finding, namely, that objective stress, as measured by the length of service, foreign service, combat experience, or being wounded, is at most only indirectly related to a man's readjustment after discharge. There were some indications that men who served for 18-23 months overseas may have been specifically handicapped in their readjustment by the effects of their long foreign service, but final judgment on this point must be delayed until we test whether this group had distinctive personal characteristics which might explain their postwar adjustment pattern. The second unequivocal finding is that the better a man's military record, the better were his prospects for readjusting successfully. Each of the indices of military performance underscored this fact—the soldier's performance rating, the grade he achieved, and his courts-martial record, if any.

The previous analysis suggests that the pattern of a man's postwar adjustment was greatly influenced not only by his personal qualities but also by the nature and severity of his disability at breakdown. It is therefore desirable to consider briefly the degree of his incapacitation for further service at the time of his breakdown and the clinical diagnosis under which he was discharged from the Army.

We found that there were pronounced differences in readjustment patterns according to the soldiers' degree of incapacitation at breakdown. Three-quarters of the men with a pattern of unsuccessful readjustment, half with a delayed pattern, and only a fourth with an early readjustment pattern had shown major incapacitation for further military service at the time of their breakdown. On the other hand, almost none with unsuccessful, an eighth with delayed, and a third with early readjustment patterns had had minor incapacitation.

The relationship between severity of breakdown and the pattern of postwar readjustment can be clearly seen in the following table.

READJUSTMENT PATTERN BY DEGREE OF INCAPACITATION, IN PERCENT

DEGREE OF INCAPACITATION	TOTAL KNOWN	READJUSTMENT PATTERN *Early*	*Delayed*	*Unsuccessful*	PERCENT WITH KNOWN PATTERN
Major	100.0	37.9	17.3	44.8	70.2
Moderate	100.0	66.7	16.1	17.2	84.0
Minor	100.0	91.0	8.3	0.7	70.1

While only 1 out of every 3 men with major incapacitation was able to make an early readjustment, 2 out of every 3 with moderate incapacitation and 9 out of 10 with minor incapacitation did so. A large proportion, 45 percent, of those with major incapacitation failed to readjust. Nevertheless, even among the most severely incapacitated, a minority did recover rapidly enough to be able to make an early occupational adjustment. However, of the soldiers with major incapacitation whose records showed clear pre-military indications of ineffectiveness, about two-thirds had an unsuccessful readjustment pattern. This finding reinforces the validity of the Army's standards for selection which, had they been implemented, would have resulted in the rejection of many of these men for military service.

The relationship between the nature of the disability which these soldiers revealed while in the Army and their civilian readjustment can be seen in the following table which presents the postwar patterns of the men by the reason for their discharge.

READJUSTMENT PATTERN BY REASON FOR SEPARATION, IN PERCENT

REASON FOR SEPARATION	TOTAL KNOWN	READJUSTMENT PATTERN *Early*	*Delayed*	*Unsuccessful*	PERCENT WITH KNOWN PATTERN
Psychoneurosis	100.0	63.5	15.5	21.0	88.7
Psychosis	100.0	26.8	16.1	57.1	85.3
Undesirability	100.0	47.8	7.6	44.6	33.8
Inaptitude	100.0	63.7	13.7	22.6	52.6

Two facts emerge from this table: nearly two-thirds of the men who had been discharged because of psychoneurosis recovered early; whereas well over half of those with a psychosis failed to adjust to civilian life. However 1 out of 4 soldiers separated with a psychosis made an early adjustment. We know about the readjustment of only one-third of the men who were discharged as undesirable. But when we recall that this group contained the highest proportion of men with major incapacitation for further service (80.5 percent), it is reasonable to postulate that the majority did in fact fail to readjust.

A substantial proportion of the inapt group were able to make an early readjustment, but it is difficult, in light of the large proportion about whom we do not have information, to make a definite statement about how well they fared after their return to civilian life. We do know, however, that many returned to the family farm or rented some land nearby where they were able to eke out a basic living for themselves and their families.

There is little doubt that the degree of a soldier's incapacitation at breakdown in the Army was indicative of how well he would readjust. Likewise the nature of his disability provided further clues. Those discharged for psychosis or for psychopathic traits (undesirability) were much less likely to readjust than the psychoneurotic and the inapt.

SOME DEMOGRAPHIC FACTORS

A related line of inquiry is to assess whether the major personal characteristics of the cohort ineffectives were significantly related to their readjustment. The first question is whether age influenced the readjustment of veterans. The following table presents the relevant data.

READJUSTMENT PATTERN BY AGE AT INDUCTION, IN PERCENT

AGE AT INDUCTION	TOTAL KNOWN	READJUSTMENT PATTERN *Early*	*Delayed*	*Unsuccessful*	PERCENT WITH KNOWN PATTERN
18-22	100.0	54.8	18.0	27.2	77.7
23-27	100.0	57.6	25.6	16.8	69.9
28-32	100.0	76.0	5.1	18.9	69.6
33-37	100.0	51.5	3.9	44.6	83.4
38 and older	100.0	73.0	7.1	19.9	54.3

Since those thirty-eight and older were a small and special group, men between the ages of twenty-three and thirty-two could be said to have made the best readjustment. Only about 1 in 6 failed to recover. The younger of these men—those between twenty-three and twenty-seven—tended to have a delayed readjustment, which undoubtedly reflected the greater stress to which they had been subjected in terms of overseas service, combat and being wounded—all factors which prolonged the period before a man was able to fit himself back into civilian life.

It is noteworthy that as many as 1 out of every 4 men in the youngest age group, those below twenty-three, failed to readjust. This probably reflects a combination of different factors: they had been less carefully screened; they were more likely to have been exposed to conditions of maximum stress; they contained a substantial proportion of men who were found to have been immature; and they tended to have the least stable work and life experience on which to build on their return.

It will be recalled that the single most important differentiating factor among soldiers with respect to their performance in the Army was their educational background. One would thus expect that a man's education would also influence his readjustment to civilian life, as in fact it did. About 3 out of every 4 men who failed to readjust had left school at the end of grammar school or before. Among those who made either an early or delayed adjustment, somewhat less than half had such a limited amount of schooling.

The following table sets out the essential relationships between education and postwar adjustment.

READJUSTMENT PATTERN BY EDUCATIONAL LEVEL ACHIEVED BEFORE THE WAR, IN PERCENT

EDUCATIONAL LEVEL	TOTAL KNOWN	READJUSTMENT PATTERN			PERCENT WITH KNOWN PATTERN
		Early	*Delayed*	*Unsuccessful*	
Less than grammar school graduation	100.0	45.3	14.7	40.0	62.1
Grammar school graduation	100.0	69.7	7.3	23.0	79.4
Some high school	100.0	63.4	16.0	20.6	81.2
High school graduation	100.0	75.8	16.0	8.2	94.2
At least some college	100.0	65.5	24.6	9.9	99.1

As the table indicates, 2 out of every 5 men who failed to complete grammar school had an unsuccessful readjustment pattern. On the other hand, just less than 1 in 12 high school graduates failed to readjust. In general, the better the veteran's educational background the less likelihood there was that he would fail to readjust. Of those among the poorly educated who did succeed a smaller proportion than among the better educated were able to make an early readjustment. Although the college group had relatively few postwar failures (about 1 in 10), they showed a definite tendency toward delayed adjustment. It will be recalled from our earlier analysis that the college group contained a high proportion of men with major incapacitation for further service in the Army which would point to difficulties in their later readjustment. That so many recovered speaks well for the support which education afforded them in reknitting the strands of their life.

A man's educational achievement helps to determine the occupation he enters and the level of work he does. In considering the following table, it is important to recall that in general the cohort ineffectives were not only poorly educated but had also been heavily concentrated before the war in farming (mostly on poor farms in the Southeast) and in unskilled and service work. However, the war helped to reduce this heavy concentration. At the time of our final evaluation only 1 in 3 was still in farming or unskilled work in contrast to 3 out of 5 before the war.

The following table presents the recovery pattern of men by their final postwar occupational area.

READJUSTMENT PATTERN BY FINAL POSTWAR OCCUPATION, IN PERCENT

TYPE OF OCCUPATION	TOTAL KNOWN	READJUSTMENT PATTERN *Early*	*Delayed*	*Unsuccessful*	PERCENT WITH KNOWN PATTERN
Farm	100.0	56.0	15.2	28.8	96.8
Unskilled and service	100.0	39.2	17.5	43.3	90.3
Semi-skilled and skilled	100.0	80.9	12.1	7.0	95.6
White collar	100.0	60.2	26.0	13.8	95.5

It is clear that those who could do no better than hold down an unskilled or service job in the expanding postwar economy tended to have more difficulty than any other occupational group with their postwar recovery: more than 2 in every 5 were rated as unsuccessful in their readjustment. Those who remained in, or moved to, a semi-skilled or skilled job tended to be most successful in their recovery; this group had proportionately both the fewest who made unsuccessful and the most who made early readjustments. The white collar group presents a more delayed recovery pattern, paralleling the pattern of the better educated group, which accounted for a large proportion of this occupational class.

There were different readjustment patterns according to race: just under two-thirds (63.1 percent) of the whites with known recovery patterns made an early adjustment and over one-fifth (22.2 percent) failed to readjust. In the case of the Negroes more than two-fifths (42.0 percent) made an early adjustment and about the same percentage (42.2) had an unsuccessful adjustment. These figures indicate that white veterans had a considerably better readjustment record than Negroes. Since education was found to be such an important factor in readjustment and since whites were on the whole considerably better educated than Negroes, the differences in the readjustment patterns of the two groups are to be expected.

In comparing the readjustment patterns of whites and Negroes of the same educational level, we found that the better educated Negroes were more successful and readjusted earlier than whites; but among the less educated the reverse was true. Negroes with less than four years of schooling had a much poorer readjustment pattern than whites. Proportionately many more Negroes than whites failed to adjust, and the Negroes who did adjust needed more time to find themselves.

In view of the lower quality of education available to Negroes before the war one might have expected that at each educational level they would have fared worse in their postwar readjustment than whites. The fact that the better educated Negro, on the whole, did much better than the whites may well have been due to their generally high motivation to succeed, especially in a civilian, non-segregated environment. Many of the better educated Negroes were from Northern states and had found little in a segregated Army to motivate them to good performance, but once they returned to civilian life their rekindled motivation facilitated their readjustment.

Although we had no reason to believe that, other things being equal, a man's religious affiliation would affect his readjustment, we made use of the available information to explore the question. Since virtually all the Negroes were Protestant, their inclusion in this analysis would have distorted the picture to the extent that they were more poorly educated and hence less likely to readjust. Consequently, limiting ourselves to the approximately 54,600 whites about whom we had information, we analyzed their recovery patterns but found no meaningful differentiation among them growing out of their religious background and affiliation.

In our earlier analysis of military performance we found that the marital status of soldiers, especially of those with broken marriages, was significantly related to the quality of their performance and the severity of their breakdown. This suggested, therefore, that we explore whether a relationship between marital status and readjustment could be found.

An overall view of the marital status of the cohort ineffectives at the time of the last available information is presented below.

POSTWAR MARITAL PATTERNS OF COHORT INEFFECTIVES, IN PERCENT

Marital Pattern	*Percent*
Remained single	12.1
Married after war—not broken	17.9
Remained married	30.2
Marriage broken after war	14.0
(Remarried)	(5.6)
Marriage broken at time of discharge	9.6
(Remarried)	(5.0)
Not stated	16.2
	100.0

Perhaps the most striking fact is that the marriages of nearly a fourth of the entire group had been broken through separation, divorce, or death. This is even more unusual since the group was relatively young; the mean age at entry into the Army was twenty-six years and our follow-up information about them after their return to civilian life covers about the next ten years. On the last reports available to us circa 1953 about 13 percent still reported a "broken marriage." According to the 1950 Census this was true of under 5 percent of the comparable age group. Thus the rate of broken marriages is almost three times larger among the cohort ineffectives than among the general population.

The proportion of single men among the cohort ineffectives was also somewhat higher than for the general population, especially if one takes into account the fact that the majority of the group for whom no postwar marital data were available had been single at the time of discharge and many would have remained so.

The following table shows the readjustment pattern of the men according to their postwar marital patterns.

READJUSTMENT PATTERN BY POSTWAR MARITAL PATTERN, IN PERCENT

MARITAL PATTERN	TOTAL KNOWN	READJUSTMENT PATTERN *Early*	*Delayed*	*Unsuccessful*	PERCENT WITH KNOWN PATTERN
Remained single	100.0	35.4	8.1	56.5	70.6
Married after war—not broken	100.0	64.0	23.0	13.0	96.8
Remained married	100.0	77.4	8.4	14.2	88.5
Marriage broken after war	100.0	49.3	24.0	26.7	91.0
Remarried	100.0	65.5	25.5	9.0	93.2
Marriage broken at time of discharge	100.0	17.8	12.8	69.4	72.6
Remarried	100.0	24.3	23.7	52.0	72.8

These figures show that among the men who remained married were the highest proportion who made an early readjustment—

about 4 times as many as those whose marriage had been dissolved prior to induction or discharge, and about twice as many as those who remained single.

Of those who remained single a large proportion failed to readjust. This was also true of those whose marriages were already broken at the time of induction or discharge: 7 out of 10 were unable to readjust to civilian life. Apparently the same factors that interfered with their making a successful marriage also interfered with their making a successful readjustment to civilian life. This is not true, however, for those whose marriages were broken after the war. Many of these veterans were able to make an early readjustment. Probably the dissolution of their marriages was more directly related to the long separation during the war than to their inherent instability.

The difference between men whose marriages were broken before their discharge and those whose marriages were dissolved after discharge is underscored in the readjustment experience of those in each group who remarried. Approximately half of those whose marriages had been broken at the time of discharge and who remarried had an unsuccessful readjustment; most of those whose marriages were broken after the war and who remarried made an early adjustment and only 9 percent failed to adjust at all.

A man's experience in entering upon and making a success of his marriage often indicates his ability to cope with other important challenges of life. Apparently the men whose marriages broke before they were inducted or while they were still in the service, including those who remarried after discharge, were severely handicapped persons. Their poor record of adjustment to civilian life, which was paralleled by the pattern of many who never ventured into marriage, sets them apart from the men who married after the war, and even from those whose marriages were dissolved after the war and who later remarried.

One of the major concomitants of the war was that a large number of young men saw other parts of the United States and other countries for the first time. The question must be asked whether this experience affected their postwar behavior and adjustment. Did many of them fail to return home and put down stakes elsewhere? We know that an individual who pulls up roots and leaves the family farm to relocate himself in an urban community a hundred miles distant is truly a migrant. His whole pattern of life is altered by his change in domicile. Unfortunately, our data do not enable us to take direct account of such intra-state migrations. We are limited, as far as geographic mobility is concerned, to facts about movements out of the state or the region. At last report 1 out of every 10 white and 1 out of every 5 Negro ineffective soldiers was residing in a state other than the one from which they had been inducted.

We know that for some time the South has been characterized by a considerable out-migration of both whites and Negroes. To the extent that we have information about the migration of whites among the cohort ineffectives, only a very few—1.4 percent—left the South in the years following their discharge from the Army. In the case of Negroes, about 1 in 13 moved out of the region. Negroes tended to migrate in two stages: from a rural to an urban community within the South and then to another urban community out of the region.

Some men move because they want to; others because they have to. The former are much more likely to be successful in relocating and readjusting than the latter. We have no way of telling how many of the cohort ineffectives who migrated did so voluntarily; how many were more or less forced off the farm or out of the community in which they had grown up. What we do know is that two-thirds of the Negroes and one-third of the white migrants failed to readjust. In contrast, only one-third of the Negroes and one-fifth of the whites who did not migrate failed.

Additional information about mobility is contained in an analysis of occupational mobility, particularly the data concerning the men who had been farmers prior to their military service. About 12,200 who had been farmers returned to farming after the war. Of those about whom we have information, a little over half made an early adjustment and more than a quarter were unsuccessful. In contrast, about 5,100 who had been farmers before the war sought other employment directly after their discharge. A somewhat smaller percentage made an early adjustment, but almost the same percentage as those who returned to farming failed. The principal difference was that the mobile group required somewhat more time to adjust.

A considerable proportion of the men who returned to farming after their discharge did not stay there, and by the time of our final evaluation they had a new occupation. Of the 7,500 who stayed on the farm, about one-third of those about whom we have information had failed to adjust by the time of the final rating. Of the 3,900 who had moved out of farming less than one-fifth had failed. The remainder had died, or we had no information about them. These figures indicate that most of the farmers who ventured to change their occupation succeeded in the effort.

More than half of the farm group about whom we have information concerning their final occupation made an early readjustment, whether they remained on the farm or left. However, the failure rate was higher among those who were farmers before the war and who stayed in or returned to farming after trying something else (29 percent) than among those who moved off the farm and stayed off (18 percent). The proportion with delayed readjustment was higher among the migrants. Moving out of an environment in which one has grown up usually presents hurdles, especially during the early years of one's relocation. But our data indicate that the men who moved were not particularly handicapped. A few tentative findings can be distilled from these fragmentary data. Since the proportion of farmers who migrated had a considerably better readjustment record than was true for all migrants, a change in residence when associated with a change in occupation was more likely to prove successful than a change in residence alone. Many of the urban migrants were "drifters" who moved from one unskilled job to another. It is likely that many who remained on the farm were marginal individuals who were able to make a minimum adjustment because of the help and protection of their families who shielded them from the more severe pressures and demands of life.

VETERANS' BENEFITS

We have now reached a point in the analysis of the postwar adjustment patterns where we can evaluate the effect of the wide range of benefits which were available to help in the readjustment of men who had been discharged as ineffective in the Army. As we mentioned in the preceding chapter, there were three major types of benefits. Men who were adjudged disabled were entitled to disability compensation. All veterans could secure medical and hospital care for service-connected illness or injury and, in many cases, hospital treatment for disabilities not directly connected with their military service. Finally, the federal government made available a large variety of educational and training opportunities. These three major classes of benefits do not by any means comprise all that were available to the veteran, but they cover the most important.

There is a widespread belief that every veteran who was prematurely separated from the service, particularly if he were separated for medical reasons, received disability compensation. In point of fact only slightly more than 2 out of 5 ineffectives initially received compensation and at the time of our final evaluation, less than 1 out of 4 was still on the rolls. Although the Veterans Administration was inclined to be relatively liberal in making its initial award, only 1 man in 6 was rated as 50 percent or more disabled. According to the 1946 scale a single man with a 50 percent disability rating would receive at least $69.00 per month. Additional compensation for dependents was not authorized until 1948, at which time a 60 percent disabled veteran who was married and had two children would receive $110.10. Effective October 1, 1957, these amounts had been increased to $100.00 and $150.00, respectively.

Expecting that the help which it extended, as well as the passage of time itself, would facilitate the readjustment of many veterans, the Veterans Administration periodically reviewed its determinations, reducing or eliminating compensation payments where indicated. At the time of our final evaluation (1953) less than 1 in 15 among the cohort ineffectives was still rated as 50 percent or more disabled.

Some experts have contended that the payment of compensation to men who were not seriously disabled would tend to delay rather than speed their recovery. Presumably they would avoid accepting a full-time job which would attest to the fact that they were largely recovered. The following table presents some relevant data to test this contention.

READJUSTMENT PATTERN BY INITIAL DISABILITY COMPENSATION RATING, IN PERCENT

INITIAL RATING	TOTAL KNOWN	READJUSTMENT PATTERN *Early*	*Delayed*	*Unsuccessful*	PERCENT WITH KNOWN PATTERN
0	100.0	67.9	12.1	20.0	60.8
10	100.0	57.9	14.1	28.0	93.4
20-40	100.0	51.9	17.2	30.9	94.3
50-90	100.0	55.6	19.2	25.2	95.5
100	100.0	22.6	23.3	54.1	83.1

Some points are immediately apparent. Two-thirds of those who received no disability compensation—either because they did not apply or, if they did, their claims were disallowed—had an early recovery and only one-fifth were unsuccessful. At the other extreme, of those who initially were rated 100 percent disabled, more than half, 54.1 percent, failed to readjust and only slightly more than one-fifth, 22.6 percent, made an early recovery. In view of the fact that a total disability rating was given only to men whom the Veterans Administration considered to be seriously incapacitated for gainful employment, it is surprising indeed to find that more than one-fifth made an early recovery. Included in this group were many soldiers who had had a psychotic episode in the Army but who started to recover even before their discharge and continued to do so rapidly after their return to civilian life. It was not long before the major symptoms of their serious disturbance had disappeared. The fact that they received liberal compensation probably removed much of the pressure that these men would otherwise have encountered during the initial period of readjustment.

As for the men who received compensation for disabilities of between 10 and 90 percent, no simple conclusions are possible about the impact of disability awards on their recovery patterns. Those who received the higher awards tended to be more heavily represented among the group with delayed readjustment, which we might expect since the amount of the award was geared to the degree of disability for gainful employment. However, more than half had an early recovery which suggests at the least that the award did not adversely affect their readjustment.

While the data do not enable us to conclude that disability compensation was of major importance in speeding the readjustment of many veterans, there is surely no evidence in support of the counter-belief that many men were unable or unwilling to pull themselves together and put forth the effort to support themselves because they did not want to lose their benefits.

As indicated earlier it was the practice of the Veterans Administration to reexamine periodically the disabled veterans and adjust the compensation ratings either upward or downward depending on the course of the disability, or to correct previous administrative errors. The extent to which the Veterans Administration reduced compensation payments to men in our sample is indicated below.

INITIAL AND FINAL DISABILITY COMPENSATION RATINGS OF COHORT, IN PERCENT

Rating	*Initial*	*Final*
0	57.7	76.7
10	14.0	10.7
20-40	11.0	6.1
50-90	11.6	3.8
100	5.7	2.7
	100.0	100.0

At the time of our final rating (1953) approximately 4,500 were receiving between 20 and 40 percent disability compensation and 4,700 were receiving more—a total of 9,200 out of 72,700. This small proportion—just about 1 in 8—is indeed surprising in view of the fact that nearly two-thirds of our sample had received medical discharges.

As long as a veteran could demonstrate the presence of even a minor degree of disability from his wartime service, even if it did not clearly interfere with his employment, the Veterans Administration was inclined to continue to give him a 10 percent disability rating. There were important advantages to a man, particularly in government employment, to have the status of "disabled veteran," and there were administrative economies to the Veterans Administration in not attempting to eliminate every rating. This would avoid multiple appeals and reexaminations and if the veteran's condition worsened, he could more easily obtain a review of his disability rating.

The following table shows the readjustment patterns of the ineffectives by their final disability rating. As one might anticipate, a distinct relationship is found to exist between unsatisfactory readjustment patterns and higher disability ratings.

READJUSTMENT PATTERN BY FINAL DISABILITY COMPENSATION RATING, IN PERCENT

FINAL RATING	TOTAL KNOWN	READJUSTMENT PATTERN *Early*	*Delayed*	*Unsuccessful*	PERCENT WITH KNOWN PATTERN
0	100.0	66.6	10.3	23.1	67.2
10	100.0	61.1	24.0	14.9	97.9
20-40	100.0	47.9	27.7	24.4	97.5
50-90	100.0	10.5	39.3	47.2	97.0
100	100.0	—	5.7	94.3	100.0

More than three-fourths of the men who at our final review were not receiving any disability compensation had successfully adjusted to civilian life. Two-thirds had made an early adjustment. A considerable number of men who were receiving no compensation had failed to adjust. For the most part these veterans were ineligible either because they were separated under conditions which were dishonorable or for a condition, such as mental deficiency, which was not considered compensable.

The proportion of those who were unsuccessful increases steadily as the disability rating increases. Virtually all who were still rated as 100 percent disabled had failed to adjust, as had nearly half who continued to be rated between 50 and 90 percent disabled. The fact that a considerable proportion who had made a delayed recovery were still drawing substantial compensation reflects either that they were still burdened with serious symptoms even though they were back at work, or that their recovery was so recent that the Veterans Administration wanted to wait a little longer before acting to reduce their rating.

The data at hand suggest that the practice of providing disability compensation shortly after discharge helped to speed the early readjustment of many veterans so that a few years later they were able to stand on their own feet. Between the initial and final ratings the original group of 20,600 men who were receiving compensation for disability of 20 percent or higher had been cut by more than half—to 9,200. It may well be that in a few instances liberal compensation acted as a deterrent to a man's recovery but these were exceptions, not the rule.

The table on the following page shows the differences in the recovery patterns of men in our sample who made use of Veterans Administration hospital services.

The first and from many points of view the most interesting finding revealed by this table is the fact that most of the veterans who made no use of the hospital made an early readjustment while such a high percentage who did make use of it failed to adjust. It was the more seriously ill who sought treatment, which in many cases was not sufficiently helpful to enable them to readjust successfully. However, about 1 out of every 4 veterans who were hospitalized succeeded in making an early readjustment and another sixth succeeded after some delay. In these cases there is good reason to believe that hospital care was a contribution to the veteran's successful readjustment.

READJUSTMENT PATTERN BY USE OF VA HOSPITAL SERVICES, IN PERCENT

VA HOSPITAL SERVICE	TOTAL KNOWN	READJUSTMENT PATTERN *Early*	*Delayed*	*Unsuccessful*	PERCENT WITH KNOWN PATTERN
Cohort not hospitalized	100.0	70.2	14.7	15.1	71.3
Cohort hospitalized	100.0	26.8	15.6	57.6	85.2
Discharged directly to hospital from Army	100.0	22.6	12.3	65.1	97.2
Subsequent treatment—mental	100.0	2.7	37.6	59.7	97.2
Treatment—other	100.0	29.0	23.7	47.3	79.1
Examination and observation	100.0	17.4	54.0	28.6	87.1

An interesting sidelight on administrative and hospital practice is the finding that 2 out of every 9 soldiers whom the Army discharged directly to a Veterans Administration hospital because of serious mental illness succeeded in making an early adjustment. As we have noted, some seriously ill soldiers recovered very quickly once they entered the discharge channel. The other side of the coin is also important: of all soldiers whom the Army sent to a Veterans Administration hospital directly, 2 out of 3 failed to adjust.

There were a number of educational and training programs available to veterans. As we noted earlier, of the 72,700 men in the sample, 27,593, or 38 percent, made use of one or more of the programs; the others did not avail themselves of any of them, although most of the men were eligible to do so.

The differences in the recovery patterns of the men who used these services and those who did not are presented below.

Whether or not a man made an early adjustment does not appear to be related to his use of these educational benefits. Roughly the same proportion of men who undertook training as those who did not made an early readjustment. We do find, however, a much higher proportion of delayed recoveries among those who used these services as well as a higher proportion of failure among those who did not use them. It can certainly be argued that these services

READJUSTMENT PATTERN BY USE OF VA EDUCATIONAL SERVICES, IN PERCENT

VA EDUCATIONAL SERVICE	TOTAL KNOWN	READJUSTMENT PATTERN *Early*	*Delayed*	*Unsuccessful*	PERCENT WITH KNOWN PATTERN
Cohort not using services	100.0	58.3	9.5	32.2	62.6
Cohort using services	100.0	60.2	20.8	19.0	93.5
Correspondence school	100.0	40.6	14.4	45.0	100.0
Institutional-on-farm training	100.0	62.2	20.5	17.3	98.9
On-the-job training	100.0	58.5	23.0	18.5	82.1
Trade and vocational school	100.0	50.4	28.4	21.2	96.4
Academic—non-college	100.0	38.6	19.2	42.2	93.7
Academic—college	100.0	54.4	31.6	14.0	100.0

aided the readjustment of many veterans. Nearly half, 48.6 percent, who made an early recovery availed themselves of their benefits and the knowledge and skills which they acquired undoubtedly contributed to their readjustment. The individual case records leave no doubt on this point. Further evidence can be found in the fact that two-thirds of the men who made a delayed readjustment used these benefits, while two-thirds of the unsuccessful did not.

The relatively high proportion of early recoveries and low proportion of unsuccessful readjustment among those who took institutional on-farm, on-the-job, or college training is in contrast to the readjustment patterns of veterans who pursued correspondence, trade school, or non-college academic courses. Many in the latter group entered training without any clear occupational objective. A study of the case records gives the distinct impression that many men (especially prior to 1948) attended trade school simply to draw the subsistence allowance. On the other hand, the veteran who took farm training, on-the-job training, or attended college usually had an occupational goal and was willing to strive hard to realize it.

The figures leave little doubt that one of the most constructive actions of the government on behalf of the veteran was to make such a wide range of educational and training opportunities available to him. Many made good use of them; it is regrettable that many others who could have thus benefited did not even enter one of the programs.

SUMMARY

It would not be possible except in a very extended summary to recapitulate the many different findings which have emerged from this detailed review of the wide range of factors that influenced or failed to influence the readjustment patterns of the cohort ineffectives. It may be helpful, however, to present a few of the more important findings which appear to be soundly grounded in the data.

The quality of a soldier's performance in the Army prior to discharge was found to be an important predictor of his performance after his return to civilian life. The better his military record, the more likely it was that he would sooner or later readjust to civilian life. Soldiers who had served in combat and had been wounded were not particularly handicapped in readjusting. Apparently they were able to absorb the stresses to which they had been exposed. Prolonged service overseas alone appeared to represent a type of stress that was a handicap in readjustment. The other important finding growing out of the review of the soldier's experiences in the Army was that the severity of his disturbance at the time he broke down provided a clue to his later readjustment. Those who were judged to be severely incapacitated for further service in the Army were the least likely to readjust in civilian life.

The fact that the different experiences which soldiers underwent in the Army were not more closely correlated with their postwar readjustment made it desirable to explore to what extent their recovery was related to their personal characteristics. Here we found that men who entered the Army in their middle thirties or in their late teens had the greatest difficulty in readjusting. The more education a man had the better, in general, his readjustment was likely to be. This fact helped to explain why Negroes had a much poorer readjustment record than whites. When whites and Negroes with similar educational backgrounds were compared, except for those with the least schooling, the differences in their readjustment patterns greatly diminished. A man's religion was not found to be significantly related to his readjustment. With reference to occupation, the most severely handicapped group were the unskilled and service workers whose postwar adjustment record was below that of all other major occupational groupings, including farmers. With regard to marriage, men who failed to marry and those whose marriages had been broken before induction or discharge were found to be the least successful in their readjustment. Those who remained married or married for the first time after discharge had the best record. Farmers who secured other employment were more successful in their recovery than those who remained on the farm, but in general migrants were less successful than non-migrants.

A review of the various benefits made available by the Veterans Administration suggested that many men who received disability compensation were aided in their readjustment; neither the data nor the case materials gave support to the widespread belief that men failed to recover because they did not want to lose their ratings. Some veterans undoubtedly benefited from the hospital care which was available to them. But the clearest finding pertaining to readjustment was the advantage that many received from the liberal educational and training opportunities which the government made available to them.

Finally, this chapter has indicated some of the characteristics of the 20,000 who failed to readjust. Men who were older than the average, with less schooling, who were in unskilled or service occupations, who had a poor performance record in the Army, who at the time of breakdown in the Army were adjudged to be severely incapacitated for further military service, who had never married or whose marriage had been broken before or while they were still in the service, who failed to make use of their Veterans Administration education and training benefits—these were the men who were most likely to fail to readjust. We will be able to learn more about them in the following chapters when we review the performance of the cohort ineffectives throughout their entire life span.

Part IV: PERFORMANCE PATTERNS

Chapter Eleven: LIFE PATTERNS OF PERFORMANCE

DURING THE WAR many speculations were advanced as to why so many young men were failing as soldiers. It was contended that men who were failing in the Army had also been ineffective prior to their military service—they were ineffective persons and that was that. The Army could do little about them but process and discharge them just as quickly as they could be identified. The same type of explanation was advanced to explain why certain men failed to readjust satisfactorily after their return to civilian life. It was maintained that the men who found it difficult or impossible to get and hold a job and to marry and settle down were the same individuals who had been poor performers before they entered the Army and who had performed unsatisfactorily while in the service.

The Army's manpower planners had based important personnel policies on this belief in continuity in performance. They sought to reject for military service any man who had ever been admitted to a mental or penal institution. They also sought to reject all who had a defect that might later cause them to perform ineffectively in the Army. Likewise, when soldiers who had been inducted began to give evidence of ineffective performance, the Army's policy at certain periods of the war was to encourage their speedy separation.

In connection with the analysis of the military performance of the ineffective soldiers prior to breakdown and the civilian performance of these men after their return to civilian life, we accumulated considerable information through which we could explore more thoroughly their life performance patterns. In addition to information about their performance both in the Army and after their return to civilian life, we also have knowledge of their performance prior to their coming onto active duty. We are therefore in a position to explore whether significant patterns of performance could be delineated up to the end of our contact with them in 1953, at which time many of them were in their thirties and a considerable proportion in their forties.

Our data have inherent limitations. In the first place, they reflect the performance of a specially selected group of men—that is, men who proved ineffective in the Army in World War II, at least in the sense of having been prematurely separated from the service. Secondly, while we were able to follow most of them for almost a decade after their discharge from the Army, we have no way of knowing how they will perform during the many years that still lie ahead of them. Finally, the materials which we have assembled about the quality of their performance, military and civilian, enable us to make only a rough estimate of the effectiveness with which they have been able to cope with life's problems. A refined analysis would require much more detail. Yet we do have a basis for undertaking a longitudinal analysis of the performance of this sizable group of men which, despite various limitations, should enable us to determine whether, and to what extent, significantly different patterns can be established to describe the consistency and quality with which these men performed.

Military administration helped to strengthen the belief in continuity of performance. When a soldier who had been properly screened and accepted for military service later broke down, those who were charged with the responsibility for processing his discharge sought to explain his failure. Inevitably they searched his background for signs of weakness which had previously escaped detection. There are few indeed, even among the fortunate who have grown up in a reasonably good environment, whose personality, upon careful scrutiny would not reveal some defects which might appear to lead to later ineffectiveness. If the members of the disposition board were able to ascertain that the ineffective soldier came from a home that had been broken by death or divorce, or that his family had been buffeted badly by his father's prolonged unemployment, or that he had been exposed to other forms of economic or social deprivation, they frequently assumed that they had determined the roots of his ineffectiveness.

Belief in the theory of continuity in men's performance was further reinforced by the realization that intelligence—which includes the ability to learn—is to a marked degree determined by heredity, and its development can be influenced by environmental opportunities, or the lack of them, only early in life. This means that a man will tend to continue to perform within limits set by his intelligence. Additional reinforcement came from the recognition that the basic personality of an adult was shaped by the experiences of his infancy and childhood. The ineffectiveness demonstrated by soldiers in World War II could be traced back in many cases to serious emotional problems within the home which had affected the soldier's childhood.

If intelligence and emotional stability are basic elements in determining the level of a man's performance and if, further, limitations and defects in each are present at birth or develop within the first few years of life, it is easy to understand why there is a widespread belief in the continuity in life performance patterns. But despite these reasons, theoretical and practical, for assuming basic continuity in life performance patterns, we have already presented in the earlier chapters a number of findings which suggest that we must consider discontinuity as well as continuity in the study of life performance patterns.

First of all, the vast majority of the men who were accepted for military service did not present any significant indications at the time of their induction examination which would have justified the Army's rejecting them. In point of fact, the composite evaluation of their pre-military performance which we undertook on the basis of the extensive information in their personnel files enabled us to conclude that the vast majority had been performing in an acceptable manner prior to their induction. Thus, their breakdown in the Army was at variance with the expectations based on their prior performance. Despite the fact that the order of demands which they faced in the Army was frequently much greater than what they had had to contend with at home, a careful evaluation of how they performed after they came on active duty revealed that once again the majority had a satisfactory performance record up to the point of their breaking down.

Moreover, in studying what happened to the soldiers who had broken down in the Army, we found that a substantial majority were able to readjust after their return to civilian life, some quickly, some only after a delay. However, approximately half of even those who failed to readjust had had a good or acceptable military performance rating up to the time of their breakdown.

These findings suggest that we must examine more carefully, and in quantitative terms, the group which shows continuity of performance—at an acceptable or poor level—and the group that does not. To do so we must enlarge the framework of our analysis to include the man's pre-military performance record and to distinguish temporary from prolonged failure to perform effectively.

The question may be raised whether such an evaluation of performance patterns may not be vitiated by the fact that we have readings about how men performed in two sharply contrasting environments—the civilian and the military. Military service during a major war presents new and unusual demands to men who have had no prior experience with fighting. Two such disparate environments as a civilian job in peace and duty in an Army at war cannot be equated. But there is no need to equate them; it is only necessary to recognize that the two have been tied together by life itself. Men are called upon to fight in war just as they are required to earn their livelihood in peace, and stress and crises are seldom completely absent from the lives of most civilians. Moreover, various organizational groups—the Army, the Veterans Administration, employers—must make judgments about how men are likely to perform based upon an evaluation of how they have previously performed, irrespective of the contrast in the environments.

Many men who had performed successfully in civilian life were not able, as we have seen, to cope with the special stresses of war. Some were not able to adjust to the Army at all while others faltered along the way. To make allowance for the special pressures of the military environment in the study of life performance patterns, we have disregarded the fact that all the men in the cohort group were ineffective in the sense of being prematurely discharged. We have included in our evaluations of their military service only the quality of their performance in the Army prior to their breakdown. The only way in which it is possible to study continuity and discontinuity in performance in a world of rapid and continuing change is to recognize that most individuals will at some time in their lives be forced to cope with special orders of stress and how they respond to such situations must be considered a significant aspect of their life performance pattern.

Our first step was to combine the multiple performance ratings about each man in the cohort group into a meaningful composite, that is, a life performance pattern. We had information about three periods in each man's life: before he entered the Army, during his military service, and after his return to civilian life. For the last period we had three different evaluations, early, intermediate, and late, but here we used only the last available rating. The maximum number of life patterns of performance based on multiple ratings for each of the three periods was twenty-four, but many of these patterns contained so few cases that we consolidated them into nine patterns, excluding the unknown group. But even this number proved too unwieldly. By combining similar patterns, such as patterns differentiated only by whether a man's military performance had been rated as good or acceptable, we were able to develop four basic patterns—adjusted, vulnerable, broken, and poor—the components of which are set out in the following table.

LIFE PERFORMANCE PATTERNS: COMPONENT RATINGS IN EVALUATION PERIODS

PERFORMANCE PATTERN	EVALUATION PERIOD *Pre-Military*	*Military*	*Post-Military*
Adjusted	Acceptable or Poor	Good or Acceptable	Good or Acceptable
Vulnerable	Acceptable or Poor	Poor or Not Rated	Good or Acceptable
Broken	Acceptable	Good or Acceptable	Poor
Poor	Acceptable or Poor	Poor or Not Rated	Poor
	Poor	Acceptable	Poor

Before briefly describing each of the four life patterns, we must remind the reader again that in assessing a man's performance in the Army we disregarded the fact that he had been prematurely discharged and used as a basis of our evaluation his performance record up to the time he broke down. No soldier would have been rated as good or acceptable, not even one who served in combat with distinction, had we used premature discharge as a criterion of military performance.

We designated as "adjusted" the life patterns of men whose ratings in both the military and post-military periods were either good or acceptable. While most of this group also had an acceptable rating of performance before the war, it included some with a poor prewar record on the assumption that they were still in the throes of finding themselves.

The second pattern, "vulnerable," included men whose performance before and after their military service was good or acceptable but whose performance in the Army was poor or of such short duration that it could not be rated. They were "vulnerable" to the stresses of military life but were able to adjust to civilian life. A few whose performance prior to entering the Army was poor were included for the same reason that men with similar prewar performance records were included in the adjusted pattern.

The third pattern, "broken," includes men whose performance

had been acceptable prior to their entering the Army, and good or acceptable while they were on active duty up to the point of breakdown, but who failed after their discharge to readjust to civilian life.

The fourth pattern, "poor," includes primarily men whose performance in the military and in both civilian periods of their life was unsatisfactory plus a few whose civilian record was poor but who performed acceptably in military service up to their breakdown and a few others whose pre-military performance had been acceptable but whose later performance had consistently been poor.

The following table summarizes the number and percentage of the cohort ineffectives who fell within each of these four life performance patterns.

DISTRIBUTION OF COHORT INEFFECTIVES BY LIFE PERFORMANCE PATTERN

Life Performance Pattern	*Weighted Number*	*Percent*
Adjusted	32,578	44.8
Vulnerable	8,979	12.4
Broken	6,201	8.5
Poor	8,499	11.7
Unknown	16,443	22.6
Cohort	72,700	100.0

The large number of "unknown" cases makes it necessary to guard against distorting the relative proportion in each pattern of those about whom adequate information is available. Men were placed in the unknown category if we did not have any information whatever about their postwar adjustment. We did, however, have considerable information about their pre-military and military performance on the basis of which we estimated their probable adjustment after the war in terms of our pattern structure (see Appendix for details). Using this estimate, the revised life pattern table is as follows:

Life Performance Pattern	*Weighted Number*	*Percent*
Adjusted	38,880	53.5
Vulnerable	13,914	19.1
Broken	7,371	10.1
Poor	12,535	17.3
Cohort	72,700	100.0

There are striking differences among the men included in each of the foregoing four patterns of life performance among which we have distributed the ineffective soldiers represented by the cohort sample. The extent of these differences will not be clear until we complete the analysis, in the following chapter, of the background characteristics, military performance, and postwar adjustment of the men within each of the life performance patterns. But even at this early stage we know that the variability in the composition of these groups will be substantial. We know from early chapters that included among the soldiers whose military service was good or acceptable—a precondition for being classified in the "adjusted" life pattern group—were men from the city and the farm, illiterates as well as college graduates, men who saw combat and others who did not, married men and single men, privates as well as sergeants.

We also know from earlier chapters that included among the men who failed to readjust to civilian life and therefore fell within the "broken" or "poor" life pattern groups were men who differ from one another in terms of their place of birth and residence, age, education, prewar occupation, marital status, military experience, and the use they made of Veterans Administration benefits.

But our earlier analysis also gives us reason to believe that there are probably significant clusterings of factors which help to differentiate the men who fall in these several life patterns. We had repeated occasion to note that men with little or no schooling found it very difficult to perform effectively in either military or civilian life. And we further noted that men who developed a psychosis in the Army not only were of no further use to the military but had no prospect of adjusting satisfactorily to civilian life unless their illness receded.

In order to illustrate the extent of the differences among men in the four life patterns, the following case histories have been selected from among white soldiers, all of whom except for the "vulnerable" example had overseas service, and all of whom were discharged from the Army because of psychoneurosis.

Adjusted

S.T. was born and brought up on a Southern farm. He had graduated from high school with average grades and had been elected vice-president of his senior class. After a brief period of employment as a general mechanic with a metal manufacturing and repair company he had entered college a few months before he was drafted.

After induction in November 1942 he was assigned to the Air Corps. Upon completion of basic training he volunteered for air crew gunnery training which he completed satisfactorily in spite of the fact that he "was in misery all the time" and when he finished he "felt doomed." Assigned to the European Theater of Operations he flew 30 combat missions as a B-17 waist gunner, and earned the Distinguished Flying Cross and the Air Medal with three Oak Leaf Clusters. Promoted to staff sergeant, he returned to the U.S. on rotation late in 1944. On a routine examination to determine his physical fitness for further aircrew duty, the medical officers noted that he was tense and anxious and complained of fatigue and insomnia. Hospitalized for several months at an AAF Convalescent Hospital, S.T. was found to be quite disturbed. He cried easily, had feelings of guilt and inferiority, tended to be seclusive and depressed. He was given a medical discharge in March 1945 after an attempt to return him to duty resulted in a psychological collapse during which he described himself as having a "sense of feeling utterly futile, helpless."

Returning home, S.T. rested and did a little work around the family farm for about a year. He re-entered college in January 1946. He started in the School of Agriculture at a neighboring university, but soon switched to the School of Business where he completed all requirements and was awarded his bachelor's degree in the spring of 1949. He then secured a job with a state commission and some time later became a field representative with increased responsibilities and a higher salary. Two years after discharge he married and at last account had one child. He claims to be in good health and considers his military experience to have been beneficial—"an experience comparable in some ways to a college education."

Vulnerable

T.U. was raised on a Midwestern farm. He completed high school in 1935, two years after he should have graduated because his family had needed him to work on the farm. When economic conditions improved he had returned to school and although "always kinda scared of school," he made fairly good grades. As a youth, he was closely attached to his parents, was somewhat shy, and did not make friends easily. In the late 1930s shortly after he married, his father set him up in a business of his own—a small hardware store in his home town, but he sold it after a few years and returned to farming.

Drafted in December 1942, he shortly thereafter went to the dispensary at the Reception Center because he was unable to eat or sleep. Since he was quite upset he was sent to the hospital for further evaluation. During a month in the hospital it became clear to the authorities that he was "so scared of Army life that he really couldn't stand it." He was depressed, confused, cried extensively during routine interviews, and had many somatic complaints as well. He was diagnosed as having a psychoneurosis, hypochondriasis, and given a medical discharge.

Returning home, he rested for a few months and then went back to farming. He now owns and operates his own farm. He claims his health is good but states that he has been afraid to have children since his wife's family has a long history of tuberculosis. His military service was too brief to qualify him for veterans' benefits under the G.I. Bill.

Broken

The youngest of five children, U.V. left his parents' Midwestern farm shortly after completing two years of high school and secured employment as a carpenter's helper in a nearby town. Married in 1937, he continued working at this trade until inducted late in 1942. Assigned to an anti-aircraft unit, he participated in the Normandy invasion and in the campaign across northern France. He was in good health and his character and efficiency ratings were "excellent."

After about two months of combat he was knocked unconscious by the blast of an aerial bomb. Because he complained of headaches, dizziness, and a "roaring in the ears," the aid station transferred him to the evacuation hospital where his condition was at first described as "mild." However, his headaches grew worse, and his dizziness was accompanied by spells of nausea and vomiting. U.V. developed increasing nervous tension, had battle dreams, and jumped at any loud noise. Five months of hospitalization in England failed to reveal any organic basis for his persistent headaches but he showed no improvement. He was evacuated to the United States where his hospitalization continued for another seven months in general and convalescent hospitals. Finally, shortly before V-J Day, he was given a medical discharge with a diagnosis of psychoneurosis, acute, severe, anxiety state.

U.V. went back to the family farm and tried to return to the carpentry trade but could not make it. He could not tolerate the noises nor could he climb ladders. Unable to work, he puttered around the farm, and received as his only cash income the 70 percent disability compensation which the Veterans Administration had awarded him. Successive examinations failed to reveal any improvement in his emotional state. He started a liberal arts course at a junior college but soon dropped out. He was not considered suitable for training under Public Law 16 until he improved.

Over the next few years he worked occasionally at odd jobs but never for long. He had difficulties in securing jobs because he detailed his symptoms and his disabilities to any prospective employer. At times, he was able to work reasonably well but either he quit or his temporary work had ended. One employer reported (in 1950) that the veteran was "an excellent painter and carpenter but that he doesn't seem able to work. He frequently blew up on a job and went to pieces." His wife had left him and later divorced him.

He is still rated as 50 percent disabled by the Veterans Administration and the last information (1953) indicates that for the past several years he had been earning some money by working as a part-time contact man for the local post of a veterans' service organization. But his supervisor reports that he could never qualify for a service representative since he appears to be incapable of assuming responsibility. Even with close supervision he had not been doing very well since he made more promises to veterans seeking help than he could possibly fulfill. In communal activities, he would start out on a new project with great enthusiasm but soon tired and moved on to something else.

Poor

A Southern farm hand before the war, V.W. started to drink steadily and heavily when he was fifteen years of age. He had a difficult time in school, attending intermittently for only three or four years, and finally left school at thirteen. He made only a marginal adjustment thereafter, working when he had to on his older brothers' or neighbors' farms. His drinking got him into numerous difficulties with the law and his record shows many arrests for drunkenness. In spite of this pattern of life he was drafted at the age of thirty-five.

In the Army he was assigned to an infantry unit and trained as a rifleman. During his first eight months of military service he stayed out of trouble but then his pattern of irresponsible behavior re-emerged. Before going overseas he had been AWOL three times, for which he was court-martialed, as well as for being drunk in uniform in a public place. In combat both in North Africa and later in Italy he performed well for a time. Following the fall of Rome, he became bothered by shortness of breath, chest pains, and lack of stamina. He was hospitalized briefly for neurocirculatory asthenia and returned to duty, this time to noncombat duty as a basic soldier with an ambulance company. For several months he performed satisfactorily, but he began to drink again, even on duty, and was again court-martialed.

A short while later he was hospitalized with a diagnosis of anxiety, tension state, chronic and moderate; he was irritable, nervous, tired, and had headaches and occasional backaches. He had difficulty sleeping and when he did he was disturbed by battle dreams. While in the hospital he obtained some alcohol and had to be confined for acute alcoholism. At one point he was diagnosed as schizophrenic because of seclusiveness, lack of normal responses, dullness, and auditory hallucinations. When he was evacuated to the States, the diagnosis of psychosis was not confirmed. For a time the authorities considered giving him a Section VIII discharge for alcoholism but because of his clear-cut anxiety symptoms he was finally given a medical discharge.

V.W. initially was rated as 50 percent disabled because of his anxiety reaction but in early 1947 this rating was eliminated. For several years following his discharge the veteran worked only infrequently on farms near his home. He continued to drink and was arrested and jailed many times for drunkenness. It was reported that after his compensation was cut off, his mother gave him a small amount of spending money. In 1950 he entered an institutional on-the-farm training program on a rented farm, but quit within three months because he could not get along with his landlord. At last report this veteran was living with his mother and an older brother and had no gainful employment beyond an occasional odd job on a farm or at the neighboring sawmill.

The four cases presented above in summary form suggest that the men with varying life patterns of performance differed from each other in personal characteristics and had to face different situational pressures in civilian and military life. In the following chapter we will seek to determine the internal or external factors which might explain, either singly or in combination, why these men revealed such different life patterns of performance. At this point it may be useful, however, to review briefly only one overriding question—the degree of continuity or change reflected in each of the four major patterns of performance.

First of all it is worth noting that nearly 39,000 men, or 54 percent, of the 72,700 men represented by the cohort sample were found to have an adjusted life performance pattern. This means that their performance before they entered the Army, on active duty up to the time they broke down, and after their return to civilian life was acceptable or good. A relatively small number of those included in this pattern had a poor record before the war, but this fact did not weigh too heavily since, as these young men matured, they became capable of meeting the demands made on them. With minor reservations, however, the basic pattern of the adjusted group is one of continuity—by and large, these men were able to cope satisfactorily with the demands made on them in civilian and military life.

Those with a vulnerable life pattern of performance show distinctly less continuity. For the most part the almost 14,000 in this pattern, or 19 percent of the total sample, performed satisfactorily in civilian life but failed in the Army. A relatively few were in the Army for such a short period of time that they could not even be rated, but their early discharge is indicative of poor performance. Since the 1930s were characterized by severe unemployment, and since many adolescents encounter great difficulty in settling down under any circumstances, the major test of adjustment to civilian life should be whether a man performed satisfactorily after his discharge from the Army. This group did. In terms of continuity and change, the performance of those in the vulnerable pattern was characterized, as the name implies, by discontinuity:

they could not cope with military life but they were able to adjust to civilian life.

About 7,400 men, 1 out of 10 in the entire group, were found to have a broken pattern of performance. This meant that while they had performed satisfactorily prior to coming on to active duty and had continued to perform satisfactorily up to the point of breakdown, they were unable to readjust in civilian life. They represent clear-cut discontinuity.

The fourth pattern was comprised of men whose life performance was characterized as poor. The majority of the approximately 12,500, or 17 percent of the entire group, had a poor performance record both in the Army and after their return to civilian life. A minority had an acceptable record either prior to induction or during military service, but the predominant trend in their performance was poor and they were therefore classified as having a poor life performance pattern.

By and large men with adjusted or poor life patterns of performance, who together accounted for 7 out of 10 in the entire group, show a high order of continuity in performance from one period of their life to another. This high percentage would drop if we subtracted from the number in the adjusted pattern those whose record before the war was poor and from the number classified as poor those who had either an acceptable prewar or military record. Together they comprised 10,230 and if they were eliminated, the percentage of men in the entire group with marked continuity in their life performance patterns drops to 6 out of 10.

Over 21,000 men, almost 30 percent of the total cohort, had life performance patterns that were either vulnerable or broken. This is the minimum number whose life performance patterns are characterized by some order of discontinuity, minor or major. At a maximum we must add the two special groups of adjusted and poor whose performance patterns contained a significant element of discontinuity. If this is done, the total with discontinuous patterns of performance amount to 31,515, or 43.3 percent.

This preliminary analysis of the life performance patterns of the cohort sample provides considerable support for the prevailing view that the performance of men is characterized by a basic continuity growing out of their fundamental strengths or weaknesses. At a minimum such continuity was found among about 6 out of every 10 men in the sample of ineffective soldiers. Among the other men who served and who were demobilized or separated for other reasons, the majority also would undoubtedly show a basic continuity in performance over time.

On the other hand, many of the men who served in the Armed Forces, and probably even higher proportions among those who were rejected for service particularly for mental or emotional reasons, would show some discontinuity in their performance. But the analysis of the ineffective soldiers alone represents a challenge to those who hold too firmly to the belief in continuity. At a minimum about 3 out of 10, and at a maximum more than 4 out of 10, show conspicuous discontinuity in their performance patterns. In the following chapter we will seek to identify and evaluate the key factors that characterize the men who fall into the different life patterns of performance.

Chapter Twelve: SUCCESSFUL AND UNSUCCESSFUL LIFE PERFORMANCE PATTERNS

SEVERAL interesting findings were distilled from the preliminary analysis of the overall data about life performance patterns presented in the preceding chapter. From this review it appeared that clear distinctions could be made among the levels at which people perform over long periods of time, which in turn could be characterized by consistency or lack of it. Some tended to perform successfully at most times; others had a consistent record of poor performance; and still others had patterns characterized by fluctuations between successful and unsuccessful performance.

The objective of the present chapter is to seek to identify some of the important factors that lie back of these different performance patterns. We start with useful clues. The first grows out of the finding that men who had encountered objectively the most severe stress in the Army—those who were in combat or were wounded—were among those who had the best recovery patterns. From this we may assume that the personal characteristics of men—their intellectual and emotional strengths—can explain in considerable measure their life performance patterns.

The second clue is the effect of an overwhelming environmental change, such as military service itself, on the performance patterns of large groups of men. We found that some who had had little difficulty in adjusting satisfactorily to civilian life had had great difficulties in adjusting to military service almost as soon as they were inducted. And still others who had performed satisfactorily prior to induction and in the service up to the time of their breakdown never recovered after their return to civilian life.

A third clue derives from the importance that various orders of support has for men who are under stress at some time in their lives. Their ability to overcome the handicaps and barriers which face them and to perform effectively may well depend on the presence or absence of adequate supports.

These clues point to the desirability of analyzing life performance patterns in terms of three distinct determinants of performances. A review of the demographic characteristics of the cohort ineffectives will help to point up the extent to which differences in their life performance reflect differences in their personal strengths and weaknesses. A consideration of their experience in the Army will throw light on the extent to which a radical alteration in their accustomed ways of life may have resulted in breaking the continuity of their established pattern of performance. And the aid which they received from the Veterans Administration should help to point up whether large-scale support provided by the community can help men maintain or reestablish a satisfactory level of performance as they shift from one environment to another.

In addition to reviewing the life performance patterns in terms of these three constellations, this chapter will also seek to explore the differences between the two groups whose life patterns proved unsuccessful—the broken and the poor, in the hope that some additional insight can be gained into the causes of failure. Such men always represent a special challenge since society is forced to assume responsibility for them and for their families.

DEMOGRAPHIC FACTORS

There were several suggestions in the earlier chapters, which considered military performance and civilian readjustment, to the effect that factors of age, education, occupation, race, and marital status, are important determinants of performance. We are now ready to explore whether they are also significantly related to life performance patterns.

The following analysis is restricted to those about whom adequate information was available for establishing a life performance pattern. As far as age is concerned youth appeared to be an advantage: in the eighteen- to twenty-two-year-old group, almost two-thirds, 63.1 percent, have an adjusted pattern while this is true of only 36.1 percent of those between thirty-three and thirty-seven. However, men with a poor life performance pattern tend to be more heavily concentrated among the youngest and the oldest groups—below twenty-two and above thirty-three. The Army's selection methods help to explain these concentrations: the examiners were inclined to accept young men if they appeared physically healthy; and they likewise were inclined to accept older men who had no dependents and were not in essential occupations, but in so doing they often overlooked serious defects which presaged poor performance later on.

Another significant finding with regard to age relates to the much higher proportion of men in the thirty-three to thirty-seven year bracket who had a broken pattern of life performance—about double the percentage of men in the lower age brackets. This suggests that the older men, once they experienced a severe breakdown, had much greater difficulty in readjusting.

The relationships between education and life performance patterns are summarized in the following table.

LIFE PERFORMANCE PATTERN BY EDUCATIONAL LEVEL ACHIEVED, IN PERCENT

LEVEL OF EDUCATION	TOTAL KNOWN	LIFE PERFORMANCE PATTERN *Adjusted*	*Vulnerable*	*Broken*	*Poor*	PERCENT WITH KNOWN PATTERN
Less than grammar school graduation	100.0	37.6	23.0	18.6	20.8	67.8
Grammar school graduation	100.0	74.9	2.6	4.9	17.6	80.5
Some high school	100.0	70.4	9.0	7.2	13.4	82.7
High school graduation	100.0	77.5	14.3	3.2	5.0	93.1
At least some college	100.0	66.6	23.5	5.4	4.5	99.1

Several points are worthy of attention. High-school graduates who did not go to college had the best record of life performance patterns—3 out of every 4 fell in the adjusted group. At the opposite extreme were men who had failed to complete grammar school: only slightly more than 1 out of 3 had an adjusted life pattern.

The group with vulnerable life patterns had a double concentration: about 1 out of every 4 of the least educated and of the best educated performed satisfactorily in civilian life but failed in the Army. The poorly educated among them tended to go back to a more or less protected farm environment; and the best educated among them were able in civilian life, where they had greater margins of freedom, to maneuver around the emotional problems which had caused them to become ineffective in the Army.

The data make it clear that those with a broken pattern were heavily concentrated among the least educated—those who had not graduated from grammar school, and who accounted for 72 percent of the total. There was a smaller proportion of the least educated among those with a poor life pattern. While the greatest proportion of the poor, 59 percent, were found among those with the least education, a considerable number who had never performed satisfactorily had graduated from elementary school or had even attended high school. Thus education appears to play a different role in each of the four life patterns.

Since a man's occupation depends in considerable measure on his education, it would be well to consider next the relationships between the occupations of the cohort ineffectives and their life performance patterns. In terms of their prewar occupations more than 8 out of every 10 in the white collar group and slightly less than 2 out of every 3 of the semi-skilled and skilled were found to have an adjusted pattern. This was true, however, for only about half of the farmers and less than half of those in the unskilled and service group. Farmers and the unskilled accounted for most of the men with poor performance patterns as well as for most of those in the vulnerable group. The semi-skilled and skilled, on the other hand, formed the largest single group — about 1 in 3 — of men with broken patterns.

When the men's most recent postwar occupations were studied in relation to life performance patterns, a few interesting shifts were discovered. Among those with adjusted patterns, there is a significantly greater proportion of semi-skilled and skilled and a smaller proportion of farmers, which reflects the fact that the more capable men among the cohort sample left the farm after the war. The farmers who moved into non-farm occupations had almost as good life patterns as those who had always been in non-farm occupations—62 percent adjusted and 15 percent poor compared to 65 percent adjusted and 10 percent poor. This was in striking contrast to those who stayed on the farm—39 percent adjusted and 25 percent poor.

Of the men with a poor performance pattern, the proportion in unskilled jobs increased substantially during the postwar years, indicating that this is a likely area in which the unsuccessful can find a job now and again. Between a fourth and a fifth of the men with broken or poor patterns of performance were not classified as to occupation because they were characteristically unemployed or unemployable.

With regard to race, approximately three-fifths of the whites but less than half of the Negroes have an adjusted pattern. Furthermore, about one-seventh of the whites but well over a sixth of the Negroes have poor life performance patterns. There are proportionately more whites than Negroes with vulnerable performance patterns but considerably more Negroes than whites with broken patterns. Limitations of developmental opportunities, especially education, and the specific barriers of adjustment which he faces because of his race are reflected in the Negro's heavier representation in both the broken and poor performance patterns.

Among the most interesting relationships are those between marital patterns and life performance patterns. These are set out in the accompanying table.

Only about 3 out of 10 men who remained single had an adjusted pattern in contrast to 7 out of 10 men whose first marriage was unbroken up to the time when we were last in contact with them. More than 1 out of every 3 single men had a broken pattern, and

LIFE PERFORMANCE PATTERN BY MARITAL PATTERN, IN PERCENT

MARITAL PATTERN	TOTAL KNOWN	LIFE PERFORMANCE PATTERN *Adjusted*	*Vulnerable*	*Broken*	*Poor*	PERCENT WITH KNOWN PATTERN
Single throughout	100.0	29.8	15.6	35.8	18.8	78.4
Married—unbroken	100.0	70.1	16.5	6.1	7.3	92.0
Broken marriage	100.0	44.9	12.6	11.9	30.6	87.4
Marriage broken before discharge	100.0	20.5	9.8	5.7	64.0	74.9
Remarried	100.0	29.8	18.7	—	51.5	73.6
Marriage broken after discharge	100.0	58.1	14.0	15.2	12.7	95.9
Remarried	100.0	66.7	21.7	2.2	9.4	95.9

almost 1 out of 5 had a poor pattern of performance. In contrast this was true of only 1 out of 16 and 1 out of 13, respectively, of the men whose marriages had remained intact.

Men whose marriages were broken at the time of their discharge from the Army had on the average a considerably worse life performance pattern than even those who had remained single. Only 1 in 5 had an adjusted pattern and approximately 2 out of every 3 had a poor performance pattern. It is interesting to note that if those who remarried in this group are studied separately, their performance patterns are still heavily skewed towards the unsuccessful: only 3 in 10 had an adjusted pattern; more than half had a poor pattern.

Those who remained married or whose marriage was broken only after the war had more satisfactory life performance patterns. Only a few had a poor performance pattern. As has been suggested earlier, marriage tends to be a positive factor in the lives of most people, helping them to perform effectively. But for those whose marriages were broken prior to or during the war, marriage did not perform this positive function. If a man has serious defects, he is unlikely to overcome them by marriage or by remarriage.

There is strong support in the foregoing to indicate that ineffective soldiers who had graduated from high school, who eventually entered white collar or skilled employment, and who married and kept their marriages intact had the intellectual and emotional qualities which enabled most of them to have adjusted life patterns of performance. On the other hand, those who had failed to graduate from grammar school, who remained on the farm or obtained only unskilled work, who failed to marry or whose marriage was broken before their discharge from the Army were much more likely to have a broken or poor life performance pattern. Apparently, they did not have the strengths required to cope with life's difficulties and challenges. It is also possible, however, that their failure was precipitated or deepened by their experiences in the Army.

ARMY EXPERIENCE

The following analysis will establish whether or not the life performance patterns of the cohort ineffectives are related to the situational pressures to which they were exposed in the Army, the degree of their incapacitation for further military service at breakdown, and the clinical symptoms which led to their premature separation.

LIFE PERFORMANCE PATTERN BY SITUATION, IN PERCENT

SITUATION	TOTAL KNOWN	LIFE PERFORMANCE PATTERN *Adjusted*	*Vulnerable*	*Broken*	*Poor*	PERCENT WITH KNOWN PATTERN
I	100.0	54.8	21.0	7.6	16.6	77.6
II	100.0	54.7	18.4	10.4	16.5	71.0
III	100.0	55.7	5.3	23.1	15.9	76.5
IV	100.0	77.9	0.4	15.7	6.0	91.5

As can be seen in the accompanying table, over 3 out of every 4 men who saw combat had an adjusted pattern, a very much higher proportion than was found among men whose military service had been less arduous. Moreover, the smallest proportion of men with poor patterns of performance is found among those with combat experience, undoubtedly a reflection of the care which the Army took to screen out from combat units those who did not look promising.

The data also point up the fact that men who performed satisfactorily in civilian life but who experienced difficulty in meeting the Army's demands came early to the attention of their officers and were discharged early in their service. Seven out of 10 men with a vulnerable pattern were discharged within one year—Situation I. Only a few, 4 percent, ever served overseas. This was also true of those with poor life performance patterns except that somewhat more, 17 percent, were sent overseas before they came to the attention of the authorities. However, a considerable proportion of the men with broken life patterns of performance, 42 percent, did serve overseas, some in combat.

The related measure of length of service is generally confirmatory. A little more than half of those who served between one and two years fell in the adjusted pattern, while for those with more than two years' service the comparable proportion was about 7 out of 10. The only exception to the general trend of a higher proportion of men in the adjusted pattern as length of service increased is the group which served from 6 to 11 months, where more than two-thirds had an adjusted pattern. This reflects the Army's easy discharge policy of 1943, which resulted in the separation of many men before they had actually proved themselves to be ineffective.

Further understanding about the relation of severity of stress to life performance patterns can be gleaned from the table below.

LIFE PERFORMANCE PATTERN BY SEVERITY OF SERVICE, IN PERCENT

SEVERITY OF SERVICE	TOTAL KNOWN	LIFE PERFORMANCE PATTERN *Adjusted*	*Vulnerable*	*Broken*	*Poor*	PERCENT WITH KNOWN PATTERN
Combat, wounded	100.0	80.1	—	16.5	3.4	97.9
Combat, not wounded	100.0	76.6	0.6	15.3	7.5	88.2
Overseas, non-combat	100.0	55.7	5.3	23.1	15.9	76.5
Zone of Interior	100.0	54.8	20.2	8.4	16.6	75.5

The findings are striking: 4 out of 5 of the wounded as well as 3 out of 4 who saw combat but were not wounded were found to have an adjusted pattern. This was true of only 5 out of 9 of those who served overseas under non-combat conditions or who never left the Zone of the Interior. Conversely, men who were wounded or at least saw combat had the smallest proportions with a poor pattern.

Another facet of military experience that may well be related to life performance patterns is the degree of incapacitation for further service that we found to exist at the time of the soldiers' breakdown. The data are presented in the following table.

LIFE PERFORMANCE PATTERN BY DEGREE OF INCAPACITATION, IN PERCENT

DEGREE OF INCAPACITATION	TOTAL KNOWN	LIFE PERFORMANCE PATTERN *Adjusted*	*Vulnerable*	*Broken*	*Poor*	PERCENT WITH KNOWN PATTERNS
Major	100.0	39.1	15.2	15.7	30.0	73.3
Moderate	100.0	70.5	12.6	12.1	4.8	85.0
Minor	100.0	76.7	22.6	—	0.7	75.6

These data indicate that the less severe a soldier's incapacitation at breakdown in the Army, the more likely that he would have an adjusted life performance pattern. The more severe his incapacitation, the more likely that he would be found to have a broken or a poor life performance pattern. The data also revealed that almost 9 out of every 10 men with a poor life performance pattern and nearly two-thirds of those with a broken pattern were at the time of breakdown severely incapacitated for further military service.

It is of interest in this connection to review the extent to which men in these several patterns who at breakdown were severely incapacitated for further military service also had pre-military indications of ineffectiveness in their records. Among those with major incapacitation in the adjusted pattern, 1 had such indications for every 3 who did not; among those with vulnerable or broken patterns the rate was roughly 2 to 5; but among those with poor patterns it was, as could be expected, reversed—5 had such indications for every 2 who did not.

Our last comparison of factors in military experience with life performance patterns is based on the reasons for separation, which is set out in the following table.

LIFE PERFORMANCE PATTERN BY REASON FOR SEPARATION, IN PERCENT

REASON FOR SEPARATION	TOTAL KNOWN	LIFE PERFORMANCE PATTERN *Adjusted*	*Vulnerable*	*Broken*	*Poor*	PERCENT WITH KNOWN PATTERN
Psychoneurosis	100.0	66.9	13.0	11.0	9.1	87.5
Psychosis	100.0	31.8	12.8	29.9	25.5	86.6
Undesirability	100.0	34.3	9.8	7.0	48.9	51.0
Inaptitude	100.0	49.3	27.3	3.2	20.2	60.9

Several interesting findings emerge. Two out of every 3 men separated for psychoneurosis fell in the adjusted pattern. Almost a third of those who had been separated for a psychosis also fell in the adjusted pattern, which suggests that they had had a psychotic episode in the Army which had no further repercussions. The second largest group among those discharged for a psychosis fell in the broken pattern, indicating that while they had performed satisfactorily up to that point in their lives, they had suffered a major breakdown in the Army from which they were unable to recover according to the latest information we have about them. The fact that they became psychotic in the Army leaves open the question to what extent, if any, their condition was precipitated by their military experience.

About 1 out of every 3 who were discharged from the Army as undesirable was found in the adjusted group, which suggests that many had been in only superficial trouble or had been discharged for reasons not directly related to their performance, such as homosexuality. But almost half of the undesirables had a poor performance pattern. Even though we were unable to develop adequate postwar information about half of this group it is doubtful that the result would have been altered had more data been available. We had rated about two-thirds of these men as poor performers prior to their breakdown in the Army and 4 out of 5 were assessed to have major incapacitation for further military service. It is doubtful that many of them, even when freed from Army discipline, would have succeeded in making a satisfactory civilian readjustment.

Those separated for inaptitude fall into three recognizable groups. Half had an adjusted pattern, which suggests that the Army had acted precipitously with regard to some of them—they were discharged before they had been given an adequate trial. About 1 in 4 were found to have a vulnerable pattern, reflecting that this group includes those with less education from the rural areas who were able to make an adjustment at home but who could not cope with the much more complex military environment. The third group are those who were found to have a poor performance pattern: limited intelligence, a major reason for a soldier's being discharged as inapt, is a serious handicap to effective performance in civilian as well as in military life. Nevertheless, it was only one-fifth of the inapt group which fell into the poor life performance pattern.

The foregoing data lend support to the contention advanced earlier that in estimating life performance patterns there are severe limitations on the reliance that can be placed on the clinical diagnoses used by the Army to separate men as ineffective. The data show that a considerable proportion of men who were psychotic, undesirable, or inapt in the Army had an adjusted performance pattern. Even less negative prognostic significance can be attached to the designation "psychoneurotic" as it was applied to ineffectives at the time of discharge. About 8 out of 10 ineffective soldiers separated for psychoneurosis had either an adjusted or a vulnerable life pattern which points to the fact that they had no special difficulties in adjusting to civilian life. And the overwhelming proportion, 84 percent, also had had a satisfactory performance record in the military up to the time of their breakdown.

An interesting additional fact emerges about the men who because of disciplinary trouble received a punitive discharge from the Army. Approximately 2 out of every 5 men with poor performance patterns were court-martialed. The rates for the other groups were 1 in 32 for the adjusted, 1 in 7 for the vulnerable, and 1 in 13 for the broken. These figures suggest that disciplinary action was largely restricted to men who fall into our poor performance pattern.

A few conclusions, some more definite than others, are suggested by this review of the relations between Army experience and life performance patterns. Men who experienced the most severe stress in the Army were not over-represented among those with broken or vulnerable patterns. In fact the reverse was true, suggesting that the characteristics of the individual rather than the external environment was the most important determinant in a man's life performance pattern.

Reinforcement for this conclusion was given by a study of the relationship between the degree of incapacitation of the soldiers at the time of breakdown and their life performance patterns. Those with major incapacitation were under-represented among the adjusted and over-represented among the broken and the poor. Moreover, only among those with poor patterns was there a disproportionately high number who had pre-military indications of ineffectiveness as well as major incapacitation for further service.

An analysis of the clinical categories under which soldiers were discharged disclosed that soldiers separated because of psychoses or undesirability had the lowest proportions with adjusted patterns, the highest with poor patterns.

The burden of these several findings is that it is the underlying strengths and weaknesses of men, more than the objective stresses and strains which they experienced, which hold the key to their life performance patterns.

VETERANS ADMINISTRATION BENEFITS

This brings us to the third complex of factors that we investigated. In what manner was the use that men made of various types of veterans' benefits—disability compensation, hospitalization, and educational and training benefits—related to their life performance patterns?

We have considered earlier the number of the cohort sample who received disability compensation. At this point we are interested in the extent to which such compensation may have been associated with various life performance patterns. It is well to remember that those separated for inaptitude were not generally considered to have a compensable defect; and those separated for undesirability were generally ineligible for compensation and most other benefits because they were discharged without honor. It was the 40,600 discharged for psychoneurosis and the 6,600 for psychosis out of the total 72,700 represented by our sample who were by and large eligible to receive disability compensation.

The following table summarizes the percentage of men within each life performance pattern who received disability compensation initially and the degree of disability that they were adjudged to have at that time.

INITIAL DISABILITY COMPENSATION RATING BY LIFE PERFORMANCE PATTERN, IN PERCENT

RATING	TOTAL	LIFE PERFORMANCE PATTERN			
INITIAL	COHORT	*Adjusted*	*Vulnerable*	*Broken*	*Poor*
0	57.7	46.8	74.1	14.8	60.8
10	14.0	16.7	15.1	19.0	15.7
20-40	11.0	14.0	8.1	25.2	9.0
50-90	11.6	18.1	1.1	24.7	5.6
100	5.7	4.4	1.6	16.3	8.9
	100.0	100.0	100.0	100.0	100.0

The table indicates that of the men with a broken performance pattern 6 out of 7 received initial disability compensation. A few had their claims disallowed; others did not apply. In contrast, far fewer of the adjusted group (only about 1 out of 2), the vulnerable (1 out of 4), or the poor (2 out of 5) were awarded disability compensation shortly after their discharge. Since a 10 percent award then amounted to $11.50 per month and reflected only a modest occupational impairment, the more important category is that which includes the men who received at least a 50 percent award. Two-fifths, 41.0 percent, of the men with broken patterns received such high initial awards, but this was true of under one-quarter, 22.5 percent, of the adjusted; under one-sixth, 14.5 percent, of the poor; and only 2.7 percent of the group with vulnerable patterns.

The relationships existing between the disability compensation which men received and their life performance patterns are quite complex. The above table makes it reasonably clear, however, that many who received no compensation whatever or only the most modest amount were found to have an adjusted or vulnerable pattern. In contrast, those who were most likely to receive compensation, including those who received substantial compensation, were men with broken life patterns. The only reasonable explanation for these differences is that some men had sufficient personal strengths to perform successfully after their return to civilian life even though they did not receive special financial support, while others with substantial compensation suffered from such serious defects that they could not perform satisfactorily. Since the Veterans Administration award of disability compensation depended, in the first instance, on whether or not a veteran's disability was caused or at least aggravated by his military service, the fact that so few of the poor and vulnerable received compensation—particularly in contrast to the broken—is most revealing. It is apparent that these two groups contain many men whose "disability" did not arise in military service but rather stemmed from long standing personal deficiencies.

There is another way of looking at these materials. Of those who received no initial compensation, over half had an adjusted and an additional quarter had a vulnerable life pattern, indicating that a substantial proportion of the cohort ineffectives were able to return to a successful level of performance in civilian life without relying on financial assistance from the Veterans Administration. Men who received substantial awards—50 percent or more—were even more heavily represented in the adjusted pattern (2 out of 3). There was a tendency for the Veterans Administration to make more liberal awards to soldiers who up to the point of breakdown had performed satisfactorily in the Army and all, except the severely disturbed (the broken), appeared to have profited from this help. Many of the latter were so disturbed that they were not able to support themselves.

It was established practice for the Veterans Administration to review the disability awards from time to time in light of the alterations in the veteran's circumstances and to pay primary attention to changes in his health and occupational status. While some whose condition had worsened might receive an increase over their previous award, thc allowances paid to most men were in time reduced or cancelled. The following table shows the percentage distribution of men with different life performance patterns by their disability compensation rating in 1953.

FINAL DISABILITY COMPENSATION RATING BY LIFE PERFORMANCE PATTERN, IN PERCENT

FINAL RATING	TOTAL COHORT	LIFE PERFORMANCE PATTERN *Adjusted*	*Vulnerable*	*Broken*	*Poor*
0	76.7	68.5	88.6	48.7	76.7
10	10.7	17.1	9.5	3.5	8.9
20-40	6.1	10.1	1.0	13.1	2.6
50-90	3.8	4.0	0.9	16.1	3.7
100	2.7	.3	–	18.6	8.1
	100.0	100.0	100.0	100.0	100.0

In Chapter Nine we noted the overall reduction between the initial and final postwar evaluation periods both in the number receiving compensation and in the level of their disability ratings. The proportion receiving compensation dropped from more than 2 in 5 to less than 1 in 4, and the proportion in each life pattern was reduced. By 1953 nearly one third, 32 percent, of the adjusted were still receiving compensation but more than half of those were drawing only 10 percent compensation, indicating that their condition was no longer seriously affecting their ability to work. Only a handful, 4 percent, were still rated at 50 percent or more disabled, but in spite of their disability they were gainfully employed although at a lower level or less effectively than had they recovered completely. Only 1 in 9 of the men with a vulnerable pattern was receiving compensation, and most of those were receiving only 10 percent. About 1 in 4 in the poor group was still receiving compensation. As one might have anticipated from the analysis of the initial compensation, those with broken patterns were still receiving compensation, and the proportion receiving 50 percent or higher had dropped only from 41 percent to 35 percent. While the prognosis for many of these men is not good, some of those who are still below the margin of acceptable performance appear to be moving in the direction of a long-delayed recovery.

Another benefit available to veterans was hospitalization. We found earlier that of the 72,700 men represented by the cohort sample, about 16,000, or 22 percent, were hospitalized at some time after their discharge from the service. The following table shows the percentage of veterans who were hospitalized and those who were not by life performance patterns.

USE OF VA HOSPITAL SERVICES BY LIFE PERFORMANCE PATTERN, IN PERCENT

	TOTAL COHORT	LIFE PERFORMANCE PATTERN *Adjusted*	*Vulnerable*	*Broken*	*Poor*
Veterans hospitalized	22.2	16.7	4.9	52.0	49.0
Veterans not hospitalized	77.8	83.3	95.1	48.0	51.0
	100.0	100.0	100.0	100.0	100.0

In addition to the strikingly low hospital utilization by the vulnerable group, explained in considerable measure by the fact that they include a high proportion of the men who were discharged for inaptitude and who once they were able to return to the farm encountered no special difficulties in taking up the threads of their former existence, the much lower utilization among the adjusted than among the broken or the poor is noteworthy.

More of the hospitalizations of men with broken or poor performance patterns were for treatment of a psychiatric condition than was the case with men with an adjusted pattern. The fact that only slightly more than two-fifths of the hospital admissions of men with an adjusted pattern were for some type of psychiatric treatment while two-thirds of the admissions of those with broken patterns were for psychiatric treatment is a further indication that the latter group contained many seriously disturbed people.

The last benefit to be discussed is educational and vocational training. Of the 72,700 men represented by the sample, 27,600 made use of one or more of these opportunities, but 45,100 did not. The following table shows the distribution of the men who used these opportunities and those who did not by life performance pattern.

USE OF VA EDUCATIONAL BENEFITS BY LIFE PERFORMANCE PATTERN, IN PERCENT

	TOTAL COHORT	LIFE PERFORMANCE PATTERN *Adjusted*	*Vulnerable*	*Broken*	*Poor*
Veterans who used benefits	38.0	55.3	41.6	32.7	33.5
Veterans who did not use benefits	62.0	44.7	58.4	67.3	66.5
	100.0	100.0	100.0	100.0	100.0

Only among men with an adjusted pattern did a majority avail themselves of the opportunity to obtain educational and vocational training. A consideration of the different types of training that men with various life performance patterns engaged in showed that the adjusted group was widely distributed among institutional on-the-farm training, on-the-job training, trade and vocational schools, and academic study at both pre-college and college levels. The vulnerable group concentrated primarily on farm training and trade schools. Very few of those with broken patterns took training on the farm; they were more heavily concentrated in on-the-job training, trade schools, and academic training. The poor, on the other hand, made heavy use of institutional on-the-farm training, but participated hardly at all in on-the-job training. Many of them entered trade schools or went back to elementary or high school.

Some men were probably too disturbed to know how to use the opportunities open to them. Others undoubtedly frittered away their opportunities. A high proportion failed to avail themselves of any of these educational and training benefits. But one fact emerges clearly: the highest percentage of veterans who used these benefits was found among those with an adjusted performance pattern. There is no reason to question that their entering upon training, and for many of them, completing a course of academic or vocational study, added to their strengths and facilitated their performing effectively during the postwar years. The broken were too severely disturbed to have made good use of these opportunities, and the poor apparently also had difficulties after long years of deprivation in knowing how to take advantage of opportunities to which they suddenly had access.

The significant fact that emerges from this review of the relation between men with different life performance patterns and their use of Veterans Administration benefits is that while many men with an adjusted pattern received liberal initial compensation awards, they had apparently less need to seek treatment for mental disorders in Veterans Administration hospitals, and they made the best use of the available educational and training benefits. In brief, they appear to have been the more capable group, a fact which made it easier for them to return quickly after their discharge from the Army to a satisfactory level of performance, since they had less need of help and made the best use of such help as was available.

SUCCESSFUL VS. UNSUCCESSFUL LIFE PERFORMANCE PATTERNS

We are now in a position to set forth in summary fashion a profile of the men with adjusted life performance patterns and to contrast it with a profile of men with broken or poor patterns. To sharpen the contrast between the successful and the unsuccessful we have ignored in this summary those with a vulnerable life pattern, that is, men whose performance was satisfactory in civilian life but who failed in the Army. The problems involved in military breakdown have been dealt with extensively earlier.

In seeking to determine whether the characteristics of men who had a successful life pattern differed substantially from those of the men who had an unsuccessful pattern, we must consider the discrete findings about the range of demographic factors which we reviewed earlier. This is what we find. Those with an adjusted pattern tended to be younger, much better educated, to be found much less frequently in farming and unskilled work at our final report, to include a higher proportion of whites and fewer men who remained single or whose marriages were broken. In each factor they had an advantage. With respect to some characteristics the margin was wider than in others, but each factor helped to differentiate the successful from the unsuccessful.

In comparing the impact of Army experience on each group, it is important to bear in mind that the group with broken life patterns had served satisfactorily up to the point of breakdown. Hence, it is not too surprising to find that those with a broken pattern served longer and had more overseas service than those with an adjusted pattern. But in most other regards, the quality of military service and the response to it was clearly in favor of the adjusted group. A higher proportion of them had been in combat, but a lower proportion were severely incapacitated for further service at the time of their breakdown. And of those with major incapacitation a much smaller proportion of the adjusted had premilitary indications of ineffectiveness. Moreover, the percentage of psychotics and undesirables among the adjusted was much smaller than among the broken and the poor. And the adjusted had fewer disciplinary cases than the group with unsuccessful life performance patterns—broken or poor.

A comparison between the adjusted and the broken groups in their use of the benefits provided by the Veterans Administration is somewhat complicated with regard to disability compensation. The more disturbed a veteran was by his military service, the greater was his disability compensation if he were discharged honorably. This explains why men with a broken pattern of performance received more compensation, both initially and finally. But this finding should not obscure another, and that is that many in the adjusted group received a high initial award which apparently helped them to readjust. The adjusted made much less use of hospital benefits. A reasonable deduction is that they had less need for this kind of therapeutic or rehabilitative help than men with either broken or poor patterns of performance. In sharp contrast, however, the adjusted group made considerably more use of educational and training benefits.

The foregoing points up two important conclusions about men with successful life patterns of performance. First, the successful group was favored by their basic strengths and their preparation for life. Secondly, these advantages made it easier for them to cope with the difficulties which they encountered in their environment and further to take advantage of such assistance and supports as were made available to them. In short, they had the essential equipment for successful performance, and they did not suffer major handicaps which interfered with their using it.

But what precisely were the others lacking? To answer this question we must probe more deeply into the life performance patterns of the broken and the poor.

BROKEN AND POOR PATTERNS

The concept of effective performance which underlies this entire analysis has several important dimensions. Ineffectiveness may have resulted when an individual was unable to meet the demands of a specific situation, such as when a soldier who suffered agonies from seasickness was assigned to duties on a crash boat. As long as he was forced to serve in this capacity, he would be ineffective. If reassigned to another type of duty, he might again prove capable of good performance.

Another kind of ineffective performance was manifested by the individual who had a good record of performance up to the point when he broke down. His period of ineffectiveness may have been relatively short; this happened with many who had a psychotic episode in the Army. Shortly after their return to civilian life they were able to achieve their former satisfactory level of performance with little or no trace of their prior ineffectiveness.

Still another dimension of ineffectiveness was presented by the relatively large numbers of soldiers whom the Army separated at the first signs of difficulty in the spring and summer of 1943 on the assumption that they would eventually prove to be unsatisfactory, even though they had not yet been found to be seriously deficient. These men were "declared" ineffective and in many instances there was nothing in their life performance patterns up to that time—or, as it turned out, later—to have justified such a verdict. The Army was in a rush and it reached quick decisions which, while justified in many cases, were without validity in many others.

These three orders of ineffectiveness—an inability on the part of the individual to meet the demands of a specific situation, a temporary inability to perform effectively, and a judgment on the part of management that a man is likely to prove ineffective in the future—are to be sharply distinguished from the ineffectiveness which characterized the men with broken and poor life patterns. Here we are confronted with an order of ineffectiveness that is either so severe or so persistent that it prevents a man from meeting the minimum demands that society places on him. This gross failure has so many serious implications for the individual, his family, and the larger community that it justifies special attention. The aim of this concluding section is to compare the two major groups with unsuccessful patterns of performance—the broken and the poor—

in the hope of identifying more sharply than has yet been possible the complex of factors responsible for their ineffectiveness.

The analysis deals with 6,201 men with a broken pattern and 8,499 with a poor pattern who together totaled 14,700 out of the 56,257 represented by the sample about whose life performance patterns we had adequate information. Considerable proportions of both groups were suffering from a psychosis at the time of our last contact with them or had previously been psychotic. Since a severe psychosis can in itself be so destructive as to preclude effective performance on the part of an otherwise capable person, we will first review briefly those with psychoses and then consider more carefully those who were not so seriously disturbed.

About one-third of the broken group and one-quarter of the poor group were psychotic at the point of our last contact or at some previous time. About 14 percent of the psychotics in the broken and 30 percent in the poor group had not been identified as psychotic at the time of discharge but were so diagnosed later on. In part this was due to nonrecognition of their condition by medical officers in the Army; in part, this means that some men became psychotic only in the postwar period.

Less than one-third of the psychotics in the broken group but as many as three-fifths of those in the poor group were "screening errors"—that is, their records contained information which if taken cognizance of at the time of their induction examination should have led to their rejection for military service.

The hospital experiences of the psychotics in the two groups differ substantially. Considerably more of the broken (2 out of 5) than of the poor (1 out of 5) had been sufficiently disturbed at discharge that the Army transferred them directly to a Veterans Administration hospital. Over half of each group had to be rehospitalized one or more times after they had been discharged from their initial stay in a Veterans Administration hospital. In addition about 35 percent of the broken and 28 percent of the poor were admitted to a Veterans Administration hospital for the first time from civilian life for one or more periods of hospitalization. More than 3 out of 4 of the broken but only half of the poor had to be hospitalized after their discharge from the Army. One out of every 4 of the broken who was hospitalized as of our last contact (1953) had been in the hospital ever since his transfer from the Army. No one in the poor group has had continuous hospitalization. The following table sets out the status as of 1953 of the men with known history of psychosis in the two groups.

STATUS OF PSYCHOTICS WITH BROKEN AND POOR LIFE PERFORMANCE PATTERNS, 1953, IN PERCENT

Status	*Broken*	*Poor*
In hospital	27.3	43.7
On trial visit or elopement from hospital	8.5	2.5
In prison (including psychiatric wards of prisons)	4.3	5.6
Incompetent, under guardianship, or cared for by relatives	33.5	20.1
All others	26.4	28.1
	100.0	100.0

The important fact that emerges is that most of the 4,000 men with a broken or poor life performance pattern with a known history of psychosis were institutionalized or under the care of relatives or guardians in 1953. Only about 1 in 4 were attempting to make their own way. While those with a broken pattern were more seriously disturbed at discharge, by 1953 a substantially higher proportion of those with poor patterns were in the hospital; this is in part a reflection of the fact that the relatives of the broken group were more willing to assume responsibility for them, but it also suggests that after the war the men in the poor group deteriorated more than those in the broken group.

The following case of A.C. is a good illustration of a soldier who developed a psychosis in the Army from which he has not recovered. His prior satisfactory performance in the Army and in civilian life places him in the broken category.

Born in 1918, A.C. grew up in a large town in the Midwest. A good student, he completed two years of a college business course, but dropped out when he suddenly lost interest. For several years he worked for a local ice cream company, then held a clerical job in the state capital for two years. He was working as a secretary for the railroad in his home town when he was drafted late in 1942. He had received one deferment because his parents were dependent on him. His father was a semi-invalid until he died in the summer of 1942. Shortly before he entered the Army, A.C.'s fiancee broke a long engagement.

After his induction A.C. was assigned as a clerk and performed satisfactorily. Promoted to technician fifth grade he served in Bombay, India, with a port of debarkation company, never near combat. Five months after leaving the United States, he was hospitalized at the request of his commanding officer, who had observed that he was no longer able to perform his duties satisfactorily and that he was acting in a peculiar manner. In the hospital A.C. first appeared only to be excessively anxious but later revealed that he believed that his food was being poisoned. These and other delusions persisted during his hospitalization, and these symptoms led to a diagnosis of dementia praecox, paranoid type.

In the summer of 1944 he was discharged and transferred to a Veterans Administration hospital. There he remained seclusive and withdrawn and still had a number of bizarre ideas. However, he improved sufficiently that year to be granted a trial visit home. He lived with his mother and uncle and helped occasionally in his uncle's grocery store. At examinations held in 1945, 1947, and 1949 his behavior and responses indicated he was still unable to pursue a gainful occupation. The Veterans Administration continued his 100 percent disability rating.

In 1949 his condition worsened and he became violent. Hospitalized for several months he underwent an extensive series of shock treatment, insulin and electric, which helped to quiet him but did not essentially improve his condition. After several trial visits home he was discharged from the hospital.

He still lives with his aging mother and uncle, occasionally puttering around the store. At times his adjustment is so precarious that hospitalization would be indicated except that he has a fear of it and his mother wants him near her. Because he is unable to travel to the nearest Veterans Administration mental hygiene clinic, he is under the care of a private physician, although the treatments are paid for by the Veterans Administration. He is not showing any improvement and if anything should happen to his mother and uncle there is little question that he would again have to be institutionalized.

The qualitative differences between men with a broken life pattern of performance and those with a poor pattern are illustrated by the preceding and following cases, A.C. and B.D.

B.D., a Negro, was born in 1921 in Louisiana. When he was an infant, his father deserted his mother leaving her to support him and an older sister. He went to school intermittently and repeated several grades; he had completed only the fourth grade by the time he was sixteen. As a child he preferred to be alone. He never exhibited any interest in girls, claiming that they talked too much. When he worked, it was usually as a yard boy but he could not hold a steady job and was arrested many times for a variety of offenses: vagrancy, drunkenness, gambling, disturbing the peace, and larceny.

Upon induction, he was assigned to a Negro infantry unit. For a few months he received satisfactory efficiency ratings. Then he began to get into difficulty. He went AWOL and broke restriction time after time. Being court-martialed and confined to the stockade had no effect on him; shortly after being released, he was in difficulty again. Finally, B.D. was given a general court-martial and sentenced to be dishonorably discharged after serving ten years at hard labor.

In confinement his confused behavior brought him to the attention of the authorities who ordered him hospitalized for observation. He complained of "agoin' and acomin' mind," and was observed to be dull, apathetic and confused, almost completely disoriented. He had auditory hallucinations (his grandfather came to see and to speak with him every night), which had apparently been present for many years. His case was reviewed and it was determined that at the time of his trial he had not been competent. After improving slightly in the Army hospital he was given a CDD for dementia praecox, hebephrenic type, severe, and turned over to the custody of a Veterans Administration hospital.

There he continued to improve and after two months was discharged, his condition deemed to be in partial remission. He continued to improve over the years; his disability compensation, initially rated at 100 percent, dropped to 50 percent in 1946 and was eliminated in 1949. Despite this improvement, he was unable to readjust economically. Initially he felt too sick to go out and stayed home with his mother; later, when he felt better he would go out with a girl friend and get drunk but would not try to work. Even though he later married, he assumed no responsibility for his wife. After his compensation had been cut off, he worked occasionally at unskilled jobs. Although he does not get along very well with his wife, he still lives with her most of the time since she is his chief means of support. A month before the deadline to enroll in training courses under the G.I. Bill, he started a course in woodworking but dropped out after a week. Since then B.D. has wandered around Louisiana and Arkansas, occasionally finding employment as a farm hand, but after a time returns home. He has had no steady work since discharge—the same pattern that he exhibited before the war.

What about the other, and larger, group of men with broken and poor patterns of performance but who had no history of psychosis? There were 4,253 in the broken group and 6,410 in the poor or a total of 10,663 with unsuccessful performance patterns, but without psychosis. They can be described most readily in terms of their personal characteristics, their environmental backgrounds, and their postwar experiences.

As to personal characteristics, the broken group was noticeably younger, had a higher level of schooling, and contained a larger percentage of men who had remained single. The contrast in marital status was striking: among the broken about 1 in 3 had remained single while this was true of only 1 out of 16 among the poor. Apparently the poor had no hesitancy to marry even when they had little or no intention of discharging their obligations. Pathological behavior ranging from persistant truancy to repeated difficulties with the law was much more characteristic of the poor (1 in 4) than of the broken (1 in 13).

In terms of environmental background, the predominant number of the broken and about half of the poor came from the South, the former from urban communities, the latter from the farm. The poor came more frequently from families where both parents had been seriously ill while the broken came more frequently from families which were characterized by severe emotional pathology, including broken homes and criminality. Such pathology was found in two-thirds of the homes of the broken but less than half the homes of the poor.

As far as their postwar performance was concerned, almost all of the broken but only three-quarters of the poor had made use of Veterans Administration benefits. Almost all of the poor but only half of the broken changed jobs at least once a year. In terms of geographic mobility about half of each group was no longer living in the community from which they had been inducted.

A striking difference existed in the racial composition of the two groups. Slightly more than half of the broken but only a sixth of the poor group were Negroes, overwhelmingly from the South. Two-thirds of the Negroes in the broken group had lived in urban communities prior to induction; four-fifths were from broken homes; and none had gone beyond grammar school. Apparently, they had been able to make a marginal adjustment before the war, but their military experience was sufficiently unsettling that they never were able to recover.

The foregoing analysis reveals important differences between men with broken and those with poor life performance patterns. The broken group is characterized by a disproportionately large number of men who came from families with serious pathology that left many of them emotionally scarred to the extent that they became excessively dependent and failed to marry. Although all of these men were initially able to perform satisfactorily in the Army, they were not able to continue after they had once broken down. It would appear that their strengths and weaknesses were in fragile equilibrium during the early years of their life, and once disturbed by the special stress of military life they did not have sufficient reserve strengths to regain their equilibrium. The nub of their difficulties appeared to be emotional. The case of U.V. in the preceding chapter is a good illustration of a man with a broken pattern of performance who was not psychotic.

The men with poor life performance patterns present a somewhat different picture. They came much more heavily from the rural South and were much more seriously handicapped intellectually. The frequency of serious physical illnesses in their families suggests that they were often neglected in childhood, which is also reflected in the haphazard nature of their schooling. They had great difficulty in holding a job and were much more given to engaging in pathological behavior such as gambling, drug addiction, bootlegging, and the like. Illustrative of such men is C.E.:

C.E. was born and raised in a Southeastern seaboard state. In school he had great difficulty in learning to read or write, with the result that he was placed in a "special room" where he completed five "grades" of instruction in manual work. He left school at sixteen and worked intermittently for the next four years as an unskilled laborer in various textile mills while he lived with an older brother. He was unable to hold a job very long—the last one he held before induction he lost after two weeks.

After induction he was immediately assigned to an infantry unit in Texas. Within two weeks he was in trouble with military authorities for disobedience and for going AWOL. Court-martial and confinement failed to affect him and he was repeatedly AWOL and into other difficulties. During training he had been AWOL six times, for periods that ranged from a few days to a month, and received one summary and three special courts-martial; he spent 174 days in the stockade serving his various sentences. In the fall of 1944 he went overseas with his division. After arriving in France his unit spent about a month in training exercises and then moved to the front. There he served as a rifleman in the attack to the Roer and was, for this brief period, considered to be satisfactory. During the attack he received a gunshot wound which factured his elbow and pulverized the bone. The wound was sufficiently severe to warrant his evacuation. Back in the United States, he went AWOL from the hospital. Returned and placed under guard, he went AWOL again. He was such a serious management problem that when his wound healed he was given a blue discharge rather than a medical discharge.

Upon his return to civilian life, C.E. applied for disability compensation. The Veterans Administration ruled that he was eligible, holding that in view of his low mental age (about 9 years) he could not be held responsible for the behavior which resulted in the Army's giving him a blue discharge. He was awarded a 50 percent disability rating. This he still has. He rarely works and when he does, it is only at odd jobs for a few days at a time. Although he had married a year after leaving the Army, he has contributed nothing to the support of his wife and children, and his wife complains that he refuses to work and "drinks up" the compensation check. She must work in order to support herself and the children. In 1950 the examining physician reported that the veteran had not worked since discharge and the veteran's wife reported the same in the reply to our questionnaire, which she filled out in his behalf. Although eligible for rehabilitative training under P.L. 16, he has never applied for it. Because of his permanently crippled right arm and since he is not trained for anything other than manual labor, C.E. will most probably continue to live on his government check (in 1953, $114.00 per month) and his wife's earnings.

The strong impression derived from a study of the men with poor life performance patterns is that they were so seriously limited by birth and upbringing that they never acquired the minimum education and skill which would have enabled them to make a satisfactory occupational and social adjustment even at a minimum level. Their low intelligence and the deprived circumstances which characterized their childhood and adolescence resulted in serious defects which were reflected in their having frequent difficulties with the law. In general they present a more seriously deprived picture than the broken group, since their limited intelligence, reinforced by the poverty of their emotional background, appears to have blocked them from the outset from acquiring the basic equipment for satisfactory performance.

Unsuccessful life patterns of performance appear to be grounded therefore in one of three basic types of conditions. Irrespective of a man's strengths, if he develops a psychosis from which he does not recover, he is likely to continue to perform in an unsatisfactory manner and he may require hospitalization for much, if not all, of his life. A second group may develop other types of serious emotional disorders which can prevent them from making effective use of such capacities and skills as they had been able to acquire prior to their illness. The third may, because of a basic lack of intellectual endowment, never acquire the skills and competences which they need to meet even the minimum demands on and off the job.

But intellect and emotion influence each other so that disturbance in one sphere is likely to be reflected in the other. The emotionally disturbed individual has difficulty in learning; and the intellectually retarded tends to become emotionally upset if he cannot meet the demands that society makes on him. When one major defect reinforces another, the two together represent a formidable barrier to effective performance.

We are now in a better position to understand some of the major factors which help to differentiate men with successful life performance patterns from those with unsuccessful patterns. The successful group was favored, as we have seen, by their basic strengths and their preparation for life. There is no question that the unsuccessful group got off to a bad start, both in terms of personal limitations, intellectual and emotional, and in terms of growing up in unstable families or in deprived environments.

The basic strengths of the successful group made it relatively easy for them, as we have seen, to overcome the difficulties which they encountered, among other reasons because they knew how to take advantage of such assistance and supports as were available to them. The unsuccessful group, on the other hand, were much more likely to be overwhelmed by adversity. Each defeat made it less likely that they would be able to meet prevailing performance standards. The successful were able to help themselves; the unsuccessful were not.

Part V: POLICY

Chapter Thirteen: PERSONALITY AND PERFORMANCE

WE HAVE CONSIDERED in this and the two accompanying volumes the major determinants in the individual, the organization, and the larger environment that singly and in combination shape the level and continuity of a person's performance. Since our study of these inter-relationships is spread over the three volumes of *The Ineffective Soldier*, it should be helpful to consider within a single chapter what we have learned about these relationships as well as the gaps in knowledge which remain and to which future research might be directed.

We have used the term *personality* throughout our analysis to encompass the totality of an individual's qualities, that is, his strengths and weaknesses which have a bearing on his ability to perform. We have used the term *performance* to refer to the individual's response to the demands that are made on him by his family, his employer, and the community of which he is a part. While the level of demands tends to be geared to the level of responsibility that individuals are able to discharge we have concentrated on exploring the reasons why large numbers of people cannot meet the minimum demands that are made on them. We know that great individual and social wastes result when talented people perform at a level far below their optimum. But a democracy, which is dedicated to the concept that the individual has primary responsibility for himself, must be even more concerned with the wastes that result when many of its members are unable to perform effectively even at a minimum level. For when this happens the community must step in and assume responsibilities that should normally be carried by the individual.

PERFORMANCE POTENTIAL

There is no doubt that an individual's personal characteristics have a bearing on his performance. This is borne out in every-day experience and is generally in accord with the many observations that we were able to make on the basis of the analysis of our materials. Yet no one characteristic can adequately explain performance except in an extreme case, such as a mentally deficient man who cannot take care of himself. When we seek to account for the successful or unsuccessful performance of a group of people, any attempt to rely solely on an analysis of their personal characteristics will generally fail. Repeatedly, we found that our expectations about how people would perform based on our interpretation of their qualities were at variance with their actual performance record.

We see, then, that there is no simple one-to-one relationship between an individual's qualities or traits and his performance except in extreme cases such as the one mentioned above. How well an individual performs depends rather on an interplay between his qualities and traits and the factors in the external environment which present him with opportunities and limitations. Therefore, instead of considering personal qualities as if they were isolated or independent factors, it would be better to recognize that the performance potential of an individual involves more than their sum. We pointed out in *The Lost Divisions* how inadequate the prediction of performance is even for groups that had been carefully studied, and certainly it is more so when based on such evaluations as were made in connection with the large-scale screening of selectees during World War II.

We did not choose the concept of performance potential because of its predictive value, but rather to stress that the individual's qualities can be properly appraised only as they are revealed in given situations, under given circumstances. In spite of this indeterminate nature of the performance potential, it is possible to single out some of the constituent factors even though they can be subjected only to a broad analysis.

PERSONAL CHARACTERISTICS

Whether an individual can perform effectively depends in no small measure on his endowment and on his life experiences, especially those during the formative years of childhood and adolescence. At one extreme are those who are so seriously handicapped that they can never acquire the minimum knowledge and skills necessary to perform at even a minimum level. Fortunately, the number in the population who are truly mentally deficient has been estimated at not more than 1 to 2 percent. In terms of the manpower of World War II this would point to a mentally deficient group of between about 200,000 and 350,000 in the age group eighteen to thirty-seven who were screened for military service. But the difference between this significant but fortunately relatively small number of truly mentally deficient persons and the ten times larger group who were rejected for service or prematurely separated from the Armed Services during World War II for mental or emotional defects points to the need of considering a much wider range of personal determinants.

Intelligence is an important determinant, but the evaluation of a man's intelligence is frequently difficult because even specially designed tests do not enable one to distinguish adequately between the individual's innate capacity and the opportunities that he has had to learn. Nevertheless, the evidence in our three volumes clearly indicates that intelligence is among the most important determinants of performance. Those with low intelligence scores and with limited schooling—the two tend to go together, although it is not always so—had a poorer performance record in both civilian and military life than men with more intellectual capacity and a greater amount of schooling. But we must be quick to add that high-school graduation or even college attendance was no guarantee that a man would perform effectively, although the odds were very much in favor of his doing so.

Effective performance implies that the individual is able to establish and maintain relationships with others, both superiors and associates, on the job and with relatives and friends off the job. Seriously disturbed individuals who do not have control over their emotions, who may not be able to differentiate between reality and fantasy, will be unable to perform effectively no matter how intelligent they may be. One must have a minimum emotional stability to be a satisfactory member of a complex society that requires every person in it to adjust his needs and desires, at least in some degree, to those of others.

But even men of intelligence and emotional stability will not always perform in an effective manner since without adequate motivation individuals do not mobilize their strengths. While most men will, by virtue of their upbringing and the pressures exerted on them by their environment, put forth the effort required to become and remain self-supporting and upright citizens, some few will not be motivated to meet society's standards and ideals.

In addition there are physical characteristics which, though they fell outside of the main concern of the study of *The Ineffective Soldier,* should not be overlooked or underestimated in their bearing on performance. What a man is able to make of his strengths, intellectual and emotional, and how well he can surmount his weaknesses depends in considerable measure on his physical condition and in particular on his stamina. This is as true in many civilian occupations as in military service. Illness is debilitating and the individual must draw upon his reserves to cope with it. The more a man is ill, the more he must use his reserves just to keep going. In contrast, the man with a strong constitution who is free of organic complaints has a distinct advantage, other things being equal. He is much more likely to be able to perform effectively because his body is his ally. If he must labor long and hard, if he is exposed to inclement weather, if he misses meals or sleep, he can take these and similar deprivations in his stride and they do not scar him easily. Moreover, he can recover very quickly. The physical condition of a person is often the crucial factor which determines whether he will be able to perform effectively or not. This is true particularly of those whose other strengths and disabilities are in precarious balance.

ORGANIZATIONAL POLICY

Years ago when most men were self-employed in farming, business, or the professions, a consideration of the factors determining their performance could be reasonably limited to their own strengths and weaknesses. Whether a man made good or failed appeared to depend primarily on whether he was intelligent, stable, well-motivated, and healthy. But the pattern of contemporary life is quite different. Most men do not work for themselves. Many are members of large organizations. This fact has a significant impact on their performance, for all men react—some more, some less—to the organizational policies to which they are exposed.

No man is indifferent to the policies which determine his specific assignment, his wages, his opportunities for promotion, the type of supervision and discipline to which he is subject, and other essential aspects of his job. Individually and in combination, these facets of his job shape his attitude towards and his performance at work. The policies pursued by the organization may result in his working more effectively or less effectively. But they cannot be without effect, even though some policies may operate in one and others in the opposite direction.

Most men must work, but how much they apply themselves and how conscientiously largely depends on the way in which they are treated by their supervisors and employers—or how they think they are being treated. Students of human behavior have long recognized that the underlying weakness of a slave society was the hidden costs involved in forcing people to work. The major challenge to management is to develop policies which encourage rather than discourage men from applying themselves to their work. Effective work must be elicited; it cannot be commandeered.

Organizational policies also affect performance by the obstacles that they place in the way or by the opportunities which they provide for people to make use of their skills and potentialities. As we have suggested, a major challenge that an army at war faces is to find the time and personnel to screen the millions of recruits in order to assign them more nearly according to their capacities and potentialities. Similar difficulties, although of a lesser order, confront every large organization. There is no way of finding out what a man can really do except by the slow and costly process of trying him out. And while measurement instruments are constantly being improved, they cannot foretell the capacity for executive leadership which a recent college graduate will eventually develop.

It is no easier to design policies which will enable men to add to their skills. Those concerned with industrial training have come to recognize that while some men are eager for the opportunity to study and grow, others will ignore the opportunities which are made available to them. But the difficulties of differentiating between those who really want to and would make effective use of learning opportunities and those who would only go through the forms should not discourage management from facing up to the important challenge to provide adequate opportunities for the continued growth of its work force.

Men resent being employed at work which does not make use of the skills which they have acquired, often arduously. They may tolerate such a situation in war or in a depression when they recognize the pressure of overriding considerations, but in peacetime such a working environment can lead only to their frustration and lessened productivity.

One important way in which organizational policy can enhance performance is through special measures designed to facilitate the indoctrination and orientation of new members. This is true for every type of organization—a college, an army, an industrial concern. The newcomer is likely to feel ill at ease as he enters a situation where he has only a hazy notion of what is expected of him and how he can meet the new demands. Even men who have performed quite well in other environments may be unsettled by a new situation. The bright high-school graduate who has never been away from home may find his first months at college very upsetting. This happens to many young men who are drafted into the Army, especially in wartime when there is a premium on their speedy conversion to soldiers. During their early weeks of active duty they are likely to be subjected to truly harassing circumstances which force them to change their habits. Although a new job in civilian life seldom represents quite such an extreme challenge, since most men continue to live in accustomed surroundings with their relatives and friends, it does imply a large number of new and frequently difficult situations. Under pressure to do well, a young man in a new job is likely to be anxious.

Since uncertainty, stress, and strain are likely to be present whenever men confront new situations, it is wise for an organization to provide orientation and indoctrination to help the newcomer better understand his new environment. Every superior has known men who showed great promise but who resigned or had to be discharged early in their employment. There is much that an organization can do to prevent such needless waste—although no program can help everybody.

Organizational policy can also contribute to the reduction, and possibly the elimination, of ineffective performance by preventing the build-up of high orders of stress. Under accumulated tension, some men who until then had performed with real effectiveness may break down, reducing their level of performance temporarily or even permanently. Although most individuals usually protect themselves if they feel that they are nearing the point of physical or emotional exhaustion, there are some situations, especially in periods of national emergency, in which men may be driven to breakdown. In the Armed Services in war this is most likely to occur when, because of lack of planning or inadequate reserves, commanders have no option but to push their troops to their maximum—and beyond—and take whatever casualties they must. But it is always preferable when possible to plan ahead for the use of manpower so as to avoid undue stresses and strains by removing men for rest and rehabilitation or reassignment before they break. Analogous situations can also be found in industry, particularly among an executive group that is confronted with a major emergency that cannot be quickly resolved.

Organizational policy that provides appropriate supports for those who suddenly encounter difficulties can help to reduce ineffectiveness. Some men who break down may become so disturbed that it is better for the organization to discharge them since there is little likelihood that they will soon again function effectively. Many others, however, may require only modest help before they can again become effective.

Some of these men may have run into conflict with their superiors or fellow workers. Others may be in emotional turmoil because of difficulties at home. Still others may be overwhelmed by an inability to cope with new responsibility. They are disturbed and therefore the quality of their performance is likely to deteriorate, perhaps at first imperceptibly, but later more noticeably. They feel tense and anxious. Frequently their fears are grounded in fact; more often they exaggerate the real situation which confronts them. Often they need only a sympathetic listener. In many cases an opportunity to talk out their problems might be all that they require. As they verbalize their problems, their difficulties may start to shrink or disappear completely. Others may not be so fortunate. They may be face to face with a realistic problem which only reassignment, additional training, or financial assistance can relieve. But if they receive such support, many of them straighten around and quickly. The wise organization will provide it.

A leadership must insure that all who are in a supervisory position clearly understand the basic principles and procedures on which the organization's operations are based. For only if the several echelons have a clear understanding of the aims and objectives of policy will they be able to use it constructively. This also indicates why the leadership of an organization must avoid instituting frequent and radical shifts in policy. For policy can realize its constructive potentialities only to the extent that it is stable. In fact, policy that is subject to frequent and large-scale changes is a contradiction in terms, for shifting principles cannot be communicated and absorbed sufficiently rapidly to serve as effective guides to action.

The burden of these considerations is that organizational policies can either strengthen or weaken the motivation of men to perform effectively; to the extent that policies facilitate a man's using his skills and adding to them, his performance is likely to be improved; policies which smooth the adjustment of new members, that prevent the accumulation of extreme stress and strain, and that provide supports for members of the organization who need them can help men to attain and maintain a satisfactory level of performance.

ENVIRONMENTAL FACTORS

In addition to the part played by an individual's strengths and weaknesses and his experiences in the organization of which he is a part, his performance will be significantly affected by conditions in the broader environment and by the pressures with which he must deal. These can affect him both directly and indirectly.

To begin with, ours is a society with certain pervasive values which help to mold the attitudes and behavior of the great majority. A man, if physically and mentally able, is supposed to work. In fact our society does not look kindly on even a wealthy man who does not work. This fundamental responsibility that is inherent in our culture provides a very strong propulsion on men to meet it.

This is reinforced by the parallel responsibility that a man has to support not only himself but his family. We had occasion to note particularly in *Breakdown and Recovery* that many men were heartened during the war by their close ties with their loved ones at home and that many others finally were able to throw off the lethargy and depression resulting from their war experience and to return to gainful employment when they saw again the need to provide for their wives and children. This is a second powerful spur to effective performance, and it is the more powerful because it goes beyond the simple question of responsibility. Many men are able to keep working at their jobs only because of the substantial emotional support that they receive from their wives or other members of their family.

It would be hard to exaggerate the importance of still another facet in the effective performance of so many men under the major stresses of war—ordinary men who had nothing of the hero in their makeup. Many kept going because they "could not let their buddies down." Unlike in some societies where the individual's responsibility does not extend beyond the confines of his family, the American soldier's behavior was greatly conditioned by his feelings of comradeship with the others in his unit.

Important as the cultural values are which spur men to assume the obligation of work or military service and to perform effectively, they cannot by themselves assure the result. It is also necessary that the environment provide an opportunity for the discharge of these obligations. The depression of the 1930s put an end to the widespread belief that a man who was willing to work would always be able to find work. In passing the Employment Act of 1946 which charged the Federal Government with taking all necessary action to establish and maintain a high level of employment, Congress underscored the new understanding which the American people had gained through adversity that a man in a modern industrial society can meet his obligations only if there are jobs available that he can fill. Whether a larger or smaller number are able to perform effectively depends on the range of opportunities available.

In a labor market in which the numbers seeking employment are far greater than the jobs available, employers will pick the potentially abler and reject those who have major and possibly even minor defects. No matter how strong their motivation for work may be, the physically handicapped, the emotionally unstable, the intellectually retarded, the former criminal, the reformed alcoholic often will be passed over not once but repeatedly. They will be barred from demonstrating that despite their handicap or record they are capable of performing effectively. Many of them will simply not have a chance.

But when jobs are plentiful it is much easier for the handicapped group to succeed, not only because employers are less critical, but because the marginal group realizes that others like them, and some possibly more handicapped, have succeeded in getting a job and performing satisfactorily. The knowledge of this fact is a substantial reinforcement of their own drive to try, and helps to still the uncertainties and doubts which might otherwise immobilize them, especially if they have been repeatedly rebuffed.

The challenge that the more seriously handicapped face is to build up and exploit their strengths to compensate for their defects. There is, however, little incentive for a man to put forth the effort if he knows from the outset that his chances of succeeding are very slim indeed. Rather than to try and fail, he prefers to let his strengths lie idle. At least he need not compound his difficulties by being rebuffed. But if he sees all about him men whom he considers no better, or perhaps even less able, than he getting and holding jobs, then the spur is great indeed. And the chances are greater that if he makes the effort, he too will succeed.

A full employment economy makes still another contribution to marginal persons. When employers recognize that the only way they can add to their labor force is by employing people who have shortcomings, they will be encouraged to restudy their jobs to see whether some of the more difficult ones might be simplified and thereby brought within the competence range of the potential working group. To the extent that this is done, the handicapped will be in a better position to find work within their competence, and if they do, they will be much more likely to perform effectively.

This comment about the matching of jobs to men points to another facet of the problem. In a country as large as the United States with such a highly diversified economy, it is exceedingly difficult for men to know the range of work which is available and for which they might qualify. Men cannot make the most of themselves and their assets unless they know about the opportunities that are available. The handicapped person who has not been regularly employed is likely to be poorly informed about the jobs that are available or are likely to become available. Yet his need for this information is the greater since he can qualify for a smaller number than a worker without disabilities.

While improved guidance and counseling services and more active employer participation in providing opportunities are required if larger numbers of marginal people are to perform effectively, they need further help. They frequently cannot meet the demands of a job without some prior medical or other rehabilitative assistance. While voluntary and governmental efforts along these lines have been expanded considerably over the past years in many parts of the country, they are still inadequate. But it must be emphasized that rehabilitation can only help a handicapped person get a job; it cannot insure that he will do so. Whether he does or not will continue to depend primarily on the total availability of jobs.

The availability of jobs and widespread information about them and how they can be secured can contribute more than any other factor to helping people become and remain effective. The more jobs there are, the easier it is for a person with a handicap to find one with which he can cope. And as more handicapped people succeed in getting jobs, others who have defects will be encouraged to make a special effort to do likewise.

The foregoing summary of the more important individual, organizational, and environmental factors that influence performance should indicate its complex nature when it is viewed as a social phenomenon. Because of this complexity we will order some of our more generalized findings around three basic concepts of performance—those of level, range, and time, the last conceived in terms of continuity. Each will be considered briefly in turn.

LEVEL OF PERFORMANCE

One of the striking characteristics of every technologically advanced society is the very wide differences in the occupational levels at which individuals perform. Contrast the man who holds down a simple laboring job which makes the most modest demands, intellectually and emotionally, with the work of Einstein who transformed for all time the world of ideas and action.

These differences in levels of performance, while reflecting in the first instance marked variations in the individuals' qualities at birth, may also mirror the external environment and the opportunities and stresses it presents. As we have noted, in the depression of the 1930s many millions of capable persons were unable to perform effectively for the simple reason that jobs were not available. And many hundreds of thousands of men who had been able to cope, by and large, with the demands of a civilian environment were unable to meet the special challenges involved in serving in an army at war.

Our industrial society with its exceedingly fine division of labor contributes greatly to enabling the maximum number of people to perform at a satisfactory, if not optimal, level by presenting such a grading of opportunities that men of vastly differing capacities, interests, and motivation can find appropriate jobs. The fact that many Americans have been willing, if not eager, to move from one region to another and from one job to another in the hope of bettering themselves has insured that they avail themselves of the advantages inherent in our increasingly differentiated labor market.

The major factor which determines the level at which an individual performs is his education and training. Every year more and more jobs in the economy are open only to men who have graduated from high school, college, or professional school. Increasingly, employers are less concerned about what a man has already learned than about his potential for further learning on the job. This is also true of the Armed Services, which have only recently sought relief from the Congress so that they would not have to accept for military service poorly educated men with little potential for learning the new skills required.

While education, skill, and the potential for acquiring further skills are the most important factors determining the level of a man's performance, they are not the only ones. One of the outstanding characteristics of present-day America is the high proportion of young people who graduate from high school—about 6 out of every 10—and the strikingly high proportion of male high-school graduates who go on to college—currently about 1 out of every 2. We will not consider here the crucial question of the relationships between the years of formal schooling and the quantity and quality of knowledge acquired; it is sufficient to note that if a high-school or college graduate is emotionally unstable or poorly motivated, his education and training will not of themselves insure that he performs effectively, surely not at a level commensurate with his preparation. Since performance makes a demand on the whole person, not only on his skills, many fail because of emotional or behavioral defects.

The fact that our society offers a great variety of jobs and patterns of life with tremendous variations in demand, however, markedly reduces the number of individuals who cannot find a level of work at which they can meet at least minimum performance requirements. Relatively few jobs make a demand on all of an individual's competences. This means that men with some kind of defect, even a serious one, may be able to perform effectively in a vast number of even demanding jobs. A minor impairment in eyesight or hearing may prevent a young man from gaining admission to West Point, but severe paralysis did not prevent Franklin Delano Roosevelt from being elected President and serving as Commander-in-Chief of the Army and Navy during the most important war in the nation's history.

Individuals will usually seek out work which will enable them to make the most of their strengths and where their deficiencies and defects will handicap them as little as possible. The freer the economy and the society and the more rapidly it is expanding, the greater opportunity individuals will have to find a niche where they will be able to perform effectively. One of the serious handicaps which encumbers an army during a period of mobilization is the pressure of time, which precludes giving soldiers an opportunity to explore where they can best fit in.

Sometimes it is not lack of time but lack of flexibility that interferes with people finding the most suitable level at which to perform. For centuries it was taken for granted that the younger sons of the British nobility had a choice only between a military career and the Church. If they had an inclination towards neither, they were likely to encounter serious difficulties in finding a career since the mores of the culture presented few, if any, alternatives.

College advisors in the United States are often confronted with a contemporary manifestation of this problem. The sons of professors often have no special intellectual aptitude or interest. Yet many of these youngsters feel that their parents and friends expect them to do well at school and enter a profession. For many years they are prevented by their family and class ties from acting to circumvent their weaknesses and building on their strengths. Some never succeed in facing up to the fact that they are not suited to an academic or professional career, but the world of business has begun to have sufficient prestige in the United States to offer most of them a suitable alternative.

While American business is constantly raising its educational and training requirements for employment, it is incorrect to assume that most jobs require a high order of mental and emotional effort. Some do, but the majority do not. No competent observer of the American scene would question the generalization that the vast majority of the population are working below, some considerably below, the level at which they are capable of performing.

Moreover, there are many millions of jobs in the economy

which are sufficiently routinized that individuals with quite modest intellectual or emotional equipment can handle them. In fact, the low order of demands built into many of these jobs makes it possible for individuals even with severe handicaps to handle them.

Historically, farming and other types of family business presented an ideal environment within which marginal persons could work. The demands of the job could be adjusted so that individuals with special disabilities could meet them. The contemporary counterpart for this historically protective environment is employment in simple service or clerical jobs. The fact that there is such a great diversity of jobs available, many of which make only the most modest demands, doubtless contributes to increasing the numbers who are able to perform at least at a satisfactory minimum level.

This diversity has another important advantage. It implies that there are many opportunities and significant rewards available for the man who wants to apply himself to his work. And while outstanding success may require talent as well as motivation, diligent application will enable many to advance.

A job helps to give structure and meaning to one's life and a person of limited strength is likely to gain considerable reassurance from the fact that others are willing to employ and pay him. As long as such a person is able to keep his place in the productive economy his self-doubts are less haunting. And the longer he succeeds in performing effectively, the less worried he will generally be about his deficiencies.

RANGE OF PERFORMANCE

A second major facet of performance is that of range: there are marked differences in the performance of individuals in similar jobs. Every supervisor knows that when he must get extra work out, there are some men on whom he can rely and others who will probably hamper the effort. In many organizations, men with the same title and the same salaries differ greatly in their actual performance. These differences often reflect varying orders of personal strengths or weaknesses. One man may be much more intelligent and well-trained than the next; and if he is also more stable emotionally, more strongly motivated, and has more physical stamina, his performance is certain to be superior.

But often differences in the range, i.e., quality, of performance reflect not individual differences so much as variation in leadership and organizational policy. Senior executives of large organizations frequently see that similar work teams have quite different production records. One is conspicuously better than the other. Inquiry usually discloses that part, and sometimes all, of the difference in the range of performance can be traced back to differences in the quality of the leadership in the two units. In one the supervisory group knows how to elicit the best that is within their work force; in the other the supervisors and the men are in conflict with the result clearly reflected in output. An outstanding example of this from World War II was when Headquarters in the European Theater had to relieve four commanders in turn before it found one who was able to get a particular division, whose men had been well-selected and trained, to perform effectively.

Sometimes differences in the range of performance can be traced more to variations in policy than to the leadership per se. For example, some hospitals in the United States have been reluctant to permit nurses and medical technicians to assume responsibilities commensurate with their training and competence. Others have been eager to delegate as much responsibility as the law will permit. Employees of the latter group are much more likely to perform at the upper range of their capacities.

The way in which an organization assigns men may also affect the range of their performance. When during World War II a Southern farmer was put into a company of tough boys from a Northern city, he felt lost. Had he been with men whom he knew and liked and from whom he could have drawn support, he would have been much more likely to have performed successfully.

Differences in the range of performance may also arise because of conditions existing in the environment which directly or indirectly influence the attitudes and behavior of men. Sometimes the environment has a positive effect, as when men are fighting on their own land to protect their homes and loved ones. It is generally recognized that the heroic defensive fighting of the Russian people during World War II against the invading Nazi armies arose out of such a situation. In sharp contrast was the depression which afflicted many American prisoners of war in the Pacific who had been captured by the Japanese early in the war and who were cut off for years from any contact whatever with the outside world. Many died because they could not make the effort required even to continue living in the face of great deprivations. The situation was so terrible that they lost the will to live.

Although the evidence is not easy to come by, many employers are convinced that in periods of prosperity when the demand for labor is very strong, many individuals slacken their efforts and their performance begins to slip. In contrast, when a recession gets under way and particularly if the numbers of unemployed should increase significantly, most members of the work force put forth additional effort and pay more attention to their work, with a corresponding gain in their output.

Another example of how the environment may affect the range of performance was the substantial testimony from the field commanders in Korea that after Negroes were integrated into combat units, most of them made a special effort to do well for they realized that they were being watched by all—white and Negro alike. Those who were prejudiced against them were sure that they would not stand up in combat. And their friends were anxiously awaiting proof that they would do as well as the next man, if not better. It soon became clear that the performance of Negro troops improved markedly when the Army began to treat them without regard to their color.

Under certain conditions the environment can encourage men to draw on their reserves and perform better than previously; in other instances it can be so depressive or overwhelming that men lose hope and their spirits flag to a point where their performance deteriorates badly. We have seen, then, that the environment, like an individual's characteristics or an organization's policy, can operate either positively or negatively to alter the range within which men perform.

CONTINUITY IN PERFORMANCE

The third important facet, that of continuity and therefore also of discontinuity, can help to clarify the relative importance of the basic determinants of performance. We have seen that if minor fluctuations are disregarded, some men tend to perform at the same level or in the same range—be it high or low—throughout most or all of their lives, while others show marked variations in their patterns of performance which follow changes within themselves or within the external environment.

While no man goes through life performing always at his highest possible level, a considerable proportion of the total population succeed in maintaining a basic continuity in their performance pattern. When crisis or illness strikes, they have sufficient resources so that they are not overwhelmed, and although their performance may deteriorate, they keep going until the difficult situation is behind them and they can again build up the resources which will enable them once more to perform effectively.

Another pattern of continuity is reflected by people who are born with or early develop such severe handicaps—physical, emotional, or mental—that they never even acquire the basic education and skills which in our society are prerequisite for effective performance. And there are others who, while they succeed in going through school and sometimes even college, develop major emotional disorders in late adolescence or young adulthood which may hold them prisoner for the rest of their lives.

Still other groups have a more or less consistently poor record of performance. They are the men with serious behavior problems who seem to be in constant conflict with the rules of society; some become alcoholics, others use drugs, and still others engage in overt criminal behavior. While some of these men do succeed in bringing their aberrant behavior under control, a high proportion are unable to do so and their record is one long story of ineffective performance.

Many individuals perform well, even with outstanding success, in certain environments but fail in others. We are not considering in this connection those whose failure is caused by a lack of knowledge and experience required to cope with the specific problems in the new environment. Our interest here lies with the individual who does not have the emotional elasticity required to meet altered circumstances. It has been noted by many historians that the man who successfully engineers a revolution seldom if ever is able to consolidate and stabilize the gains. To take another example: the British public questioned Churchill's skill for peacetime leadership, but they had correctly estimated his potentialities for taking the helm in war. Much less spectacular examples were the many members of the Regular Army and National Guard who had excellent and sometimes even superior ratings in peacetime, but who failed when confronted with the exigencies of war. Apparently they could perform well in the stabilized environment of peace, but were overwhelmed by the speed and flux which characterized the emergency.

Individuals perform differently in different circumstances but the change in their performance is often a reflection of internal factors. Acute observers have noted that certain individuals appear to do better under the severe stresses of modern war when their life is endangered than in the normal pursuits of peacetime. This happens, but it is the exception. We also called attention to the more typical situation where individuals who perform effectively in the normal pursuits of life may fail to do so if they are forced to confront a new and strange set of circumstances. Both of these instances involve individuals who sometimes perform effectively, and at other times do not.

The more supportive and rehabilitative services which a society provides, the larger will be the proportion of those who have failed who can later succeed. We noted earlier that large organizations are likely to be able to provide various kinds of support which will reduce the toll of ineffectiveness and which will speed the recovery of those who break down. But voluntary and governmental agencies also have a major responsibility. Many types of assistance go far beyond the resources of even the largest employer. For instance, since many become ineffective because of the onset of a serious emotional disorder which requires hospitalization, the nature and speed of their recovery will depend in the first instance on the quality of the mental hospitals in the community and their follow-up services. There is increasing agreement among experts in the fields of medicine and rehabilitation that the crucial time for helping people who become emotionally disturbed is at an early stage of their illness before their ties with the world of work become severed. After a man has tried several times to return to a self-supporting status and failed, he is likely to develop an adjustment to his disability that will prove very difficult to reverse. Society has a major stake in providing sufficient services to help all those who begin to fail so as to prevent a permanent adjustment to failure.

Fortunately, the factors responsible for the onset of ineffective behavior in many individuals prove to be self-limiting and these people are usually able to reknit their lives with little or no assistance from the outside. This may be the case when ineffectiveness is precipitated by a major personal crisis, such as the death of a spouse or the recurrence of emotional depression. In such cases time may bring relief and provide the basis for recovery. As his depression lifts, the individual again feels capable of coping with the demands of reality and can again perform effectively.

These findings about continuity in performance point to four major life patterns of performance. Some people tend to perform effectively almost all of the time. Others tend to do well most of their lives but experience a period of ineffective performance when in a new environment or because of an emotional disturbance. If they can escape from the difficult environment, their difficulties may largely disappear. And, if their ineffectiveness results from an emotional disturbance that is not too deep, time is also likely to bring a change for the better. Still other men perform satisfactorily for some period of their lives but then encounter a situation which appears to "break them." They are unable to recover from this experience or rather from what was touched off by it. Finally, there are some who never perform effectively.

Chapter Fourteen: THE MANAGEMENT OF MEN

UNDERSTANDING is a prerequisite for effective action. In the preceding chapter, we considered the relationships between personality and performance with regard to the individual's assets and liabilities, the impact of organizational policy and of environmental factors, and the level, range, and continuity in performance. In this concluding chapter we shall search out the more important actions that can be taken by the various sectors of our society to control and reduce ineffectiveness.

Since ours is a pluralistic society, no single institution—not business, not government, nor community agency—can exert more than a limited influence on the performance of individuals and groups. No matter how hard it strives, no matter how powerful it may be, the fact remains that the power and influence of any institution is limited. Its actions alone can never fully determine the outcome. This limitation on the scale and scope of action which attaches to even the most powerful institutions in our society means that a comprehensive consideration of policy must make provision for at least three major sectors—the organizational, the governmental, and the societal. Individually, each sector can do much to improve the level of performance, but the greatest gains can come about when the three reinforce one another.

THE ORGANIZATIONAL SECTOR

We will begin our consideration of how policy can contribute to the more effective performance of men by setting out the problems and potentialities for action that confront management in large organizations. As we had occasion to note earlier, more and more of the activities of modern man take place in large organizational structures where the element of size presents both opportunities and limitations.

The range of actions which the management of large organizations can take to control ineffective performance can be reviewed in terms of the need to plan, the stability of policies, and the specifics of policies and procedures. Large organizations have a clear need to plan ahead, for their very size means that they face serious costs if they are forced to improvise. One of the major advantages of largeness is the opportunity that it provides for decentralization and specialization of function. However, changes can be effected only within a framework of organizational objectives, policies, and procedures that are well understood and accepted by all echelons. In attempting to effect change without long-range plans, a company will be forced to solve each problem as it arises. Those at the top may have a sufficient overview of a reorganization but lower levels of management will be confused and uncertain during any change, and this can only result in a serious reduction in their own effectiveness and that of their subordinates.

But long-range planning alone is not enough: the key to success is the quality of these plans. The more management can at least delineate the range of its future requirements, the more likely that its long-range plans will be sound. In recent years more and more large corporations as well as voluntary organizations have sought to forecast their future personnel requirements, especially for key people, by developing replacement schedules which identify the important positions that are likely to become available as a result of death, retirement, and other losses. But for every instance where the analysis of future requirements has been ventured, there are tens and hundreds of illustrations of a failure to act until pressure or even a crisis has arisen. While some sort of a solution can always be worked out in an emergency, an improvised solution will generally be inferior to one which has been worked out over time. Alternatives tend to disappear as deadlines approach.

One major reason underlying the need of large organizations to plan ahead in light of their future requirements is that they are likely to encounter difficulties if they rely exclusively on the market for meeting their personnel requirements. Their very size makes it likely that the market will not have the numbers and more particularly the types of individuals that the organization will require if it is forced to replace within a short period many of its key personnel or if it must expand rapidly. The only buttress for the market is the constructive use of time when time is still available to recruit and train so that future requirements can be met more nearly from within the organization.

The extent to which planning is successful depends in large measure on the quality of the people assigned to the planning functions. Historically, the Army and the Navy assigned its staff personnel in the following descending order—the best to operations, followed by supply, intelligence, and finally personnel. Business and voluntary organizations have followed a somewhat similar practice; they pay much less attention to their manpower and personnel posts than to such functions as finance and production.

As President Eisenhower remarked during one of his 1958 press conferences, no plans are likely to prove adequate in a world characterized by constant and unexpected changes, but the fact that an effort is made to plan will usually result in a better outcome than if no effort is ventured. It is not possible for a planning group to forecast the future, but it is often possible for them to take into consideration some of the more important contingencies that may arise. The more experience they have in planning, the more sensitive they will be in recognizing the contingencies that they must include in their future plans.

The better the quality of planning the better the level of future performance. If an organization has the foresight to take action in time to acquire resources essential to its future work, if it avoids making commitments that are likely to reduce its future flexibility unduly, if it has considered and weighed the relative advantages of responding to possible emergencies, its level of performance will be noticeably better than if it has failed to do any of these things.

A second way in which organizational action bears directly on effective performance is through stability of policy. To illustrate this point, let us consider for a moment the results that are likely to flow from a marked instability in policy. We noted earlier that one of the major advantages of large organizations is their opportunity to rely on specialization and decentralization in order to integrate the work of large numbers of people for a common purpose. But this can be done effectively only through established plans and procedures. It is not possible to rely on the personal direction and relationships which can exist in small organizations. When members of a large organization, frequently stationed hundreds or thousands of miles from headquarters and with little or no personal knowledge of the leadership, are confronted with frequent changes in policy, they are likely to conclude that the top executives do not know what they want. Such a deduction, justified or not, will be certain to have an adverse effect on their own performance and in turn on the performance of those who report to them. Having seen a radical shift in policy first in one direction and then in another within a short period of time, they are likely not to respond to the next shift, assuming that it, too, will be reversed before long.

The crucial importance of a basic stability in policy can be further illustrated by noting the impact of an organization's policy on the individual's expectations and motivation. When men know what to expect, when they understand what management considers important and what unimportant, when it will reward and when it will discipline, they will make an effort to perform as management would like them to perform. They stand to gain from this and to lose if they fail to comply. However, if the policy emanating from the top is subject to frequent change, individuals in the lower echelons cannot know what is wanted of them, and even less how they can gain favor, and therefore they do not put forth special effort. In fact, if they work for long in a situation where the objectives and standards are constantly being altered, they are likely to become indifferent, which in turn will be reflected in poorer performance.

Another important reason why management must avoid too frequent major changes is the difficulty, even in the absence of the resentment and hostility mentioned above, of conveying to the many different groups in a large organization the aim of the new policy and the plan for its implementation. To be effective, policy changes must lead to changes in behavior. These in turn can come about only if the individuals who are to learn a new technique, a new approach, have sufficient time to learn and to practice the new. A management that changes its policies too often cannot be in effective control of the organization for the simple reason that the people who are to carry out the new policies will never be able to keep up with them. As we pointed out in an earlier study, *Effecting Change in Large Organizations*, this underestimation of the time required to understand new policies and to implement them is among the most serious errors that management tends to make in instituting programs of change.

There is still another reason why management should avoid frequent changes in policy. No one can ever know all the consequences that are likely to result from replacing an established policy with a new one. The responses of the members of the organization can only be estimated. One way that management can reduce undesirable repercussions to a new policy is to take the time and effort to explore in advance how different groups are likely to receive it. There is, of course, a limit to how often and how thoroughly management can engage in such pre-testing.

Thus, management can achieve and maintain effective performance throughout the organization by introducing effective personnel planning and maintaining stability of policy. In addition to these general approaches there are specific approaches. These will be briefly considered. With regard to selection, there is a danger in establishing minimum standards which are either too high or too low or which are purely arbitrary. There is a natural inclination on the part of management to establish standards as high as possible, but this is usually an error. If the requirements which are established have no realistic relationship to the work that needs to be done, now or in the future, as when a large department store in the depression of the early 1930s hired only Ph.D.s for salesmen, the outcome is likely to be a low level of performance. Frustration and resentment are the inevitable results when people cannot make use of their training and skills.

The obverse is easier to recognize. Management stands to gain if it sets its standards sufficiently high that it rejects the less capable among those who are seeking employment.

Yet the selection process is frequently faulty because management often knows little about the true requirements of the jobs which it is seeking to fill or about the abilities and limitations that characterize the potential supply of manpower. In recent years it has sought to avoid this problem by contending that since it is concerned not only with the employee's capacity on the entry job but with his capacity for growth, there is little or no danger in setting high standards. But if the opportunities to move ahead are limited, as they must inevitably be in any organization, large as well as small, disappointment and frustration, leading to lowered effectiveness, are likely to develop when the gap between potentialities and requirements is wide.

Closely related but still distinguishable from the foregoing is the establishment of arbitrary standards which bear no relationship to the requirements of the job. It is easy for management in this as in the earlier instance to rationalize such arbitrary standards, especially if they have widespread acceptance in the community or the industry. But unless the costs of deviating from established patterns entail serious and manifold consequences—which they seldom do—the advantage is likely to be with the employer who refuses to be bound by tradition and who will consider in setting his selection standards only relevant factors such as skill and experience and not, as so frequently happens, those which more often than not are likely to be irrelevant such as age, sex, or racial or ethnic origin.

Another misconception that permeates many selection procedures should be pointed out. Many managements search for individuals who are free of any disability. As we have stated, a particular advantage of a large organization is its ability to break down its principal functions into many specialized subdivisions so that it is easier to match men who are available with the work that needs doing. But the personnel staffs in many organizations are loath to employ anybody with a clearly recognizable handicap; this policy ignores the fact that no man is free of shortcomings and that the real challenge is to know both the job and the man so as to be able to decide whether a particular disability is relevant or not.

Even if selection were more scientific and reliable than in point of fact it is, management would still have to direct considerable resources to training. The larger the organization and the more specialized its functions—and the two tend to go together—the less likelihood there is that the market will be able to supply people with all of the types of skill that are required. During the past decade, an increasing number of large business organizations have recognized this fact and have expanded and improved their training. And more effort is now being made by large voluntary organizations to do likewise since only thus can they hope to secure the number of qualified people they require.

Many of the recent efforts in training have been concentrated on formal programs, both intramural and extramural, and it is likely that much of this has been of sufficiently good quality under sufficiently favorable conditions that the effort has been justified by the results. But there is ground for believing that in the first flush of enthusiasm insufficient attention has been paid to such basic questions as who should be selected for training, how he should be trained, and for how long, and what standards can be used to measure the effectiveness of the training which he has received.

The stress on formal classroom training has also tended to divert attention from the inevitably close relations among work assignments, the quality of supervision, and training. A man is most likely to learn by doing. To learn he must have both the responsibility for a specific assignment and the authority to make the requisite decisions. Unless he can make mistakes and be held to account, he is unlikely to learn any more than a child could learn to walk without being permitted to fall. And if a man is kept at his assignment long after he has thoroughly mastered it, his acquisition of new knowledge and skill will inevitably be retarded. Thus, effective training depends on the overall effectiveness of the personnel system in which formal training can at best play only a small part.

This brings us to the next consideration—the way in which the assignment system can contribute more to effective performance. We have just pointed out the close connections between training and assignments. Here we must note the dilemma that organizations frequently face in balancing the additional training that they would like their staffs to acquire and their need to get their present work out speedily and efficiently. There is no simple resolution of this conflict between the present and the future, but a wise management knows that the price of making the most productive use of its people in the present is too high if it will lead to a weakened organization in the future. It must stand ready to remove men who are performing excellently in their present positions sometimes to give them, sometimes to give others, a chance to grow.

The assignment process can also contribute to effective performance by insuring that a reasonable balance is established and maintained between the organization's needs for generalists and specialists. One of the consequences of the continuing technological advances is the inevitably larger number of specialists that every large organization requires. But at the same time the men at the helm of a large organization can manage successfully only if they have a real understanding of many different sectors of the organization. They can have this only if they are periodically moved from one to another assignment rather than being left to become expert in one.

There is another aspect of this problem that goes beyond establishing and maintaining a proper balance between the generalist and the specialist. Since many men by inclination or necessity will have to remain specialists, and since many of them will frequently make very important contributions to the success of the organization out of their specialized knowledge, it is important for management to keep under constant review whether the incentive and reward structure has been appropriately adjusted to take cognizance of the growing importance of the specialist.

Assignments can also be used to motivate men to do better work and thus contribute to the overall management objective of effective performance. It is well known, although management frequently fails to act on the knowledge, that some men are strongly motivated to work, others only slightly. A large organization is particularly able to learn more about the motivation of its work force and then to make use of its wide range of assignments to exploit this knowledge. While the performance of men over time will usually enable management to differentiate between the strongly and the poorly motivated, this knowledge can be secured more quickly and with less expense if an organization permits men to choose from among different types of jobs that fall within their competence. There is much more room for self-selection than most managements are willing to grant.

No organization, surely no large organization, can hope to prosper unless it establishes and adheres to a set of rules governing discipline, promotion, and discharge. Large organizations are under the special necessity to govern through policy rather than through persons. Whatever actions it takes or fails to take with respect to a specific individual must be considered and weighed in the larger context, that is, with regard to how its action will be interpreted by the whole group. Since in a large organization, there cannot be personal relations between most of the work force and the management, the integrity of the people in responsible positions can be tested only by the way they act in the face of concrete situations involving members who have performed well or poorly.

If promotions do not go to those who have earned them, or if punishment is not meted out to those who have broken the rules, others in the organization are not motivated either to strive to perform effectively or to abide by the regulations. They have nothing to gain and nothing to lose—at least nothing that they can count on. The fact that management reveals itself to the members of the organization only through the policies which it establishes and enforces makes equity that much more important. For policies and practices grounded in equity instill confidence—and confidence, or the lack of it, will surely be reflected in performance.

It is particularly difficult to establish sound promotion policies. Many large organizations tend to rely heavily if not exclusively on seniority, in the hope of gaining at least the advantage of following an objective criterion—of moving men ahead in terms of length of service. But few organizations have found it possible to rely solely on seniority or any equivalent objective factor. The nub of the difficulty here is the need to provide more incentive for men who are capable of and willing to perform above the average. While some men will do their best in the absence of special recognition and reward, many need the spur of knowing that their efforts will be singled out for special rewards.

It is not easy to reconcile the necessity to handle promotions objectively with the necessity to identify and reward those whose performance has been above average. The fact that it is very difficult to assess performance objectively and that, in a large organization, it is very hard for those at the top to have adequate personal knowledge of the people scattered throughout the organization only compounds the difficulties. But there is no escaping the problem: effective performance depends on a system of promotion that can soundly and objectively relate effort to reward with proper weight given to length and faithfulness of service.

Associated with this problem is management's need to establish and maintain reasonable discipline; supervisors must see to it that men do their jobs and on time and that they suffer penalties and even discharge if their performance remains unsatisfactory. Management must take corrective action when individuals perform poorly, for otherwise even larger numbers in the organization will disregard established standards and try to "get away with" as much as or more than the next man. While management must avoid arbitrary or punitive actions which are likely to lead to disturbance that will be reflected in lowered performance, proper enforcement of discipline is an essential function of management.

This brief consideration of the several approaches through which large organizations can influence performance has called attention to the positive contributions possible in personnel planning, stability of policy, and general principles in the selection, training, assignment and promotion of personnel. Much is known about the way in which these several approaches can contribute to effective performance, but much remains to be learned. For instance, the proper balancing of the rate of technological improvement with additional efforts to raise the skill level of those who must manage, operate, and maintain the increasingly complex structures warrants further study. So too does the problem of work motivation. We are only at the beginning of understanding the marked differences between the strongly and the poorly motivated in the world of work. We also need new knowledge about how the individual, his immediate work group, and the larger organization can be more effectively integrated so that performance can be improved.

GOVERNMENT

Although ours is a society that has long prided itself on getting most of its essential work done through the voluntary efforts of individuals, from the beginning of its history it has relied to a considerable degree on the intermediary of government—local, state, and federal—to undertake directly or to assist indirectly in accomplishing many important social objectives. Today government spends about one-quarter of our national income and provides direct employment for almost one-sixth of the labor force.

There are two ways of looking at government from the point of view of manpower. Government is by far the largest employer in the nation and as such shares many of the problems of other large employers. This means that the approach in the preceding section is specifically relevant to government. But government also exerts a unique influence through its many different programs and policies on the development and utilization of the nation's human resources. To this we now turn.

In our tradition government has long assumed the principal responsibility for providing adequate educational opportunities which are essential if people are to develop their potentialities. Over the decades government has constantly broadened the scale and scope of its educational program, recognizing that elementary instruction is no longer adequate preparation for work and life in a modern age. While only about 6 out of every 10 young people currently graduate from high school, state governments are constantly expanding their support for post-high-school education with the result that about 30 percent of the men eighteen and nineteen years of age are now attending college, and about 60 percent of these are in public institutions.

Education up to the present has been a responsibility of local and state governments, although the federal government has been increasingly involved through the G.I. Bill, construction loans for college dormitories, fellowship programs, research grants, and many other ways. And this involvement has recently increased as a result of the passage of the National Defense Education Act.

Education and performance are related in several important ways. We have seen that this nation's security is jeopardized when localities and states fail to support their schools adequately. Large numbers of men must be rejected for military service or they will fail to perform adequately because they lack an adequate educational background. Since many men, if they are to find work, must leave the localities where they were born and brought up, they carry their educational deficiencies to other regions. This means that they can be at best only marginal members of the labor force in the communities to which they have migrated. The entire nation pays a considerable part of the price of inadequate education in particular states and regions.

The third important tie between education and performance derives from enforced education: the prolongation of schooling is no nostrum. If an adolescent is uninterested in what is going on in the classroom and remains there only because he is forced to, he will not be properly prepared for work and life. Compulsory schooling beyond the middle teens can have a deleterious instead of a constructive effect on a young person's development. There is a pressing need for communities throughout the United States to experiment with new methods and approaches, such as combined work-study programs, to give these young people a better start in life so that they will be able to perform effectively as adults.

Important as education is as a prerequisite for effective performance, it frequently is not enough. A man with serious physical or emotional defects may be very well educated yet be unable to perform effectively. The past decades have seen spectacular advances in medicine with the result that many who in earlier times would have been lucky to survive can now reach maturity and function effectively as an adult.

The challenge to government here is to see that those in the population who do not have adequate financial means to secure essential medical care can obtain it nevertheless. No responsible society dares tolerate a situation where the poor, or even the improvident, are denied access to essential medical care or, even worse, where their children go without it.

In addition to making more adequate provision for medical care for the indigent and the near indigent, government has another responsibility in this connection and that is to invest liberally in medical research and education. Future progress depends on research; and adequate medical care depends primarily on the availability of trained personnel.

These several responsibilities in the area of medical care do not rest on government alone but they cannot be adequately met without the active participation of each level of government. While progress in recent years has been notable on each front—availability of care, research, and training of personnel—and government has played an important part in the progress, more needs to be done.

From many points of view the challenge to government to assist those with physical illness or injury is easier to meet than the challenge to contribute to the emotional health and well-being of the population which, as we have had repeated occasion to note, was so frequently responsible for ineffective performance.

The federal government has taken the lead in raising the level of psychiatric care just as it has played the leading role in recent years in many other areas affecting the nation's health and well-being. The outstanding improvement in the Veterans Administration psychiatric services, inpatient and outpatient, after World War II contributed markedly to helping many veterans get back on their feet. While some were too seriously ill to be helped, many others benefited from the psychotherapy which they received.

Undoubtedly the major efforts of the federal government to provide a high level of psychiatric care for soldiers and veterans had an impact on the community at large, with the result that state governments have in recent years been encouraged to increase their support for mental hospitals and mental hygiene clinics. At the same time voluntary groups have also become much more active in the mental health field. The monetary costs of mental illness to the American people have recently been estimated by Rashi Fein to amount, on an annual basis, to between 2 and 3 billion dollars.

While money still remains a major lack, the problem goes deeper. Despite recent advances in chemotherapy and the earlier advances in insulin and electric shock therapy we know very little about the causes and cure for serious mental illness. And we are still seriously handicapped in treating individuals with neuroses because the origins of their difficulties are so deeply imbedded in their personalities and are reinforced by reality situations which often can be changed, if at all, only with the greatest difficulty. Despite these real limitations to psychiatric treatment, it is generally agreed that many who develop emotional difficulties can, if they receive help early, regain sufficient stability so that they are able to bring their strengths to bear on their problems and once more perform effectively.

Among the important lessons that World War II should have taught us is that most people want to perform effectively and to be self-supporting, and that in the absence of satisfactory alternatives, government should at least provide essential rehabilitative services for those in need. Sound social accounting would always justify an effort to rehabilitate even individuals who had only modest assets on which to build in the hope that some would make the grade. It is much less expensive for a society to invest liberally in rehabilitative efforts in order to help handicapped people, especially the young, to perform effectively than to conclude that there is no hope, and thus leave these people to be maintained in one way or another by the community.

There is, however, a warning in the experience of World War II that should be heeded. The supports that are made available should not be permitted to weaken the individual's motivation to recover. This is what happened as the result of the difference between the comforts, security, and relaxation of discipline that soldiers experienced in Army hospitals and the dangers and deprivations they were forced to endure at the front. It is generally agreed that a liberal annual sick-leave policy, which in essence is a sound health measure, may in organizations with poor morale be seriously abused by encouraging some workers to stay home from work when they are only slightly indisposed. The system may operate to weaken rather than strengthen motivation to work.

The foregoing recommendations concerning actions that government and other agencies of society can undertake to increase the proportion of the population who are able to perform effectively have been developed without explicit consideration of whether jobs are available for all who want to work. In our economy, however, the will to perform is not enough; a job must be available. Hence the Employment Act of 1946, which recognized the responsibility of the federal government to maintain a high level of employment, must be viewed as a major advance. It is questionable whether any national objective, other than peace itself, has a right to more consideration from a modern state. It should be a constant challenge to government to devise means of enabling all members of the community who are able and who want to work to do so, even if some of them require a protective environment. For instance, it is difficult to see how the mentally ill, or other people who may be institutionalized, can be successfully rehabilitated without the opportunity and rewards of work. Admittedly special problems must be solved before many more of them could benefit from an opportunity to work. First, care must be taken to avoid their being exploited. Next, it is exceedingly difficult in our society to provide the type of special environment which would help them to mobilize their assets without exposing them to excessive pressures. But in view of the great personal, social, and financial costs of caring for the mentally ill, efforts to help them perform effectively, even in a controlled environment, would represent a major gain.

The same holds true for prisoners. While competition between free and prison labor presents problems, they are not so serious that they should continue to prevent prisoners from engaging in useful work and adding to their skills. To confine a man behind bars and further to deprive him of the opportunity to work is cruel and inhuman punishment and can lead only to his demoralization and increase his difficulty of readjusting.

A further responsibility of government is to give all people an opportunity to develop their full potentialities. Among the principal handicaps from which large numbers suffer are those growing out of place of residence, low income, and race. With respect to each, the government can be of assistance. Many are born and grow up in regions where there is little prospect of productive employment. The best opportunity for young people who live in these areas is to migrate, but they are much more likely to make a successful readjustment if they receive proper occupational guidance and employment help.

Improved guidance is required by many others in the society, especially young people from low income homes whose parents are unable to give them good advice about the new opportunities that are opening up or how to prepare for them. Congress recently took cognizance of this need by providing in the new National Defense Education Act for strengthening guidance and counseling services.

Another major barrier to full development and effective performance grows out of the deep-seated prejudice that still exists in American society against various minority groups, particularly Negroes. In recent years every level of government has taken active steps to eliminate various forms of discrimination based on race, color, creed, or national origin. In this regard the record of the Armed Forces has been outstanding. While the gains have been significant the roots of discrimination are so deep and the ramifications so great that it will require sustained effort on the part of governmental and voluntary agencies before their substantial eradication can be accomplished.

Responsible under the Constitution for national defense and the general welfare, the federal government has the primary responsibility for acting on new problems growing out of the international situation and developments in science. Specifically, the nation has need for new kinds of talents and skills and for individuals who will devote themselves to work that has a high national priority. The government must see that able people are trained in sufficient numbers to meet the requirements in these new and important fields; and it also must see that there are employment and career opportunities available which will attract and hold competent individuals in these essential fields. While the federal government has been steadily expanding its support of postgraduate training, particularly in those scientific fields that are closely related to defense, and to a lesser degree in fields related to welfare, such as medical training, it has not yet responded wholeheartedly to these challenges. There is no other instrumentality of our society that has the resources necessary to initiate and support large-scale programs, though government alone cannot do the job.

One of the important responsibilities of government, especially the federal government, is to undertake logistical studies of manpower that will help the nation determine its needs and the priorities required to meet them. First of all, the government itself uses so much trained manpower that it must seek to estimate its own future needs and to relate them to the potentially available supply. Moreover, as the major collector of statistical information, it is best able to make essential information available to professional, educational, and business groups that have a direct concern with particular segments of the nation's manpower. A recent instance of government's assuming this type of responsibility was the establishment by the Surgeon General of the U.S. Public Health Service of a top level committee to review the nation's needs for physicians. If the United States requires more physicians there is need for speedy action since it takes approximately ten years from the planning stage of a new medical school until the first student graduates. Even if state governments and voluntary groups are to carry much of the responsibility for expanding medical education, they need overall guidance.

Finally, government is in a unique position to study various manpower problems either by undertaking the research itself, or by facilitating, through financial grants and other means, the research efforts of outside groups. The increasing awareness that manpower sets the limit on our national strength and well-being carries with it the implication that we should seek to increase our knowledge of the characteristics and qualities of the nation's human resources in order to develop and utilize them more effectively. And in such an expanded effort government has a logical leadership role.

THE SOCIETAL SECTOR

A democracy faces a special challenge when it comes to programs and policies that involve people directly, for they are at once the means and ends of a free society. What such a society can accomplish depends on its members; at the same time a major objective of a free society is to enrich and strengthen the lives of its citizenry. Even a totalitarian leadership cannot espouse certain programs because it knows that the masses will oppose them, passively if not openly.

A virile democracy constantly aims to remove the barriers and obstacles that remain in the paths of individuals who are seeking to develop their full potentialities, for only in that manner will it be true to its basic obligations to broaden opportunities for all. As it succeeds in eliminating its shortcomings, it provides a sounder basis for realizing its major objectives. Justice and opportunity alone provide the foundation stones for a stable social order.

The specific policies that organizations—private, voluntary, or governmental—can develop are bounded by the attitudes and values held by the citizenry who must both accept and implement them. The success or failure of new policies will be largely determined by the skill of the leadership in mobilizing the positive and overriding the negative influences embedded in the body politic.

To illustrate: a management that indicates to its employees that it has little interest in helping them to acquire additional skills and to rise in the organization will soon meet recalcitrance, for advancement as a reward of effort has become a basic expectation of men in the United States. Similar opposition will face a government that indicates to the voters that it is little interested in helping those in need of help. In fact, a lack of action to help people to help themselves can jeopardize the position of the United States in world affairs because so many nations, old and new, are now trying to help their people achieve a better life. They cannot do this alone; they need help. The United States is being weighed by most of mankind according to its willingness to help the underdeveloped nations in their struggle to emancipate their people from disease, poverty, and ignorance.

A second important value of our society that can be ignored only at the risk of failure is the need to balance efficiency with equity. Men insist on being treated fairly, or as nearly fairly as possible, in war as in peace. This means that a management which focuses solely on efficiency is likely to precipitate serious trouble. Men who have served an organization long and faithfully feel that they are entitled to special consideration. They do not believe that they should be required to meet the performance standards of the exceptionally able man, and if necessary they will act to protect themselves. These attitudes are reflected in the behavior of trade unionists and executives alike, in government and in private business. In all sectors the rule of seniority must be respected by management, even if it is not followed slavishly in promotions and layoffs. The sharing of risks and rewards as a value is deeply ingrained in a democratic society that views each man as worthy of respect and consideration for what he is as well as what he is able to do.

Closely related to the foregoing are the limitations that a wise government or management must place on itself in the enforcement of discipline. A democratic people will balk at discipline that is arbitrary or excessively severe. While restraints and punishments will be acknowledged as prerequisite for effective organizational and social performance, punitive action will be resented and will fail as policy. For people who work in fear of the exercise of arbitrary power by their leaders will become disturbed and will perform less effectively than in a more secure environment.

One other significant way in which a democracy's value structure sets limits on manpower policies is its insistence that the sick and injured be treated considerately. Illness excuses ineffective performance. However, those in control of policy must take care not to establish conditions that will encourage the sick individual to hold on to his symptoms. The advantages and rewards must always be clearly and unequivocally in favor of the man who performs effectively.

Another attitude of a democratic society is that men who fail are entitled to a second, and even a third, chance and that there is no gain in blanket condemnations. For as long as men know that even if they fail they will have another chance, to that extent will they be encouraged to draw on their latent resources and try to meet the prevailing standards. Some will not try and some who do will fail a second time—but many will succeed. But if men are not expected to perform effectively they will not even try.

These then are some of the major values characteristic of a modern democratic society that dare not be ignored in the formulation and implementation of manpower and personnel policy—broadened opportunity, the balancing of equity and efficiency in the establishing of rewards, moderation in discipline, consideration for but not indulgence of the sick, and the desirability of affording all who fail at least a second chance. The more these underlying values are respected and acted upon, the more likely it is that men will respond by performing effectively.

A democratic society is a society based on concert, not compulsion. What the majority approves, it can accomplish; what the majority disapproves will fail. Having recognized the important role that both institutions and values play in determining performance, the key question that remains open is how people can understand more clearly the connections between their own fulfillment and the general welfare. As long as these links are only dimly perceived, many will see little point to doing their best. But as men and women perceive more clearly that their own welfare—and that of their children—is indissolubly tied up with the welfare of the nation and that of the nation's with the world, many more will be willing to do their best. Understanding is antecedent to commitment and commitment is the foundation of effective performance.

THE LESSON

IN TIMES of major crisis such as World War II, a people's strengths and weaknesses come to the fore. Although unprepared, spiritually and militarily, the United States was able to build up in record time the most powerful Armed Forces that the world had ever known and, with the assistance of its allies, to defeat utterly two most determined enemies.

Remarkable as this achievement was, the war also revealed serious defects in our national fabric. Of the 18 million young men who were screened for military service, 2.5 million were either rejected or prematurely separated because of a mental or emotional defect.

In any large population failures are inevitable. But most of the young men who failed in World War II although normal at birth had suffered serious deprivations in childhood and adolescence. And others, whose development had not been seriously handicapped, were the victims of faulty organizational policies.

The majority of the ineffective soldiers were able to adjust after their return to civilian life where conditions were less demanding and the margins of freedom greater. They were aided by liberal benefits provided by an appreciative people and by the full employment which characterized the economy and which meant that there were jobs available for them. A small minority, most of whom had never performed effectively, failed to adjust and remained dependent on their families or the community.

No society can afford to ignore the fact that one out of every seven men was judged to be mentally or emotionally incapable of serving effectively in its armed forces in time of war; or that a significant, if much smaller, proportion cannot support themselves in time of peace. The cost of failure not only to the individual but to his family, to business, and to the larger community is too high to be tolerated by a responsible democracy.

APPENDIX

THE FOLLOWING PAGES present a more detailed explanation than was feasible in the text proper of our sampling procedures, how the degree of a soldier's incapacitation for further military service was determined, the criteria used for evaluating a man's civilian and military performance, and the method we followed in constructing the readjustment and life performance patterns.

This volume, while it makes use of some data which pertain to all the ineffective soldiers of World War II and which were reported in detail in *The Lost Divisions*, deals primarily with the group of men who came on active duty with the Army during the last four months of 1942, either as selectees or as enlistees or reservists, and who were subsequently separated, as enlisted men, for ineffectiveness as defined in this study. These men are referred to throughout the text, generally, as "cohort ineffectives." The sample was limited to male enlisted personnel of the Army and excludes the relatively small number of men who entered the Army as enlisted men during the cohort period and who were later commissioned and subsequently separated, as officers, for ineffectiveness.

Sampling Procedure

To have drawn a sample directly from among the more than 12 million personnel files of enlisted and officer personnel who served during the war, which are maintained at the Army Personnel Records Center, would not have been feasible. Fortunately, however, the Army had made out a punched card each time a soldier changed his status—from the day he was inducted until he was finally separated. These final status cards, or, as they are more generally referred to, the separation cards, were retained temporarily after the war, but the problem of storing them was so great that all but a five percent sample were eventually destroyed. This sample of separation cards, which provided a key to the detailed personnel and medical files, was made available to the Project staff for research purposes by the Adjutant General's Office (AGO).

As indicated in *The Lost Divisions* and in Chapter Two of this volume, our own experience during the war reinforced by a preliminary analysis of the available statistics led us to begin with an operational definition of ineffectiveness based on the Army's discharge categories. We defined an ineffective soldier as one prematurely separated from the Army for mental, emotional, or behavioral reasons—specifically, for psychoneurosis, for psychosis, for undesirable habits or traits of character, or for inaptitude.

The AGO separation cards, while containing adequate demographic and military service data to provide guidelines for setting up the sample, had one major drawback. They indicated whether the soldier had received a Certificate of Discharge for Disability (CDD) but did not specify the medical diagnosis. The Surgeon General's Office (SGO), however, had their own file of punched cards, which included detailed medical data on each soldier who had been given a CDD. The two sets of cards had in common the name, rank, and serial number of the men. By means of a complicated matching process, the psychiatric diagnoses were obtained from the SGO cards for the men in the AGO sample who had received CDDs, and a new deck of cards was punched incorporating the appropriate psychiatric diagnosis with the other data from the AGO cards.

The tabulations of the information contained on the cards of soldiers separated during the years 1942 through 1945 formed the basis for much of the analysis in *The Lost Divisions*. These tabulations also provided guidelines for setting up the sample used in this volume. Additional guidelines were provided by an analysis of about 250 case records randomly selected from special strata of the total wartime five percent sample of ineffective soldiers. These special stratified samples included, for example, men separated for psychosis after only a few months' service; men separated for psychosis after having served several years; high-school graduates and college men separated for inaptitude or for undesirability; top ranking noncommissioned officers separated for inaptitude or for undesirability; psychoneurotics who had served overseas, and others who had not; and other special rosters.

The analysis of these statistical materials and case records, together with the insights we had gained from our study of the 400 cases used in *The Uneducated*, convinced us that a cohort approach would be the most fruitful for this study of the ineffective soldier. We decided on a cohort period to include September through December 1942 for the reasons given in Chapter Two. We then asked the AGO to furnish us complete rosters of all men in the five percent sample who had entered the Army during this period and who were subsequently separated for ineffectiveness. The total number of these men was 3,867. In order to differentiate the nature of their military service, the men in the cohort were grouped into four distinct Situations as follows:

I. Zone of Interior duty only, under one year
II. Zone of Interior duty only, one year or more
III. Overseas duty, not in combat
IV. Overseas combat duty

Although, on the basis of the data punched on the separation cards, we could distinguish between men who had served only in the United States (ZI) and those who had served overseas and further among them by length of service, there was no notation on the card of whether a soldier had been in combat. Consequently, an intermediate step was necessary. The separation card did identify the branch of the Army in which the soldier served. Therefore, to assure a representation of both combat and noncombat cases, the overseas group was split into three rosters: those who had served in one of the ground combat arms; those who had served in a service branch; and those who had served in the Air Corps. Then, on the basis of information in the individual case records supplemented by reference to the histories of the military units with which the soldiers served, men with overseas service were placed in Situation III or Situation IV according to whether or not they had been in combat. For our purposes, combat duty was defined as being directly under enemy fire for any length of time.

Once the rosters had been prepared by cause of separation and by Situation, random sampling techniques were used to select the cases for analysis. Names on the printed rosters were numbered consecutively, and a table of random numbers was used to select the cases; for one large roster which was composed of punched cards, we used the last two digits of the men's serial numbers to provide a random sample. The total sample consisted of 534 cases, divided among the four Situations as follows: Situation I, 152 cases; II, 97 cases; III, 168 cases; and IV, 117 cases.

For reasons of time and economy, we decided to draw a specified number rather than a percentage of cases from each roster (whose numbers varied from several hundred to over a thousand). The number drawn from each roster was determined by our experience in analyzing the earlier cases and also by the degree of homogeneity that we found to exist among the cases in any one roster. Provision was made for drawing additional cases from each roster without affecting the randomness of the sample, if, as the analysis proceeded, the number of cases proved to be too few.

This sampling procedure, while permitting us to use the raw case values in analyzing the data by Situation, necessitated weighting the cases when the four Situations were combined in order that the entire cohort could be analyzed. After taking into account minor variations between the AGO five percent sample and the entire group of Army ineffectives, we assigned each case a weighted value which was determined by the total number of cases in the roster. On the basis of the five percent sample we calculated that 72,700 of the 1,764,900 men who had entered the Army as enlisted men during the last four months of 1942 were subsequently separated for psychoneurosis, psychosis, undesirability, or inaptitude. The 534 cases were weighted accordingly.

While the percentages reported in this volume apply to the expanded group of 72,700 or to specified parts of it, tests of significance (principally chi square analyses) were based on the N of 534. Care was taken throughout the analysis not to draw any conclusions from the data when the number of raw cases falling within a particular cell or cells proved to be too few. Moreover, in the study of readjustment patterns and life performance patterns, the percentage of known cases is always indicated.

To provide the staff with further points of reference and a better understanding of the case materials, nearly 300 additional cases, not included in the materials analyzed in this volume, were reviewed. These included special rosters of soldiers separated for epilepsy or other neurological disturbances that were sometimes grouped under the heading of neuropsychiatric illness but which we decided to exclude from our definition of ineffectiveness; and additional rosters of men who did fall within the definition, such as men separated for enuresis or for homosexuality. They also included rosters of men separated to accept a commission or who were demobilized. While the analyses of these additional case materials were not incorporated in this volume, they proved of great help in providing perspective on the cohort sample.

In Chapter Five reference was made to the fact that the cohort sample, in contrast to the five percent sample of all ineffective soldiers, had a disproportionate number of men who served only in the Zone of the Interior. As we have shown in *The Lost Divisions*, the period of the cohort intake (late 1942) was followed the next year by a lowering of the criteria for discharge. Consequently, men who were in the Army in 1943, especially if they were still in the Zone of the Interior, had a better chance of being separated early than soldiers who were inducted at times when discharge policy was more stringent. The cohort sample therefore contains relatively more men with no overseas service. It should be noted, however, that the distribution of the cohort ineffectives who served overseas, according to their branch of assignment and time of departure for overseas duty, compared with a similar distribution of all Army ineffectives as a group indicates that the cohort ineffectives did not have combat experience significantly different from the group as a whole.

Evaluation of Degree of Incapacitation

In order to evaluate the case materials we had to develop a method for analyzing the effects of three major determinants of performance—individual characteristics, situational stresses and supports, and organizational policies—acting alone or in combination with one another. In view of the varying relative importance of these several factors in most, if not all cases, it would not have been appropriate to rely on any one of them to categorize the cases. And to weight and combine the several factors in each case would have been unduly complicated, even if the case materials had been sufficiently detailed to permit us to do so. Consequently, we developed a different approach.

As each case was received from the Records Center, it was evaluated by the staff and the findings were summarized on a one-page evaluation sheet that had been designed for this purpose. Preliminary assessments included whether or not the soldier fell below the then prevailing standards for induction; the major factors precipitating his breakdown or poor performance in the Army; what the Army had done to assist him prior to his breakdown or, possibly, to contribute to his breakdown; whether the Army could have salvaged him and, if so, by what means; whether he could have served in any capacity in the Army if the manpower situation in the country had demanded the use of every possible man.

While these preliminary evaluations proved valuable in the early phases of the analysis, they did not provide a satisfactory basis for categorizing the cases. We decided that it was not only feasible but necessary to develop a single measure which could be graded, which could be applied to all cases, and which would result in a group of categories which would be mutually exclusive and yet permit the distribution of every case in the sample. The measure determined upon was an estimate of the degree of a man's incapacitation for further military service at the time of his breakdown. Three gradations were established—major, moderate, and minor—and appropriate criteria were developed to distinguish among them. In establishing the criteria cognizance was taken of Army personnel policy, the facilities generally available in the Army for support, therapy and rehabilitation of soldiers who broke down, and the impact of the stage of the war on manpower utilization requirements. In applying the criteria, the man's entire history—before, during, and after his period of service—was reviewed for relevant information.

Major incapacitation for further military service was defined as an individual condition (psychiatric illness, physical disability, personality defect, or habit or trait) which unquestionably rendered a man unfit for further military duty in the setting of the American Army during World War II. To be classified in this category a man's record had to reveal that his condition was in fact disabling as indicated by the medical description of his symptoms as well as the summary diagnosis, evidence of its effect on his prior performance, and its severity and chronicity as revealed by the state of the soldier's health and performance after discharge. The condition may have been present at induction, or it may have first manifested itself during his military service. Included in this category were men with mental deficiency, psychosis, or severe psychoneurosis that precluded even minimal performance; men with confirmed histories of chronic alcoholism, homosexuality, enuresis, or irresponsible behavior; and some who had disqualifying physical disabilities.

As indicated in Chapter Two, the category of major incapacitation was further refined into four sub-categories which are described in the text. A distinction was made as to whether the man's condition clearly existed prior to his induction or whether it first manifested itself in the Army. While it was the Army's practice to state whether or not the condition leading to discharge existed prior to entry (EPTE), we did not rely on the Army's determination alone. No man was placed in Category 1a unless the record itself revealed clear-cut evidence of the existence of a disqualifying condition before he entered military service or unless the condition, although appearing shortly after induction, could be presumed to have existed earlier, as in cases of severe mental deficiency and certain psychotic reactions. The other sub-categories are explained in the text and do not require amplification here.

Moderate incapacitation for further military service was defined as a condition which was sufficiently severe that the man's further value to the Army was questionable, particularly if he did not receive substantial supports, such as extensive therapeutic measures or such special organizational adjustments as modified assignments, which could not be readily provided by the Army during wartime. We placed in this category soldiers who did not reveal any evidence of major ineffectiveness before entering service and who did show evidence, either in the Army or before entering military service, that they had been able to perform effectively.

Minor incapacitation for further military service was defined as the absence of any individual conditions which would have placed a soldier in one of the other two categories; and, more importantly, it was used when the soldier's discharge appeared to reflect an easing in the Army's manpower requirements rather than the soldier's personal deficiencies. The soldier's performance up to the time of his separation might have been marginal or it might have been good. Some men had deficiencies which, although not serious enough to have warranted their rejection for service or even their separation from service at other times during the war, nevertheless impeded their performance to an extent that the Army decided to separate them in view of its overall manpower position at that time and of the investment that might have been required to utilize them effectively. Their personal deficiencies, however, might have been overcome with the special assistance or therapeutic measures which the Army made available to men with similar disabilities at other periods of the war. In short, the men included in this category were essentially logistical losses. This conclusion is reinforced by our rigorous application of the criterion of presumptive usability to those men whose records revealed no evidence of prior ineffectiveness or no indication that the Army had attempted to salvage them through special training, outpatient treatment, change of assignment, discipline, or merely returning them from the hospital to full duty when one or more of these alternatives was clearly called for.

In evaluating the cases to determine the degree of incapacitation for further service, we searched first for evidence that would place a soldier in Category 1 (major incapacitation). If there was no clear evidence that he belonged there, the record was reviewed to ascertain whether there was any evidence, direct or implied, that he was a logistical loss and belonged in Category 3 (minor incapacitation). If the decision was again negative, the case was tentatively placed in

Category 2 (moderate incapacitation). Hence to some degree this latter category is a residual one, but all cases that were placed in Category 2 were carefully evaluated. As pointed out in the text, there was no difficulty in distinguishing between men who belonged in Categories 1 and 3, but uncertainties arose on the borderlines between Categories 1 and 2 and between 2 and 3. Doubtful cases (where the evidence was not clear-cut) tended to be placed in Category 2; each case was evaluated by several of the staff and the classification of doubtful cases was decided in conference.

Criteria Used for Evaluating Performance

The performance of each man in the sample was evaluated on the basis of pertinent information contained in all of his records—the abstract of official military records; detailed clinical histories; evidence presented at military board hearings; information elicited by Veterans Administration psychiatrists during rating examinations; occupational histories compiled for VA rating boards; histories prepared by social workers; VA training records; and the statements of the men themselves as reported in their records or as contained in their replies to our questionnaire. Each man's performance was rated independently for each of three major periods: the time prior to his entering the Army; during his military service up to the time of his breakdown; and the period after his discharge from the Army. The rating for each period was made without reference to the ratings in other periods, and the cases were evaluated separately by two or more staff members. The following criteria were developed and pre-tested.

Pre-military performance of the man was rated as either acceptable or poor. His performance was rated as acceptable if the record revealed nothing which would have justified a rating of poor. If he met any one of the following criteria his pre-military performance was rated poor:

a) Continued poor school performance as indicated by retardation of three or more years for reasons other than economic or a record of continued difficulty such as very low grades, truancy, or infractions of discipline. This criterion was not applied to men who had three or more years of satisfactory work experience after leaving school.

b) Imprisonment for a year or more; two or more convictions for felonies; or a record of clear evidence of continuing difficulty with law enforcement authorities or of frequent arrests for misdemeanors.

c) A history of being fired from three or more jobs because of poor performance or inability to accept work discipline; or labor force participation of two years or longer without being able to hold any job for at least six months.

d) Clear evidence that the man had been a hobo for three or more years and had worked only intermittently in different parts of the country; or unemployment for at least half of the year preceding his induction into military service, if his previous work record had been marginal.

e) Indication in a verified social history that the man characteristically performed poorly throughout the period of his labor force participation or had worked only at extremely simple jobs in a highly protective environment.

Military performance was rated as good, acceptable, or poor, except in the case of men whose total military service was less than 90 days or who had been in training or duty assignments for less than six weeks. These men were not rated. In order to be rated good, the soldier had to meet *all* the criteria for good performance listed below; to be rated poor, the soldier needed to meet only *one* of the criteria for poor performance listed below. However, if he met four of the criteria for good performance while meeting but one under poor, he was rated as acceptable; a soldier was also rated as acceptable if he met none of the criteria for poor performance while failing to meet all of the criteria for good.

The criteria for good military performance were:

a) No courts-martial other than summary for minor infractions of rules.

b) Time lost under Article of War 107 did not exceed one week per year of service. (AWOL, in stockade, or incapacitated due to own misconduct.)

c) No unsatisfactory efficiency ratings.

d) Effective (full duty status) service up to breakdown of at least 90 percent of the time.

e) Achieved and retained minimum grade of corporal; or was awarded the Bronze Star Medal, its equivalent, or higher award. Bronze Star Medals awarded solely on the basis of the soldier's having the Combat Infantry Badge were not credited in this connection.

The criteria for poor military performance were:

a) One general court-martial; two or more special courts-martial;

four or more summary courts-martial; or equivalent combinations thereof.

b) Time lost under Article of War 107 exceeded 30 days per year of service. (AWOL, in stockade, or incapacitated due to own misconduct.)

c) Unsatisfactory efficiency ratings for a period of two months or longer per year of service, unless the record contained unequivocal evidence to the contrary.

d) Effective (full duty status) service up to breakdown of less than 70 percent of the time.

e) Two or more reductions in grade during service with grade at discharge that of private.

Post-military performance of a man was rated, where the case materials provided sufficient basis for reaching an evaluation, as being good, acceptable, or poor. Each veteran's post-military history was divided into three periods: the first two years following his discharge, the last two years for which information was available, and the intervening period (which was rated if it covered a year or more). The man's performance during each period was rated according to the criteria given below. To be rated as good he had to meet *all* the criteria appropriate to his occupational or training status for good performance listed below; he was rated as poor if he met any *one* of the criteria for poor performance listed below; he was rated as acceptable if he met none of the criteria under poor but failed to meet all the criteria under good.

The criteria for good post-military performance were:

a) Constantly engaged in either employment or training, except for brief periods of job-seeking or school vacation. A maximum of three months of inactivity following discharge from the Army was ignored.

b) If employed, worked for at least half the rating period in a position clearly above the level of his highest regular pre-war level; in the case of farmers and other self-employed, expanded the nature or profitability of the enterprise in which engaged.

c) Pursued training programs or courses of study related to his occupational field or of such a nature as to improve his occupational or self-employment status. An unfocused training program or one pursued merely for the sake of obtaining subsistence allowance from the Veterans Administration was not considered an adequate basis for a good rating.

d) Changed jobs only to improve his position or to make necessary adjustments to personal or family circumstances; did not drop out of any training program except to accept fulltime employment or to make necessary adjustments to personal or family circumstances.

e) No evidence of poor work performance or of excessive absenteeism (loss of three or more working days per month on the average was considered excessive); or if in training, no record of unsatisfactory performance or of excessive absenteeism.

f) Not fired from any position or dropped from any training program.

g) No arrest and conviction of any felony and no evidence of other serious trouble with the law.

The criteria for poor post-military performance were:

a) Not employed or engaged in educational or training activity for at least 70 percent of the period. In computing this, we ignored the first three months following discharge if the veteran was inactive, normal school vacation periods, employment time lost due to strikes or to seasonal layoffs.

b) Fired from two or more positions for poor performance or inability to adhere to work discipline; failures in or forced dropping from training programs or educational courses were treated as firings.

c) Failure to hold any job or to continue with any training program for at least six months.

d) Clear indication in the social history that the veteran was characteristically a poor performer or worked at his job only intermittently.

e) Arrest and conviction for a felony or for repeated misdemeanors.

Construction of Performance Patterns

As indicated above, the performance of each man in the sample was rated for three separate periods following his discharge from the Army. With four ratings possible for each period—good (G), acceptable (A), poor (P), and not rated (N)—a total of 64 separate combinations resulted. We grouped these 64 detailed patterns into a number of sub-patterns for preliminary analysis, and then combined various sub-patterns into the three *readjustment patterns*—early, delayed, and unsuccessful. These are presented and analyzed in the text (Chapters Nine and Ten). The following outline indicates how the detailed patterns were grouped by sub-pattern, and in turn, by the three readjustment patterns.

Readjustment Pattern	*Sub-Pattern*	*Detailed Pattern*
1. Early	a. Stable, good	GGG, GGN, GNG, NGG
	b. Stable, acceptable	AAA, AAN, ANA, NAA
	c. Improved from acceptable to good	AGG, AAG, ANG, AGN, NAG
	d. Declined from good to acceptable	GGA, GAA, GNA, GAN, NGA
	e. Variable, good and acceptable	GAG, AGA
2. Delayed	f. Improved from poor to good	PGG, PAG, PPG, PNG, PGN, NPG
	g. Improved from poor to acceptable	PAA, PPA, PNA, PAN, NPA
	h. Variable, one poor period, final period good	GPG, APG
	i. Variable, one poor period, final period acceptable	GPA, APA, PGA
3. Unsuccessful	j. Stable, poor	PPP, PPN, PNP, NPP
	k. Deteriorated from acceptable to poor	AAP, APP, APN, ANP, NAP
	l. Deteriorated from good to poor	GGP, GAP, GPP, GPN, GNP, NGP
	m. Variable, final period poor	AGP, PGP, PAP
4. Unknown	n. One period good	GNN, NGN, NNG
	o. One period acceptable	ANN, NAN, NNA
	p. One period poor	PNN, NPN, NNP
	q. All periods unknown	NNN

The *life performance patterns* were constructed by utilizing each man's pre-military performance rating (acceptable or poor), his military performance rating (good, acceptable, poor, not rated), and his last post-military performance rating (good, acceptable, or poor). These ratings resulted in 24 detailed patterns which were initially grouped into 9 sub-patterns for preliminary analysis and then consolidated into the four life performance patterns which are presented and analyzed in the text (Chapters Eleven and Twelve): adjusted, vulnerable, broken, and poor. The following outline indicates how these life patterns were developed.

Life Performance Pattern	*Sub-Pattern*	*Detailed Pattern*
1. Adjusted	a. Stable, good	AGG, AGA, AAG
	b. Stable, acceptable	AAA
	c. Poor only before entering service, acceptable thereafter	PGG, PGA, PAG, PAA
2. Vulnerable	d. Acceptable civilian, poor military	APG, APA, ANG, ANA
	e. Acceptable veteran, poor soldier and pre-military	PPG, PPA, PNG, PNA
3. Broken	f. Acceptable up to breakdown, poor veteran	AGP, AAP
4. Poor	g. Stable, poor	PPP, PNP
	h. Poor civilian, acceptable military	PGP, PAP
	i. Acceptable pre-military, poor soldier and veteran	APP, ANP
5. Unknown as veteran	j. Acceptable through military	AGN, AAN
	k. Poor through military	PPN, PNN
	l. Variable	APN, PGN, PAN, ANN

Utilizing a man's final post-military performance rating rather than his readjustment pattern in constructing the life performance patterns had two advantages: it enabled us to make use of the most recent information about his performance; and by relying on a single post-military evaluation it reduced the number of unknown life performance patterns. As we have indicated in Chapter Eleven, the unknowns were allocated among the four life patterns in order to provide an estimate of the total number of cases in the cohort sample that fell within each. Unknown cases were distributed among the four patterns on the basis of the established prior ratings (pre-military and military) of all those whose performance as a veteran was unknown and on the probability of their having a given post-military performance rating as determined by the distribution of similar known cases. A comparison of the various background and military service factors of the unknown cases thus distributed and of the cases already in these patterns assured us that this procedure resulted in a reasonable estimate.

SELECTED BIBLIOGRAPHY

Ahrenfeldt, Robert H. *Psychiatry in the British Army in the Second World War.* New York, Columbia University Press, 1958.

Allport, Gordon W. *Personality.* New York, Henry Holt, 1937.

Arensberg, Conrad M. and others (ed.). *Research in Industry.* New York, Harper & Brothers, 1958.

Baier, D. E. "The Marginally Useful Soldier," *American Journal of Mental Deficiency,* XLVIII (1943), 62-66.

Bailey, Pearce and others. *Neuropsychiatry,* Vol X of the series, The Medical Department of the United States Army in the World War. Washington, D.C., Government Printing Office, 1929.

Bartemeier, Leo H. and others. *Report of Special Commission of Civilian Psychiatrists Covering Psychiatric Policy and Practice in the U.S. Army Medical Corps, European Theatre, 20 April to 8 July, 1945.* Washington, D.C., Office of Scientific Research and Development and Office of the Surgeon General, War Department, 1945.

Beebe, Gilbert W. and John W. Appel. *Variation in Psychological Tolerance to Ground Combat in World War II.* Washington, D.C., National Academy of Sciences – National Research Council, 1958.

Berlien, Ivan C. "Alcohol and the Soldier," *Quarterly Journal of Studies on Alcohol,* V (1944), 405-13.

Bond, Douglas D. *The Love and Fear of Flying.* New York, International Universities Press, 1952.

Boulding, Elise. "Family Adjustments to War Separation and Reunion," *Annals of the American Academy of Political and Social Science,* CCLXXII (1950), 59-67.

Bradley, Omar N. *A Soldier's Story.* New York, Henry Holt, 1951.

Brill, Norman Q. and Gilbert W. Beebe. *A Follow-Up Study of War Neuroses,* VA Medical Monograph Series. Washington, D.C., Government Printing Office. 1955.

——. "Some Applications of a Follow-Up Study to Psychiatric Standards for Mobilization," *American Journal of Psychiatry,* CIX (1952), 401-10.

Bühler, Charlotte. *Der Menschliche Lebenslauf als Psychologisches Problem.* Leipzig, S. Hirzel, 1933.

Carp, Louis. "The Battle of Grand Central Palace: Observations at an Induction Station," *Military Surgeon*, IV (1948), 285-91.

Chein, Isidor. "The Environment as a Determinant of Behavior," *Journal of Social Psychology*, *XXXIX* (1954), 115-27.

Dollard, John. *Fear in Battle*. Washington, D.C., Infantry Journal Press, 1944.

Dornbusch, E. C. (comp.). *Histories of American Army Units: World Wars I and II and Korean Conflict, With Some Earlier Histories*. Washington, D.C., Department of the Army, Office of the Adjutant General, 1956.

Dubin, Robert. *Human Relations in Administration*. New York, Prentice-Hall, 1951.

Eisenhower, Dwight D. *Crusade in Europe*. Garden City, N.Y., Doubleday, 1948.

Fein, Rashi. *Economics of Mental Illness*, Monograph Series No. 2, Joint Commission on Mental Illness and Health. New York, Basic Books, 1958.

Fritz, Charles E. and Eli S. Marks. "The NORC Studies of Human Behavior in Disaster," *Journal of Social Issues*, X (1954), 26-41.

Ginsburg, Ethel L. "Veteran into Civilian: the Process of Readjustment," *Mental Hygiene*, XXIX (1945), 7-19.

Ginsburg, Sol W. "The Mental Health Movement: Its Theoretical Assumptions," in Ruth Kotinsky and Helen L. Witmer (ed.), *Community Programs for Mental Health*. Cambridge, Mass., Harvard University Press, 1955.

——. *Psychiatric Needs in Rehabilitation*. New York, New York City Committee on Mental Hygiene of the State Charities Aid Association, 1948.

——. "Values and the Psychiatrist," *American Journal of Orthopsychiatry*, XX (1950), 466-78.

Ginsburg, Sol W. and John L. Herma. "Values and their Relationship to Psychiatric Principles and Practice," *American Journal of Psychotherapy*, VII (1953), 546-73.

Ginzberg, Eli. *Human Resources: The Wealth of a Nation*. New York, Simon & Schuster, 1958.

——. "The Occupational Adjustment of 1000 Selectees," *American Sociological Review*, VIII (1943), 256-63.

Ginzberg, Eli and Associates. *The Negro Potential*. New York, Columbia University Press, 1956.

——. *Occupational Choice*. New York, Columbia University Press, 1951.

——. *The Unemployed*. New York, Harper & Brothers, 1943.

Ginzberg, Eli and James K. Anderson. "The Shape of Military Manpower Policy," in William Haber and others (ed.), *Manpower in the United States*. New York, Harper & Brothers, 1954.

Ginzberg, Eli and Douglas W. Bray. *The Uneducated*. New York, Columbia University Press, 1953.

Ginzberg, Eli, John L. Herma, and Sol W. Ginsburg. *Psychiatry and Military Manpower Policy*. New York, King's Crown Press, 1953.

Ginzberg, Eli and Ewing W. Reilley. *Effecting Change in Large Organizations*. New York, Columbia University Press, 1957.

Glass, Albert J. "Psychiatry in the Korean Campaign," *U. S. Armed Forces Medical Journal*, IV (1953), 1387-1401, 1563-83.

——. "Psychotherapy in the Combat Zone," *American Journal of Psychiatry*, CX (1954), 725-31.

Goldberg, Samuel. *Army Training of Illiterates in World War II*. New York, Bureau of Publications, Teachers College, Columbia University, 1951.

Goldhamer, Herbert and Andrew W. Marshall. *Psychosis and Civilization: Two Studies in the Frequency of Mental Disease*. Glencoe, Ill., Free Press, 1953.

Grinker, Roy R. and John P. Spiegel. *Men Under Stress*. Philadelphia, Blakiston, 1945.

——. *War Neuroses*. Philadelphia, Blakiston, 1945.

Guttmacher, Manfred S. and Frank A. Stewart. "A Psychiatric Study of Absence Without Leave," *American Journal of Psychiatry*, CII (1945), 74-81.

Hanson, Frederick R. (ed.). *Combat Psychiatry*. Washington, D.C., Government Printing Office, 1949.

Herma, Hans (John L.). "The Unconscious," in Hans (John L.) Herma and Gertrud M. Kurth (ed.), *Elements of Psychoanalysis*. Cleveland & New York, The World Publishing Company, 1950.

Hill, Reuben. *Families Under Stress*. New York, Harper & Brothers, 1950.

Hollingshead, August B. "Adjustment to Military Life," *American Journal of Sociology*, LI (1946), 439-50.

Hollingshead, August B. and Fredrick C. Redlich. *Social Class and Mental Illness: A Community Study*. New York, John Wiley & Sons, 1958.

Kardiner, Abram and Herbert Spiegel. *War Stress and Neurotic Illness*. New York, Paul B. Hoeber, 1947.

Kinkead, Eugene. *In Every War But One*. New York, Norton, 1959.

Kinsey, A. C. and Associates. *Sexual Behavior in the Human Male*. Philadelphia, W. B. Saunders Company, 1948.

Kubie, Lawrence S. "Motivation and Rehabilitation," *Psychiatry*, VIII (1945), 69-78.

Lemkau, Paul V. "Prevention of Psychiatric Illness," *Journal of the American Medical Association*, CLXII (1956), 854-57.

Lewis, Nolan D. C. and Bernice Engle (ed.). *Wartime Psychiatry: A Compendium of the International Literature*. New York, Oxford University Press, 1954.

Lohman, Joseph D., Lloyd E. Ohlin, and Dietrich C. Reitzes. *The Combat Adjustment of Felons Paroled to the Military Service*. Illinois Division of Correction, date unknown.

Magnuson, Paul B. "Medical Care for Veterans," *Annals of the American Academy of Political and Social Science*, CCLXXIII (1951), 76-83.

Malberg, Benjamin. "Mental Disease in Relation to Economic Status," *Journal of Nervous and Mental Disease*, CXXIII (1956), 257-61.

——. *Social and Biological Aspects of Mental Illness*. Utica, N.Y., State Hospital Press, 1940.

Marshall, S. L. A. *Men Against Fire*. Washington, D.C., Infantry Journal Press, 1947.

——. *The River and the Gauntlet*. New York, William Morrow, 1953.

Menninger, William C. *Psychiatry in a Troubled World*. New York, Macmillan, 1948.

Merton, Robert K. and Paul F. Lazarsfeld (ed.). *Continuities in Social Research: Studies in the Scope and Method of "The American Soldier."* Glencoe, Ill., Free Press, 1950.

Metcalf, Henry C. and L. Urwick (ed.). *Dynamic Administration: The Collected Papers of Mary Parker Follett*. New York, Harper & Brothers, 1942.

Millett, John D. *The Organization and Role of the Army Service Forces*. Washington, D.C., Government Printing Office, 1954.

Miner, John B. *Intelligence in the United States*. New York, Springer Publishing Company, 1957.

Miner, John B. and James K. Anderson. "Intelligence and Emotional Disturbance: Evidence from Army and Veterans Administration Records," *Journal of Abnormal and Social Psychology*, LVI (1958), 75-81.

Mira, Emilio. *Psychiatry in War*. New York, Norton, 1943.

Myrdal, Gunnar. *An American Dilemma*. New York, Harper & Brothers, 1944.

Newcomb, Theodore M., Eugene L. Hartley, and others (ed.). *Readings in Social Psychology*. New York, Henry Holt, 1947.

The OSS Assessment Staff. *Assessment of Men*. New York, Rinehart, 1948.

Palmer, Robert R., Bell I. Wiley, and William R. Keast. *The Procurement and Training of Ground Combat Troops*. Washington, D.C., Government Printing Office, 1948.

Peterson, Donald B. "Boards, Certificates, and Psychiatric Reports," "*U. S. Armed Forces Medical Journal*, II (1951), 959-70.

The President's Commission on Veterans' Pensions. *Veterans' Benefits in the United States: Findings and Recommendations.* Washington, D.C., Government Printing Office, 1956.

Rees, John R. *The Shaping of Psychiatry by War.* New York, Norton, 1945.

Rioch, David McK. *Problems of Preventive Psychiatry in War.* Washington, D.C., Army Medical Service Graduate School, Walter Reed Army Medical Center, 1954.

Roethlisberger, F. J. and William J. Dickson. *Management and the Worker.* Cambridge, Mass., Harvard University Press, 1949.

Rosenzweig, Saul and Douglas W. Bray. "Sibling Deaths in the Anamneses of Schizophrenic Patients," *Archives of Neurology and Psychiatry*, XLIX (1943) 71-92.

Ryan, Francis J. *Relation of Performance to Social Background Factors among Army Inductees.* Washington, D.C., Catholic University of America Press, 1958.

Schneider, Alexander J. and Cyrus W. LaGrone. "Delinquents in the Army," *American Journal of Psychiatry*, CII (1945), 82-91.

Shaffer, Laurance F. "Fear and Courage in Aerial Combat," *Journal of Consulting Psychology*, XI (1947), 137-43.

Singer, H. W. *Unemployment and the Unemployed.* New York, Chemical Publishing Company, 1940.

Smuts, Robert W. "The Negro Community and the Development of Negro Potential," *Journal of Negro Education*, XXVI (1957), 456-65.

Stern, Frederick Martin. *The Citizen Army.* New York, St. Martin's Press, 1957.

Stouffer, Samuel A. and Associates. *The American Soldier: Adjustment during Army Life; The American Soldier: Combat and its Aftermath*, Vols. I and II of Studies in Social Psychology in World War II. Princeton, N. J., Princeton University Press, 1949.

U. S. Department of the Army. Office of the Surgeon General. *Medical Statistics of the United States Army* (Annual Report of the Surgeon General), various years. Washington, D.C., Government Printing Office.

U. S. Department of the Army. Office of the Surgeon General. Neuropsychiatric Consultants Division. *Annual Reports to the Surgeon General*, 1943, 1944, 1944-45; *Reports of the Service Commands to the Surgeon General*, 1945. Washington, D.C.

U. S. Department of Defense. Research and Development Board and Personnel Policy Board. *Report of Working Group on Human Be-*

havior Under Conditions of Military Service. Washington, D.C. Government Printing Office, 1951.

U. S. Selective Service System. *Reemployment and Selective Service,* Special Monograph No. 13. Washington, D.C., Government Printing Office, 1949.

U. S. Senate. Committee on Military Affairs. *Demobilization of the Armed Forces: Hearings on S.1355, A Bill to Provide for the Speedy Return of Veterans to Civilian Life, for the Immediate Military Needs of the United States, and for other Purposes,* September 12, 13, 17, 18, and 19, and October 17 and 18, 1945. Washington, D.C., Government Printing Office, 1945.

U. S. Veterans Administration. *Annual Report of the Administrator of Veterans Affairs,* 1943-1957. Washington, D.C., Government Printing Office, 1944-1958.

——. *Schedule for Rating Disabilities.* Washington, D.C., Government Printing Office, 1945.

Waller, Willard. *The Veteran Comes Back.* New York, Dryden Press, 1944.

Additional relevant books and articles are given in the bibliographies of the two companion volumes in this series, *The Lost Divisions* and *Breakdown and Recovery.*

INDEX

www.ingramcontent.com/pod-product-compliance
Ingram Content Group UK Ltd.
Pitfield, Milton Keynes, MK11 3LW, UK
UKHW020221290926
15470UKWH00001B/316

9 780837 184692